OFFICE SKILLS

Also by Thelma Foster and published by ST(P):
Telephone and Reception Skills

OFFICE SKILLS

Thelma J Foster

Senior Lecturer, Business Studies Department,
Worcester Technical College

Stanley Thornes (Publishers) Ltd

First published in 1981 by Stanley Thornes (Publishers) Ltd, Educa House, Old Station Drive, off Leckhampton Road, Cheltenham, Glos, GL53 0DN

Reprinted 1982 twice

British Library Cataloguing in Publication Data

Foster, Thelma J
    Office skills
    1. Office practice
    2. Clerks
    I. Title
    651.2'74   HF5547.5

ISBN 0 85950 459 X

Text typeset by Quadraset Ltd, Combe End, Radstock, Bath
Printed and bound in Great Britain at the Pitman Press, Bath

Contents

Preface

I have written this book in the hope that young people will enjoy reading it. My experience of teaching the subject over the past 20 years has shown me that pupils in schools and students in colleges will not read their textbooks unless absolutely obliged to do so and I have tried to make this one interesting, attractive, funny (in places), and, perhaps most important, simple – especially when dealing with points which I know very well young people find confusing.

Ideally, Office Practice should be correlated with Commerce, Economics and Accounts – not to mention typewriting, but I know this is a counsel of perfection and difficult to achieve. What I hope this book will do is to enable teachers in schools and colleges to make Office Practice as practical as possible; even where equipment is inadequate, it is possible to organise supplies of forms so that the lessons can be interesting and imaginative. Typewriting lessons could be used for this purpose, once some degree of proficiency has been reached.

Technology is bringing changes in offices, as elsewhere, but the fundamental principles of storing and finding information, dealing with visitors to firms and answering the telephone, will remain for many years to come and study of Office Practice can only be of use to the office workers of the future.

Office Skills will be especially useful for pupils in schools studying the CSE syllabuses on Office Practice, and also for students in Colleges of Further Education working towards the Secretarial Studies Certificate. BEC/General students should also find much of this book relevant.

My most heartfelt thanks are due to my husband for his patience and help, to my colleagues for their interest and encouragement and, especially, to all those students who have worked painstakingly through the exercises and shown me the error of my ways. I should also like to acknowledge Mr Tony Edwards, who made helpful comments and suggestions on the first draft, and the staff of Stanley Thornes (Publishers) who turned the final draft into a book.

Finally, I am grateful to the Bank of Education, the Post Office and ROSPA for permission to use some of their material.

THELMA FOSTER
Worcester, 1981

Notes on Second Printing

The author would like to take this opportunity to thank Pitman Books Ltd for granting permission to reproduce an exercise on the franking machine control card (see Exercise 32, p. 179). This exercise was inadvertently copied from *Practical Office Exercises* by John Harrison.

The publishers wish to make it clear that the book *Office Skills* is not in any way derived from or connected with the magazine of the same name published by Pitman Periodicals Limited.

A number of errors have come to light since the first printing and these have been corrected. In particular, there were a number of incorrect figures in Chapter 15 due to a misunderstanding of VAT Regulations. These have been amended and a note has been added on p. 303 to clarify the situation. Amendments have also been made in the light of the separation of British Telecom from the Post Office. However, changes in both organisations are occurring rapidly as this printing goes to press, and it is difficult to keep completely up to date. In particular, the *British Telecom Guide* has already gone out of production, though some of its information will be found in the *British International Services Guide* which is to replace it. Teachers would be well advised to supplement *Office Skills* with whatever additional information they can obtain from their local post offices.

Finally, there is now available an *Office Skills Answer Book*. Further details may be obtained from the publishers.

List of Topics For Your Folder

*The cartoon 'What's Wrong?' is reproduced by kind permission of the Royal Society for the Prevention of Accidents.

List of Exercises

SECTION A   THE OFFICE WORLD

CHAPTER 1

The Departments of a Company

Introduction

Most companies are divided up into departments, with a manager to take responsibility for each one. The managers report to the managing director who in turn works in close cooperation with the board of directors and the chairman.

The organisation chart below shows the responsibilities of each manager, including the manager in charge of office services.

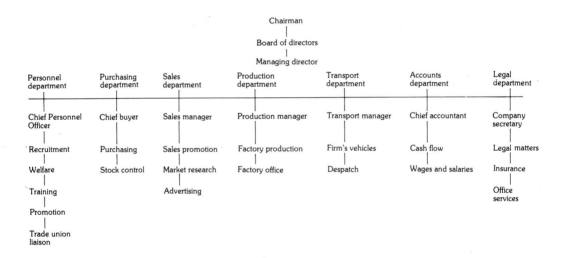

A typical organisation chart. The exact structure of any firm will of course depend on the particular type of business being conducted

A separate chart shows what office services consist of, with each department controlled by a supervisor under the authority of the company secretary. The supervisors have the responsibility of ensuring that the work of their staff is carried out efficiently, accurately and promptly.

The Purpose of the Office

An 'office' is a place where any clerical work is done, and the word 'clerk' means any office worker – typist, computer programmer, receptionist, for example. Offices exist in firms mainly to receive, record and find information. In a small one-man business, separate office services will not be necessary. The manager can receive and give information himself. In larger businesses the managing director cannot deal personally with all inward and outward communications (see pp. 115–23); nor can he supervise everything that takes place. The office services are there to carry out these functions on his behalf.

The Key People

THE CHAIRMAN OF A COMPANY

The chairman is the most important member of the board of directors (and is usually elected by them). He represents his company both outside the firm to the public (shareholders, for example) and in the firm – he may make presentations to employees with long-service records or who have given exceptional service. He takes the 'chair' (i.e. presides – see p. 123) at board meetings and presents the annual report on the company's progress to shareholders. The chairman depends upon his fellow directors for information and advice – no single individual could be expected to know every detail of what is going on in a large firm.

BOARD OF DIRECTORS

Each director may be responsible for a particular section of the business – production, sales or buying, for example – but they are also responsible to the managing director and have to accept the board of directors' decisions.

MANAGING DIRECTOR

The managing director's chief responsibility is to see that the decisions made by the board of directors are carried out. He works in close cooperation with the chairman; in order to achieve this he also spends a great deal of time with the managers (known as 'executives') of the various departments. It is through the managing director that important matters are passed to the board of directors for discussion and decision.

THE COMPANY SECRETARY

The company secretary is mainly responsible for making sure that his company does not break the law (taking care of legal matters). He also acts as a link between the company and the shareholders and sends them information about their shares, and the company's financial position (i.e. how much profit or loss it has made in the previous 12 months). The company secretary is responsible for keeping an account of proceedings at all meetings (minutes: see pp. 124–5) and that the company keeps proper records of its financial transactions (buying, selling, borrowing, paying wages). The company secretary works closely with the chief accountant. As well as legal matters, the company secretary handles insurance matters. In many firms he is responsible for the office services. In all firms he is the link between the board of directors and the office staff.

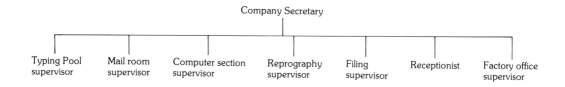

The organisation of office services in a typical large firm may look like this

The People and Departments in a Large Firm

We now look at the departments in a large firm and see 'who does what'.

THE PERSONNEL DEPARTMENT

The word 'personnel' means 'the persons employed in any service', and the main duties of the staff working in a personnel department are connected with people. Such duties may include:
- Advertising vacancies for jobs.
- Training employees; promoting them.
- Transferring employees from department to department.
- Keeping staff records.
- Looking after the welfare of staff.
- Organising negotiations with trade unions.
- Dealing with resignations and dismissals.
- Helping to run social events and 'public-relations' exercises such as open days for visitors.

The first step towards obtaining a job in a large firm is usually taken by completing an application form for the personnel department. This may be a general form (suitable for any vacancy in the firm) or a specialised one – perhaps (say) suitable for office staff only. A completed application form will tell the firm whether an applicant is suitable enough to be interviewed. If so, he or she is put on what is called a 'short list'.

EMPLOYMENT APPLICATION FORM (Office Staff)

Surname (in CAPITAL letters, please) . . . .

Forename(s) . . . . Mr/Mrs/Miss

Address . . . .

. . . .

Date of birth . . . . Nationality . . . .

Education

	Name	From	To
Last school attended	. . . .	. . . .	. . . .
Further education	. . . .	. . . .	. . . .

Examinations passed

Subject	Board	Grade
. . . .	. . . .	. . . .
. . . .	. . . .	. . . .
. . . .	. . . .	. . . .
. . . .	. . . .	. . . .
. . . .	. . . .	. . . .
. . . .	. . . .	. . . .

Previous office experience

Name of firm	Position held	From	To
. . . .	. . . .	. . . .	. . . .
. . . .	. . . .	. . . .	. . . .
. . . .	. . . .	. . . .	. . . .

Any other work experience

. . . .	. . . .	. . . .	. . . .
. . . .	. . . .	. . . .	. . . .

Hobbies and other interests

. . . .

. . . .

Please tick any of the positions below in which you are interested and for which you consider you would be suitable. Number them in order of interest and suitability.

☐ Audio-typist   ☐ Receptionist

☐ Book-keeper   ☐ Secretary

☐ Copy-typist   ☐ Shorthand-typist

☐ Filing clerk   ☐ Switchboard operator

Signed . . . . Date . . . .

An application form for employment

This list will give the names of the half-dozen or so really first-class applicants for a particular post.

After interview, and appointment, details on an application form are transferred to a staff record sheet. In the one shown this will go on to the left-hand side; the right-hand side is for information relating to the employee's career with the firm and this will be kept up-to-date continuously. Some employees stay with one firm all their lives, and obviously one staff record would not be large enough to contain all the relevant information, so after a number of years there could be a series of such sheets.

Personnel records contain a great deal of information which is confidential and must be filed in lockable cabinets, which should never be left open when the office is unattended. Staff working in a personnel department have to be trustworthy and discreet – never passing on information about staff to anyone outside or inside the firm.

STAFF RECORD SHEET

Name . . . . First name(s)	Department . . . .
. . . .	Position . . . .
Address	Salary (starting) . . . . Date . . . .
. . . .	Salary increases . . . . Date . . . .
	. . . . Date . . . .
Tel No . . . . Nationality	. . . . Date . . . .
Next of kin . . . . Address	. . . . Date . . . .
Tel No	Date of appointment . . . . Age on appointment . . . .
Date of Birth . . . . M/F Married/single	Transfers or promotions: . . . . Date . . . .
Children	. . . . Date . . . .
. . . .	. . . . Date . . . .
Education: To/From To/From	. . . . Date . . . .
Secondary . . . . Further	Training Record:
	In the firm: To: From . . . .
Qualifications:	Day Release To: From . . . .
Subjects Examining Boards Dates	Block Release To: From . . . .
. . . .	Additional qualifications gained: Date
. . . .	. . . .
. . . .	. . . .
. . . .	Periods of illness
. . . .	From: To: Nos of days absent . . . . . Reason . . . .
. . . .	From: To: Nos of days absent . . . . . Reason . . . .
	Absences for reasons other than illness:
Previous employment	Date Cause
Firms Positions held Dates	. . . .
. . . .	. . . .
. . . .	. . . .
	Pension scheme Joined . . . . . Due to retire . . . .
National Insurance No	Retired . . . .
Referees given:	Date of leaving . . . .
. . . .	Reason (other than retirement) . . . .

A staff record sheet

PURCHASING DEPARTMENT

The purchasing department is the responsibility of the purchasing officer (sometimes called the 'chief buyer'). The chief buyer carries out three important duties:

- He must make sure that value for money has been received.
- He must make sure that accurate records of money spent are kept by his department.
- He must authorise all payments made on behalf of his department.

The purchasing department arranges for the buying of raw materials to be used by the production department, as well as office equipment, stationery and possibly the food and other requirements of the canteen. Frequent visitors to the purchasing department are salesmen from other firms, hoping to be given orders for the goods they are trying to sell. Invoices from suppliers are sent to the purchasing department for checking, after which they are sent to the accounts department for payment. Other forms used are orders and enquiries. Another important responsibility of the purchasing department is stock control.

Stocktaking

The 'stock' in a firm consists of supplies of everything likely to be needed, and it costs money, so it is very important to make sure that too much stock is not piling up on the shelves. Money can earn interest – idle stock on shelves which is not likely to be required for months earns nothing. The supervisor in charge of stock control has to arrange security for the goods in store so that they cannot easily be stolen, and he also has to prevent stock being wasted. Stock record cards (see p. 199) enable him to see at a glance how much of any article is in stock, and who is 'requisitioning' it from him. Stock requisitions (see pp. 199–201) are forms completed by employees requiring goods from the stores.

SALES DEPARTMENT

The work of the sales department is very important because without sales a firm would go out of business. A large sales department may be divided into two – one for supervising sales overseas (export market) and one for supervising sales in this country (home market). The organisation of the sales department is carried out by the sales manager who may attend directors' meetings at which sales policy is decided. The sales manager also supervises his assistant managers and sales representatives. An advertising section often forms part of the sales department, and its main job is to arrange sales 'promotion' – to bring the products of the firm to the attention of the public by free offers, advertising in magazines, newspapers, on television and arranging exhibitions and special campaigns. Other ways of advertising are by 'direct mail' – sending circulars through the post to people living in a selected area or having a particular interest. Market research (interviewing passers-by in the street or calling at their homes in certain neighbourhoods and asking them to fill in questionnaires) enables the advertising section to find out what the public wants to buy.

Clerical workers in the sales department spend part of their time sending out catalogues and price lists to customers, and typing invoices.

Customers' complaints may also be dealt with by the sales department, and in some firms, this department provides a repair service to customers for goods they have purchased from the firm.

PRODUCTION DEPARTMENT

The production manager is responsible for the factory which manufactures the goods sold by the firm. A works manager is usually in direct control of the factory, and the factory office is the link between the factory and all the other departments in the firm. When an order is received by the sales department, it is sent to the factory office, and the factory office must ensure that orders are correctly delivered without delay.

The production manager may also be responsible for the maintenance in a firm – repairing roads, buildings and machinery in the factory. This work is carried out by supervisors with technicians and workmen under their control.

TRANSPORT DEPARTMENT

The manager in charge of transport has the responsibility of arranging for the goods manufactured by the firm to be delivered to the customers. This may be done by the firm's own vehicles – vans or lorries – or by British Rail or transport firms. The transport manager has to decide upon the safest, quickest and cheapest methods. If the firm's own vehicles are used, he also has to make sure that they are always in a good state of repair and that there are always some available when required. Company cars, mini-buses and coaches may also be the responsibility of the transport manager.

The transport manager and the works manager have to work closely together.

ACCOUNTS DEPARTMENT

The chief accountant is the head of the accounts department, which is one of the most important in the firm. It is the job of the accounts department to see that all the bills sent to the firm by its suppliers are paid promptly and, similarly, that all bills are sent out punctually to the customers of the firm, and that they are also paid promptly.

At the end of the 'financial year' (this is often the income tax year: see pp. 323–4) the records kept by the accounts department are checked by an independent outside accountant (this is known as an 'audit').

A copy of the audited accounts is sent to the shareholders. These audited accounts enable the accounts department to produce a 'balance sheet' which shows how much profit or loss the firm has made during the preceding financial year.

Payment of wages and salaries is often a part of the accounts department's responsibilities, and it may be dealt with by a separate section. Employees in the wages section are busy working out the amounts due to workers each week, or each month, and what amounts have to be deducted for income tax, national insurance and other deductions (see pp. 321–2). The busiest time in the wages section is towards the end of each week – most firms pay out wages on Thursdays or Fridays. Since much of the work in this section is concerned with figures, much of it today is completed by machines – for example, calculating machines and computers (see pp. 138–40).

FOR YOUR FOLDER

1. THE DEPARTMENTS OF A COMPANY

Write these notes in your folder, filling in the missing words and phrases.

1) An organisation chart shows the responsibilities of each _____ in a firm.

2) An 'office' is a place where any _____ work is done.

3) The word 'clerk' means any _____ worker – typist, computer programmer, receptionist.

4) Offices exist in firms mainly to receive, record and _____ information.

5) The chairman _____ his company both inside and outside the firm.

6) The chairman is usually _____ by the board of directors and is the most important member of this board.

7) The managing director's chief responsibility is to see that decisions made by the _____ are carried out.

8) The company secretary is mainly responsible for legal and _____ matters.

9) In many firms he is also responsible for _____ services. In all firms he is the link between the board of directors and the _____.

10) The main duties of the staff working in the personnel department are connected with _____.

11) Staff working in a personnel department have to be _____ and _____.

12) The purchasing department arranges for the _____ of raw materials to be used by the production department, as well as many other requirements of the firm.

13) Documents sent out by the purchasing department are _____ and _____.

14) Another important responsibility of the purchasing department is stock _____.

15) Forms used in connection with this are _____ record cards and _____.

16) The sales manager organises the sales department and also supervises _____ and _____.

17) An _____ section often forms part of the sales department.

18) Clerical workers in the sales department spend part of their time sending out catalogues and price lists to customers and typing _____.

19) The production manager is responsible for the _____ which manufactures the goods sold by the firm.

20) A works manager is usually in direct control of the factory and the _____ office is the link between the factory and all other _____ in the firm.

21) The transport manager has the responsibility of arranging for the goods manufactured in the firm to be delivered to the _____.

22) The transport manager has to decide upon the safest, quickest and _____ methods of transport.

23) The head of the accounts department is the _____.

24) It is the job of the accounts department to see that all the bills sent to the firm by its suppliers are paid promptly and that all bills are sent out of the firm punctually to the _____ of the firm.

25) Each year, the records kept by the accounts department are checked by an independent accountant – this is known as an _____.

26) Also part of the accounts department's responsibilities may be the payment of _____ dealt with by a separate section of the department.

Exercise 1

QUESTIONS ON THE DEPARTMENTS OF A COMPANY

1) Describe the work of the personnel department.

2) What is the purpose of an office?

3) What is the importance to a firm of the chairman, board of directors and managing director?

4) Explain the importance of stock control in a firm.

5) What is 'sales promotion' and 'market research'?

6) The transport department and the production department have very important links. What are they?

7) Explain what a 'balance sheet' is and its importance to the shareholders in a firm.

Office services

The tendency in many large firms is towards centralisation of office services. There are many advantages of centralisation:

- *Reduction of noise.* All noisy equipment such as typewriters can be located away from staff who need quiet in order to concentrate.
- *Economy.* When work is centralised it is carried out by clerical staff who are specially trained in that type of work more efficiently and quickly.
- *Better equipment.* It is worth spending more money on better equipment because it is being shared by many.
- *Efficiency.* The work is done under experienced supervision.
- *Spreading the work.* The work load can be spread evenly, perhaps reducing the need for overtime.

The disadvantages of centralisation are:

● Work can become monotonous.
● No training is given in any other type of work – promotion prospects may be lessened.
● There is a loss of personal contact with staff engaged on other work, as most communication is done through the supervisor.

TYPING POOL

This is an example of centralisation, where all the typing, audio-typing and shorthand-typing carried out in a firm is done in one department under a trained supervisor. The typing pool provides an excellent training for the school or college leaver, as working directly under experienced supervision is of great benefit to beginners. The work in a typing pool consists of typing circular letters, form letters, schedules, ink stencils, envelopes or letters. Word processors are beginning to take the place of copy-typists in some large firms, but audio-typists and shorthand-typists are still in great demand.

MAIL ROOM

In many firms, all the mail is collected and dealt with by a centralised mail room, who also distribute incoming mail after it arrives in the mornings. Many school-leavers are first appointed to work in the mail room, which gives them an opportunity to get to know their way around a large firm and to find out who works where.

COMPUTER SECTION

The computer section has to be housed in special air-conditioned rooms, as the equipment is affected by changes in temperature. Computers are used in large firms to work out the payroll, sales account records, stock control and production planning. Clerical workers in the computer section include 'programmers' – people trained to work out a set of instructions for a computer to perform a complete operation (see pp. 138–9).

REPROGRAPHY DEPARTMENT

The reprography department is where all the duplicating and photo-copying needed in the firm is centralised. The workers in a reprography department may produce a wide variety of jobs – staff handbooks, price lists, instruction sheets, office stationery, internal telephone directories, copies of minutes and agenda.

They work closely with the typing pool in many large firms. The equipment used in reprography includes: photocopiers, ink duplicators, spirit duplicators and offset-litho duplicators (see Chapter 12). Clerical workers in the reprography department have an opportunity to become familiar with all these machines.

FILING DEPARTMENT

In many firms, one department is responsible for the sorting and filing of all the papers in the firm which are required to be stored for future reference. Centralised filing saves space, ensures a uniform method of filing and makes better use of both filing staff and equipment, but papers may be out when required, and the filing department may be some distance from many of the offices, thereby causing a waste of time when clerical workers go to borrow files.

RECEPTIONIST

The receptionist is almost the first person callers see when they come to a firm and therefore her job is most important. She must be pleasant, polite, tactful and well-groomed; in addition she should learn all she can about her firm and what it does so that she can answer callers' questions. To learn about reception work, a school or college leaver should look for a job as an assistant receptionist (see Chapter 4).

FACTORY OFFICE

Clerical workers in the factory office have to work closely with the factory workers (the people actually engaged in making the firm's products). The factory office keeps records of all manufacturing and production operations – the factory office is the link between the factory and all the other departments in a firm.

FOR YOUR FOLDER

2. OFFICE SERVICES

Write these notes in your folder, filling in the missing words and phrases.

1) The department where all the typing, audio-typing and shorthand-typing carried out in a firm is done under one trained supervisor is the _____.

2) The department which deals with all outgoing letters and parcels, as well as the incoming ones, is the _____.

3) Clerical workers in the computer section trained to work out a set of instructions to a computer are _____.

4) The department where all the duplicating and photocopying is carried out is the _____ department.

5) Centralised filing saves _____ ensures a uniform method of _____ and makes better use of both filing staff and _____.

6) The receptionist's job is important because she is almost the _____ _____ callers see when they come to a firm.

7) The factory office is the _____ between the factory and all the other departments in a firm.

8) Centralisation of office services has many advantages; economy, reduction of noise, better equipment, efficiency and _____.

9) Disadvantages of centralisation are: monotony, fewer promotion prospects and _____.

CHAPTER 2

Today's Office

Health and Safety

Most offices today, even those in old, inconvenient buildings, are warm in winter, well-lit and have up-to-date equipment and furniture. If office staff are uncomfortable, they will soon look for another job.

It was not always so. Until 1946 there were no regulations at all for the protection of office workers and many firms failed to provide even the most elementary standards of lighting, heating or adequate space for their office staff. The description in Dickens' *Christmas Carol* of the office where Scrooge was the employer could almost have been true of many offices in the twentieth century! Factory workers and mine-workers had been protected by law since 1802 – it took over a century and a half for anything to be done for office workers.

The Industrial Injuries Act of 1946 provided a scheme of insurance against accidents at work for *all* employees, including office workers, and this was at least a beginning. Seventeen years later, in 1963, the Offices, Shops and Railway Premises Act was passed. This Act laid down conditions for lighting, heating, washing and toilet facilities, as well as minimum space (400 cubic feet) for each office worker. Regulations about first aid and safety were also laid down in this Act – firms employing over 150 people had to arrange for one person to be trained in first aid. The Offices, Shops and Railway Premises Act did not, however, apply to schools and colleges – and these have office workers, too.

First aid box needed!

Workers in many small offices continued to endure miserable conditions – larger firms had more money and provided better facilities. Eventually, the shortage of office workers forced employers to improve working conditions – even a generous salary does not compensate for shivering through the winter or stifling in the summer.

The formation of Trade Unions for office workers has also influenced their conditions and helped to improve them.

The most recent and important development in office workers' conditions is an Act passed in 1974 called the Health and Safety at Work Act, which includes all the regulations in the Offices, Shops and Railway Premises Act of 1963 but which is much more comprehensive and also applies to schools and colleges. HASAWA (for short) lays responsibility on employees as well as employers, especially for safety and security.

Accidents can be caused in offices (as in homes) very easily by carelessness or thoughtlessness, and it is now the duty of everyone, from the executives to the youngest employees, to help to prevent accidents in offices. HASAWA makes it plain that although employees now have rights, they have duties, too.

The following is a list of suggestions for office workers to help to make their places of work safer for all:

- Gangways between desks should not be blocked with boxes, files or wastebins.
- Fire exits must be kept clear, too.
- Fire doors must be kept closed (not propped open).
- Filing cabinet drawers must be closed after use, it is easy to trip over an open bottom drawer.
- Smouldering cigarette ends are one of the main causes of fire, and smokers should observe non-smoking rules.
- Electric appliances must be unplugged and switched off at the end of each day.
- Adaptors and trailing wires are dangerous and should be avoided. Any faulty electrical equipment must be repaired by an expert electrician.
- Tops of high cupboards should not be stacked with files and boxes.
- Torn or frayed floorcovering should be reported to a supervisor and then barricaded off until it has been repaired.
- First Aid boxes must be clearly displayed and contents replenished frequently.
- Unguarded electric fires must never be used.
- All employees should be familiar with the use of fire extinguishers and know the firm's fire drill – fire drills are usually carried out regularly in most firms. If they are not, they should be.
- Any cupboards containing valuables (see p. 287) should be locked at the end of the day, and filing cabinets with confidential documents also. Office doors should be locked and windows firmly

secured – this will not prevent a burglar gaining entrance if he really is determined to, but it will make it more difficult for him.

Employers, office staff, trade unions – all have to work together to improve the safety of their places of work.

FOR YOUR FOLDER

3. SAFETY FIRST!

How much do you remember about safety. Look at the picture below and list 'what's wrong'. Remember to avoid these hazards if you go to work in an office!

What's wrong with this office?

Location of Offices

The location of offices is very important to different types of office workers for many reasons:

- Their special type of work may require peace and quiet.
- They may need to be accessible to frequent outside callers or to staff from other departments.
- Privacy may be necessary – some interviews with other members of staff should not be overheard.
- Good lighting is essential for all office workers.
- Ventilation is vital too – in summer and winter.

The siting of firms comes before the location of the offices inside them and here it is important to take into account:

- Nearness to public transport (trains, buses).
- Nearness to shops, banks and post office, cafés and restaurants.
- Allocation and provision of adequate parking space.

Once the building has been completed, it is then necessary to decide where the various offices shall be located inside.

Obviously the reception area and receptionist's desk must be near the main entrance, so that visitors can easily find them (see Chapter 4). Also, the personnel department should not be too far away from the main entrance, as they will have many callers from outside – people coming for interviews for instance. The buying department, too, will have representatives calling from other firms, so should not be far from the main entrance.

It makes good sense to site on the ground floor any department using heavy machinery – the reprographic department, for example.

Services which are centralised in many firms – mailroom, filing, typing pool, messenger, reprographic, wages and accounts – should be central and convenient to other departments, not on the top floor which necessitates all staff wasting time and energy unnecessarily. (And lifts do not always work!)

There must be toilet and cloakroom facilities on every floor, and fresh drinking water should be available, as well as hot water for washing. The canteen and surgery ought to be close to offices to avoid staff having to walk long distances in cold or wet weather.

The Layout of an Office

PLANNING OFFICES

Siting of office buildings and location of offices inside the building is important to those who work in them; just as important is the right type of furniture and equipment, but, before this is chosen, another decision has to be made – the layout of each office.

CELLULAR OFFICES

The traditional type of office is rectangular, similar to a medium-sized room with doors and windows, and is known as a 'cellular' office.

The advantages of cellular offices

- They are lockable, providing security for anything confidential or valuable.
- They are private.
- There is peace and quiet for work which requires concentration.
- Special conditions can be provided for equipment which needs controlled temperature and humidity (e.g. a computer).

The disadvantages of cellular offices

- They require more space in a building, because of partitioning, doors and windows.
- They are more expensive to maintain – redecoration, heating, lighting.
- More supervision is required as each office operates behind its own walls.

OPEN-PLAN OFFICES

An open-plan office is where a large space is furnished as one integrated whole, with or without the use of screens (sometimes provided by plants in pots or plant stands). It generally accommodates several grades of staff from typists and clerical workers to managers and directors.

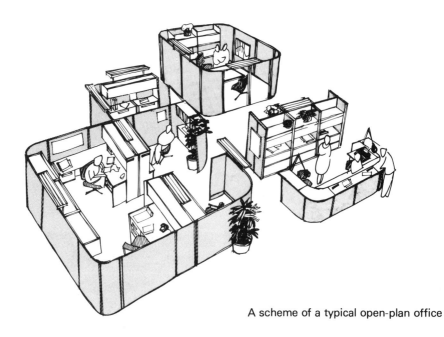

A scheme of a typical open-plan office

20

The advantages of open-plan offices

- They are easy to supervise, as all the staff are on view.
- Communication between sections and departments can be carried out without delay, since everyone is on view.
- Flow of work is speeded up since it is from desk to desk rather than from office to office.
- They enable centralisation of office services to be organised easily.
- Managers and senior staff are in constant contact with the work of all staff.
- They are cheaper to maintain – there is more economical use of space, heating, and lighting, and cleaning is straightforward.
- Layout in certain areas can be changed quickly if required.

The disadvantages of open-plan offices

- They are noisier, because of the lack of partitions.
- Workers are distracted, because of people passing to and fro.
- Security is reduced because there are no lockable doors.
- Privacy is difficult to obtain.
- Infections (coughs, colds, 'flu) spread more quickly.
- Some office machines are noisy (typewriters, duplicators) and unsuitable for an open-plan area.
- Senior staff prefer their own offices which they regard as status symbols (marks of seniority).
- It is difficult to arrange lighting and ventilation for all tastes.
- The atmosphere is impersonal – many people like their own office walls on which to hang pictures, photographs etc.

CENTRALISATION

This is an arrangement in firms where services used by all departments are under the control of one or two supervisors – e.g. the typing pool, the mail room, the filing and reprography departments and the wages and accounts departments.

The advantages of centralisation

- The work load can be spread more evenly among specially trained staff.
- All noisy machinery can be contained in one area and away from other staff.
- Expensive equipment is not installed in many offices in several departments.
- A more efficient service can be provided by the specialist staff.

The disadvantages of centralisation

- Centralised services may be a long way from some offices and time is wasted while staff walk to and fro.
- The staff engaged on work in a centralised office may find it monotonous.
- Contact may be lost with staff in other departments.

Office Furniture

Well-designed office furniture, suitable for the work of the user, helps health and efficiency. The heights of desks and chairs should be appropriate to avoid slumping and discomfort.

A manager's desk and chair

Steel furniture is less of a fire risk than plastic, which causes suffocating smoke within seconds after the outbreak of a fire.

For typists L-shaped modules provide a working and a typing area, and a swivel chair enables both areas to be used easily. The height of seat and back should be adjustable. Footrests should be available for all typists and clerical workers.

A typist's swivel chair

A special desk and chair for the drawing office

Specialised furniture is required for workers in the drawing office and artists in the advertising department.

The reception area has special furniture for people waiting so that they may relax comfortably (see Chapter 4).

FOR YOUR FOLDER

4. TODAY'S OFFICE

Write these notes in your folder, filling in the missing words and phrases.

1) The Industrial Injuries Act of _____ provided a scheme of insurance against accidents at work for all employees, including office workers.

2) In 1963, the Offices, Shops and Railway Premises Act was passed, which laid down conditions for lighting, heating, washing and toilet facilities as well as minimum space for _____.

3) The Offices, Shops and Railway Premises Act did not, however, apply to _____.

4) The formation of trade unions for office workers has also influenced their conditions and _____.

5) The most recent and important development in office workers' conditions was passed in 1974 and is called the _____.

6) The location of offices is very important to office workers for many reasons:
   > peace and quiet
   > privacy
   > good lighting
   > ventilation

   _____.

7) Reception area and personnel department should be near the main entrance as also should the _____ department.

8) Any department using _____ machinery (such as the reprography department) should be on the ground floor.

9) Centralised services, such as mail room, filing, typing pool, messenger, reprographic, wages and accounts should be central and _____ to other departments, not on the top floor which necessitates staff wasting time and energy.

10) The traditional type of office is rectangular, similar to a medium-sized room and is known as a _____ office.

11) Where a large space is furnished as one integrated whole, with several grades of staff (typists, clerks and managers) is an _____ office.

12) A very large area with a minimum of 50/100 occupants is a _____ office.

13) Open-plan offices are not always popular, because they are noisier, there is more distraction for workers, security is reduced and _____ spread quickly.

14) Centralisation in firms is an arrangement where _____.

15) Two examples of centralisation are _____ and _____.

16) The advantages of centralisation are the spreading of a more even workload and _____.

17) The disadvantage of centralisation is _____.

18) Well-designed office furniture helps _____ and _____.

19) Typists' chairs should have seats and backs which are _____.

20) Specialised furniture is required in drawing offices and for artists in advertising departments. The _____ area also has special furniture for people _____.

Exercise 2

PLANNING AN OFFICE LAYOUT

Make a plan to scale (¼ inch to 1 foot).

Mark doorways and windows.

Decide on furniture and equipment.

Cut out templates of all furniture and equipment to scale.

Arrange templates on plan.

Mark in names of workers, telephones etc.

Submit for approval.

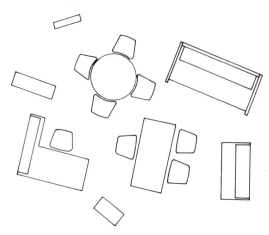

Exercise 3

QUESTIONS ON TODAY'S OFFICE

1) Compare the Offices, Shops and Railway Premises Act of 1963 with the Health and Safety at Work Act of 1974.

2) Explain six ways in which office workers can help to make their places of work safer.

3) What five factors have to be taken into account when deciding on the site of an office?

4) Why do many senior members of staff prefer their own offices? Explain two reasons why open-plan offices are not popular with office workers.

5) Make a plan to scale of an office, with furniture, equipment and staff, remembering that 40 square feet is the allowance of space (minimum) laid down by law for office workers.

CHAPTER 3

Finding a Job and Starting Work

Types of Job in the Office

OFFICE JUNIORS

Some firms will employ school-leavers as office juniors. An office junior will learn to do many different sorts of job and will often be asked to help out a department if it is short of staff – perhaps because of sickness or holidays or when someone has recently left the firm. The junior may even be asked to make the tea – see Appendix 1, pp. 369–70!

AUDIO-TYPISTS

Someone new to the office may be introduced to 'audio' typing. An audio-typist listens to a cassette through headphones and types what she hears. She has to be very good at spelling and punctuation because she has nothing to guide her.

An audio-typist

COPY-TYPISTS

Copy-typists type from handwritten or corrected typescript. Their typing speeds range from 35 words a minute (a junior copy typist) to about 60 words a minute (an experienced copy typist). A junior typist may also be sent on a day-release course to the local college to learn shorthand and improve her typing speed.

SHORTHAND-TYPISTS

A shorthand-typist has to have a good typing speed (50 words a minute) and also be able to write shorthand at about 100 words a minute. In addition her English must be very good, because she is typing from shorthand not longhand.

A shorthand-typist

FILING CLERKS

Some office workers specialise in filing, an important job which requires great care and efficiency (see Chapter 13).

A filing clerk

RECEPTIONISTS

Many school-leavers are attracted by the idea of becoming reception-ists. A receptionist in a firm is the first person a caller may speak to and her speech, manner and appearance are very important. Usually, a firm's receptionist will be around 20 years of age, but in a very large firm she will need an assistant and a school-leaver could be considered for this job. Some receptionists also look after switchboards and are able to type. There is more about receptionists later on in the book (Chapter 4).

A receptionist

TELEPHONISTS

Another important key post in a firm is that of the telephonist or switchboard operator. Many of these are trained by British Telecom before going to work in a firm as they must be efficient, polite, tactful, calm and helpful. There is much more about telephonists in Chapter 5.

In some firms the jobs of receptionist and switchboard operator are combined and done by one person.

A switchboard operator

SECRETARIES

A secretary is a very good shorthand-typist or audio-typist (or someone who can do both audio and shorthand-typing) who has worked in a firm, or several firms, and gained experience of what the firm does and of her employer's duties in the firm. She is thus able to take over much of the day-to-day running of the office, screening callers on the telephone and personal callers, organising the diary, making travel arrangements, taking minutes at meetings and finding information for her employer, so saving him time and enabling him to work without interruption in his own specialised field. Many good shorthand-typists or audio-typists become excellent secretaries when they have gained sufficient experience to use their initiative in this way.

A secretary dealing with callers

FOR YOUR FOLDER

5. TYPES OF JOB

Write these notes in your folder, filling in the missing words and phrases.

1) An audio-typist has to be very good at spelling and punctuation because she listens through _____ and then types what she has heard.

2) A book-keeper in a firm works with accounts. Although in a large firm much of this work is done on accounting machines or computers, a book-keeper would have to be very good at _____.

3) Copy-typists type from handwritten or corrected typescript. Their typing speeds range from 35 words a minute (a junior copy-typist) to about 60 words a minute (an experienced copy-typist). More important than speed, however, is _____.

4) A filing clerk spends most of her time putting away letters and other documents so that they can be _____ quickly. She must be an especially careful worker, as looking for missing papers is a waste of valuable time.

5) A receptionist's speech, manner and appearance are very important, as she is likely to be the first person to whom a caller will go when he visits a firm. In a small firm, she may look after a switchboard as well as looking after all the _____ to a firm.

6) A shorthand-typist has to have a good typing speed and also to be able to write shorthand at about 100 words a minute. In addition, her English must be very good, because she is typing from _____ and not words.

7) A secretary has to have good typing speeds and be able to write shorthand at over 100 words a minute. She must also have very good English. In addition to these qualifications, she needs several years' _____ in a firm so that she is able to help her employer with a great deal of his office work.

8) A switchboard operator may be trained by the British Telecom before she goes to work for a firm, as she has the very important job of dealing with all the incoming and outgoing _____ calls, and she must be efficient, polite, tactful, calm and helpful.

Exercise 4

QUESTIONS ON TYPES OF JOB

1) Explain the difference between a shorthand-typist and a secretary.

2) Why do audio-typists and shorthand-typists have to be especially good at English?

3) In some cases, who trains switchboard operators?

4) A switchboard operator must be very efficient. What else should she be?

5) In a small firm, one member of the office staff might look after a switchboard as well as doing another job. What other job would this be?

Vacancies

The employment exchange run by the Government's Manpower Services Commission is known as a Jobcentre. There is one in most towns and cities. There is also a Careers Advisory Centre for school and college leavers. Employers may notify Jobcentres of vacancies they wish to fill.

There are also employment agencies run by private firms. They keep a register of people who are looking for jobs, and put them in touch with firms who have vacancies. There is *no charge* to the people looking for jobs — it is the firms with the vacancies who pay, when the job is taken.

Advertisements in local papers are another source of information about vacancies.

RECEPTIONIST/ TYPIST

Hours 3 p.m.-7 p.m., Monday-Friday evenings; one Saturday morning in four 9 a.m.
1 p.m.
Salary at age 21 plus £2,625 pro rata, per annum. Box 891

Sometimes there is a box number in place of a firm's name, so that the applicant does not know *where* the job is when she applies. The reason for box numbers is to prevent people calling at firms instead of writing in the first place.

Another way of finding out about vacancies is to write to firms and enquire if there are likely to be any in the near future. If you are especially interested in working in a building society, a bank, an estate agent or a travel agent, for instance, the addresses are in the Classified Trade Directory (Yellow Pages) and a letter can be sent to them, with brief details of education etc. Calling personally is not a good idea as firms are too busy to cope with you and you will be politely asked to write in, anyway.

Letter of application

Ideally, this should be typed, but often this is not possible. The letter should, therefore, be written as neatly and clearly as possible, with spelling checked and double-checked! It is a great saving of time and of considerable help to a prospective employer if a letter of application is short, with most of the details set out plainly on a separate sheet. This separate sheet should be headed 'curriculum vitae' (this means 'life history'). Curricula vitae can be duplicated (if possible) or typed with five carbon copies, so that they are ready for sending with letters applying for jobs. These letters (known as 'covering letters' since all the information is on a separate sheet) must be written or typed for each firm applied to. Making carbon copies of curricula vitae, or duplicating them, saves time when several jobs are being applied for, and also avoids the possibility of omitting an important piece of information, but the 'covering letter' must *not* be a carbon copy. This would not give a good impression to the firm reading it.

Application forms

Many firms send these to applicants for jobs, even though full details have been supplied to them on a curriculum vitae. An application form must be completed and returned to the firm as quickly as possible, with a brief 'covering letter' simply stating that the completed application form is enclosed.

Exercise 5

APPLICATION FORM

Copy out the application form opposite and fill it in with your own personal details.

For which of the jobs listed is typing not required?

For which jobs is good English important?

FOR YOUR FOLDER

6. SITUATIONS VACANT

Collect advertisements for office jobs from your local paper and put them in your folder.

EMPLOYMENT APPLICATION FORM (Office Staff)

SURNAME (in CAPITAL letters, please) ....

Forename(s) .... Mr/Mrs/Miss

Address ....

....

Date of birth .... Nationality ....

Education

	Name	From	To
Last school attended	....	....	....
Further education	....	....	....

Examinations passed	Subject	Board	Grade
	....	....	....
	....	....	....
	....	....	....
	....	....	....
	....	....	....
	....	....	....

Previous office experience

Name of firm	Position held	From	To
....	....	....	....
....	....	....	....
....	....	....	....

Any other work experience

....	....	....	....
....	....	....	....

Hobbies and other interests

....

....

Please tick any of the positions below in which you are interested and for which you consider you
would be suitable. Number them in order of interest and suitability.

- ☐ Audio-typist
- ☐ Book-keeper
- ☐ Copy-typist
- ☐ Filing clerk
- ☐ Receptionist
- ☐ Secretary
- ☐ Shorthand-typist
- ☐ Switchboard operator

Signed .... Date ....

The Right Way to Apply for a Job

> JUNIOR TYPIST required for busy office in local firm
> centrally situated. Shorthand not necessary but good standard
> of English essential—'O' level or CSE equivalent. Apply by
> letter to: Office Manager, Millard & Perkins Ltd. St
> Christopher's Trading Estate, Bromswood B95 8BT.

Below you can see how Margaret Atkins applied for this job. She has
typed her letter nicely and sent in a very useful curriculum vitae – so
naturally she hopes to get an interview.

---

8 Rose Crescent
Garden View Estate
BROMSWOOD
Essex
G45 8TA

Telephone: 432 990

30 June 198–

The Office Manager .
Millard & Perkins Ltd
St Christopher's Trading Estate
BROMSWOOD, Essex
G45 5TB

Dear Sir

Re: Vacancy for Junior Typist

I am interested in your advertisement in today's issue of
the "Daily News" for the above vacancy, and enclose
details of my education and training, together with a
photocopy of my latest school report.

I am 16 years of age and have finished my examinations,
so should be able to leave school at any time.

If you would like me to call for an interview, I shall
be pleased to do so on any day and at any time to suit
your convenience.

Yours faithfully

Margaret Atkins

Margaret Atkins (Miss)

Encls

The letter of application

```
Name:      ATKINS Margaret        Nationality:  British

Address:   8 Rose Crescent        Marital status:  Single
           Garden View Estate
           BROMSWOOD
           Essex
           G45 5TB

Tel.       432 990

Date of birth:   16 May 1965

EDUCATION:   St Mary's Comprehensive School, Bromswood.  1976 - 1981

QUALIFICATIONS:     (Examination results not yet known.)
                    'O' Level

                    English
                    Mathematics
                    History
                    Geography

                    CSE

                    Typewriting
                    Office Practice
                    Commerce
                    Home Economics

EXPERIENCE:   Working on Saturdays for Nevinson's Stationers, High St,
              Bromswood - typing envelopes, filing, helping in the shop
              at busy times. Also dealing with incoming and outgoing post
              and paying money into the bank.

              From August 1980 to the present day.

HOBBIES:      Swimming, gymnastics, hockey, cooking.

OTHER INTERESTS:   Raising money for muscular dystrophy (have helped to
              organise a sponsored walk), disco-dancing.

REFERENCES:   These may be obtained from:

              Headmistress                    The Manager
              St Mary's Comprehensive School  Nevinson's Stationers
              Bromswood                       High Street
                                              Bromswood
```

A curriculum vitae

Interviews

Many applications for jobs do not result in an interview. One of the reasons is that the applicant has not read the advertisement properly and has applied for a job for which she is totally unsuitable. Points to check especially are: age, experience, skills needed. The other main reason for no interview following a letter of application is that the letter was badly spelt and untidily written and set out or did not supply the information requested (unlike the one written by Margaret Atkins!).

BEFORE AN INTERVIEW

If you are successful with your application and receive a letter asking you to attend for an interview, there are several things which will improve your chances of success before you even set out:

1) Find out what you can about the firm – its history, what it makes or what it does, when it was founded, how many people it employs etc. (The local library may have some books or they may be able to help if you ask an assistant. Alternatively you may be able to talk to someone already working at the firm.)

2) Locate the building beforehand, so that you know exactly where it is, and find the main entrance and the reception area. This will save valuable time on the day of the interview.

3) Check bus and/or train times making sure that you will arrive near the firm with time to spare. You can always 'kill time' near the firm taking a walk or having a cup of coffee in a snack bar.

4) Make a list of suitable questions to ask your interviewer – his job is to try and get you to talk to him so that he can find out more about your personality; he already has the basic facts in your letter of application and curriculum vitae. Some topics for you to ask about could be:

- What other duties would be involved besides typing
- What sort of typewriter – electric or manual
- Any possibility of further training or day release
- Pension scheme
- Promotion and pay increases – on merit or automatically
- Welfare and medical service
- Social activities and sports clubs
- Canteen
- Hours of work
- Holidays
- Pay (if not mentioned by interviewer – this is why you are going to work, after all).

Before an interview try to think of the questions you may be asked. One question frequently asked is 'Why do you want to come and work here?' A sensible answer to this might be 'I have always been interested in banking (or travel, or whatever the firm's type of business is)'. Another question will almost certainly be about any hobbies or special interests mentioned on your curriculum vitae, so it is important to be honest when mentioning these and not just to try and impress. It's no good, for example, listing 'horse-riding' if the only time you mount a horse is once a year when you're staying with a friend, or 'reading' if you only glance through weekly magazines.

Finally, on the day of the interview:

- Dress carefully – smart but not startling and above all, comfortable.

- If it's a hot day, wear something loose and cool in preference to a very new outfit which is really too heavy for a summer's day.
- If it's very cold, wrap up warmly – arriving looking blue and shivering will not create a good impression.
- Wear comfortable shoes – those 4" heels are fine for the evening but not for tottering into a strange building with unfamiliar stairs and (possibly) polished floors.
- Pay especial attention to hair, hands, shoes and tights.
- Be prepared for a typing test and take with you typewriter eraser and a backing sheet; a ruler may be useful.
- Take the letter asking you to come to the interview with you.

DURING THE INTERVIEW

The interviewer's job is to make you feel at ease, so you will be pleasantly surprised to find that you stop feeling nervous quite soon. Sit down when you are asked to do so. Talk naturally and avoid 'you know' – nervous people often use this phrase out of sheer fright. At the end of the interview, the interviewer will usually say 'we will let you know' – it is not often that a decision is given there and then. If you decide that you don't want the job anyway, don't say so – you might change your mind later on, or the job may not even be offered. Thank your interviewer for seeing you and say 'Goodbye' with a smile – the last impression is just as important as the first.

Making you feel welcome

SUCCESS OR FAILURE?

If you receive the long-awaited letter offering you a job, reply at once by letter accepting it, or, tell them you have decided not to accept it, if that is the case. You may receive a letter telling you you have not been successful. If so, do not be too discouraged – every interview and interviewer is different and adds to your experience. Next time you will have a great deal more confidence.

FOR YOUR FOLDER

7. FINDING A JOB

Write these notes in your folder, filling in the missing words and phrases.

1) A 'curriculum vitae' is a _____.

2) It is useful to have several ready to send with letters of application for jobs because _____ and _____.

3) Questions may be asked at an interview about hobbies or interests listed in a curriculum vitae so it is important to be _____.

4) Before attending for an interview, it is a good plan to find out what you can about a firm, visit it beforehand to locate it exactly and _____ so that you will not be late.

5) A list of suitable questions to ask the interviewer could include:

   a _____
   b _____
   c _____
   d _____
   e _____

6) You may be given a typing test as part of an interview for a typist's job. It will create a good impression if you take with you _____ _____.

7) It is also important to have with your letter _____.

8) At the conclusion of an interview, you should _____ – the last impression is just as important as the first.

9) If an important letter arrives offering you the job you should _____.

10) If after all you have decided you do not want the job, you should _____.

Exercise 6

QUESTIONS ON FINDING A JOB

1) There are several ways of finding out about job vacancies. Explain three of them.

2) What is a 'box number' and why do firms use them?

3) On Margaret's curriculum vitae (p. 35) she gave 'date of birth' and not her age. Why was this?

4) What was the distinction between her 'hobbies' and 'other interests'?

5) Why did she include two names of people to whom application could be made for references?

6) Write a letter to the Office Manager, Millard & Perkins Ltd, accepting the post in the advertisement.

7) Write a letter to the Office Manager, Millard & Perkins Ltd, explaining that you do not wish to accept the post. You do not have to give a reason.

8) Write a letter to the Office Manager, Millard & Perkins Ltd, in reply to his asking you to come for an interview on Monday 1 July 198—, explaining that you are ill and unable to come on that day, but would be pleased to come a week later.

9) Draw a map showing the way to a firm in your town, marking any landmarks such as a river, bridges, cathedral, railway and bus stations, with bus and train times.

10) Find out what you can about this same firm on the lines suggested in this chapter, and type (or write) it out in a suitable form to take with you to an interview (A5 paper, so that you could slip it into pocket or handbag for quick reference during an interview if needed).

Starting Work

CONTRACT OF EMPLOYMENT

If you are offered a job, you will sooner or later get a contract of employment.

This may be in the form of a letter of appointment, or it may be oral, in which case the terms of appointment must be set out in the form of a notice on the wall of the office, so that employees are aware of the conditions of their contract of employment.

The contract of employment must set out the following details and must be supplied by your employer within 13 weeks of your starting the job:
- Rates of pay (and whether paid weekly or monthly)
- Hours of work
- Sick pay
- Pension
- Holidays and holiday pay
- Length of notice to be given by either side
- The right to belong to a trade union of choice
- The right *not* to belong to a trade union
- The person to whom a grievance can be made
- Date of commencement of employment.

The minimum periods of notice which must be given to employees are based on length of service:

After four weeks' service – one week's notice *and then*
one week's notice for each completed year of service up to a maximum of 12 weeks' notice.

THE FIRST DAY

Your first day in an office is very important, and also rather alarming to contemplate. It helps to get ready the evening before. What to wear should be decided, clothes laid out, shoes cleaned, and alarm clock set – it would never do to be late on the first morning!

Many firms have what is known as an induction course for new employees.

An induction course is actually an introduction to the firm, its departments and its organisation and procedures. Many firms have a printed handbook which will be given to you to keep with all this information contained in it.

An induction course will normally occupy most of the first morning, so it will be after lunch before you get down to finding out what you actually have to do in the firm's office where you are to work. By this time you will have found out where the canteen is, where the cloakrooms are and whether you clock in and out when you leave. It is also important to remember where the sick room is, in case you feel ill at any time. Some firms arrange a medical inspection for each new employee, either just before or just after they start work.

WHAT TO TAKE WITH YOU

A National Insurance number is necessary for your first job and this is obtainable from the Department of Health and Social Security. Your National Insurance contributions will be deducted along with your income tax by your employer. If you have not worked before, you will not have a P45 form, which is a record of income tax deducted by your previous employer. You will be given an emergency code until your income tax form (Claim for Allowances) has been completed by you (see Chapter 16).

You will be introduced to the person to whom you will be responsible and who will tell you what your duties will be. An office junior, straight from school, without any training in office routine or typewriting, may be shown how to collect the mail from the other offices and take it to the mail room. She may be given messages to take around the firm (so it is important to remember how to find your way around); she may be shown how to collect filing and pre-sort it (see Chapter 12); she may make tea or coffee for other people in the office – or fetch it from vending machines for them. One day a week may be spent at the local college learning to type and write shorthand – this is a 'day-release course'. The firm itself may run a training section of its own.

CLOTHES AND MAKE-UP

The right clothes give you confidence. This is particularly important for a new job. Also, an outfit must be comfortable when you are going to wear it all day.

All large firms have centrally heated offices and it is not necessary to wear thick clothes indoors, in the winter.

Trousers, well-pressed and part of a matched outfit look smart, but any old jeans and T-shirt will *not* do.

Warm summer days may have chilly mornings, so a cool dress with a matching jacket is useful.

Long skirts *look* pretty and feminine but can easily cause an accident while going up or down stairs carrying files.

High heels and platform soles can also cause accidents. Besides, they are tiring to wear all day, especially as some office jobs involve hours of standing or walking. A spare pair of shoes with lower heels kept at the office may be the answer to the footwear problem.

What is wrong? Why did she fall?

Jewellery worn to the office should be simple and inexpensive.

Leave anything really precious at home. Long dangly ear-rings or necklaces may be caught up in typewriters or other equipment which could be dangerous.

Hands and nails are conspicuous when typing, answering the telephone or filing, and should be well-cared for. Dark nail varnish is attractive but it must be unchipped and perfect (all part of the good grooming). A paler vanish is easier to keep in a good state of repair as it needs replacing less often. Filing nails a little shorter than usual is sensible as this avoids tearing them on a typewriter or other office equipment.

Scent is pleasant – in moderation. A light toilet water and matching talc is ideal.

Personal freshness should be an automatic part of the day's grooming routine, but it is worth remembering that in a centrally heated office during a busy day, a deodorant may need re-applying.

A spare make-up kit containing everything necessary for a quick repair job to face and nails should be kept in your office drawer. This, together with aspirins, tissues, plasters, needle, cotton and scissors, and a spare pair of tights, will enable you to cope with most minor emergencies, as well as that exciting unexpected date!

Good grooming is essential, and a simple, basic plan is a great help, because it means you arrive at the office looking your best *every* morning. Spending the first 15 minutes in the cloakroom putting on make-up is not a good idea – it is no better than arriving late at the office – and will soon get you a reputation for being slack.

Hair should be shining clean and if short or medium length, well-cut so that it looks its best with very little trouble. If it is long, experiment with taking it up, or back, so that it does not obscure your view during the day.

Finally, a word for young men. A jacket, trousers, shirt with collar and tie are the right wear in an office, with the alternative of a polo-necked sweater under a jacket if the weather is wintry. Shoes must shine, please!

Jeans and T-shirts are *not* suitable.

Not an ideal hair-style for a typist!

FOR YOUR FOLDER

8. OFFICE CLOTHES

Either: trace a winter and summer outfit from a magazine

or: (if you can draw) design a summer and winter outfit.

Complete all these drawings with suitable shoes for wearing in an office.

Some Do's and Don'ts

Do Arrive a little early – this helps you to feel calm and relaxed.

Do Try to learn your way around a firm as quickly as possible. Draw a rough plan of the various buildings and write their names on it.

Do Try to remember people's correct names and titles. Use names when you say 'good morning' or 'good afternoon'. It sounds polite and efficient.

Do Make sure you do everything you have been asked to do before you go home. Keep a little notebook so that you can jot down any points you may forget, and cross each job off as it is completed. This will avoid anything being overlooked.

Do Keep your desk, desk drawers and area around you neat and tidy, not like the office squirrel below. You cannot work in a clutter nor can you find anything quickly when you are asked for it.

Clocking in

The office squirrel!

Don't

Be a clock watcher and vanish at the first stroke of the hour you are allowed to leave. Finish off any work which you know may be needed. Some firms operate what is known as flexible working hours and you are able to 'save' extra time and take a half-day off when you have sufficient time in the 'bank' (there is more information about this on p. 45. To operate this system it is necessary to clock in and clock out so that your employer knows exactly when you arrived and when you left.

Don't Gossip. What you hear may not be true and will only hurt someone's feelings if they hear it.

Don't Criticise. If you can't think of anything nice to say, say nothing. This is known as 'being tactful'!

Don't   Take your troubles with you to the office. Try to forget them and concentrate on your job. You may find that by the time you go home your problems will not seem nearly as bad as they did in the morning.

Don't   Sit and look bored when you have finished all the work you have been given to do. Keep busy by cleaning your typewriter or tidying desk drawers. Later on, when you are more experienced, you will be able to see what else needs doing, without being told. This is known as 'using your initiative'!

Don't   Forget to let your employer know, before 9 o'clock if possible, that you will not be coming to the office (if you are ill, for instance). This is known as 'being polite'!

Don't   Regard small items of stationery, such as pencils, ball-point pens, envelopes, erasers, rubber bands, paper clips, or typing paper, supplied to you at the office, as being yours to take home.

Don't   Be disloyal to your employer. This means that you do not discuss what you may consider to be his faults with anyone, either in the firm or outside it.

Exercise 7

CROSSWORD ON STARTING WORK

Make a copy of the crossword square below and see if you can solve it.

Across

1   You may be wearing the wrong kind of shoes if your feet _____ (4)

3   Some firms require their workers to clock _____ and out (2)

5   Hands and _____ are so much on view they must be well-cared for (5)

6   People who criticise without thought _____ tactless (3)

7   If you have work to do when it is time to go home _____ a little later to get it done (4)

10   Spending the first 15 minutes of each morning in the cloakroom to put on make-up is as bad as arriving _____ (4)

11   As well (4)

Down

2   Taking home small items of stationery is not _____ (6)

3   If you are _____ you must let your employer know (3)

4   Arrive at the office a few minutes _____ if you want to start the day calm (5)

8   It may be your job to make this! (3)

9   Should long hair be styled so that it is off the face in an office? (3)

Flexible Working Hours

This is a system whereby office workers can vary their starting and finishing times to suit their own convenience, so long as they work an agreed minimum number of hours per week. They may prefer to start early (0800 hours) and finish early (1600) to fit in with family commitments (children at school, for example) or start later (1000) and finish later (1800) to avoid rush-hour traffic.

There are usually periods when all workers have to be in the office. One is in the morning (perhaps 1000–1200) and the other in the afternoon (perhaps 1400–1600). These periods are known as 'core time'. The lunch hour may be taken at any time between the two core periods. Different workers may choose different lunch hours so that, for instance, the reception desk always has someone in attendance (see pp. 57–8).

Time may be 'banked' by working overtime – hours in addition to the agreed minimum and half-days taken by arrangement with the firm. Banked time is generally limited to a certain number of hours per week.

Clocking in and out is an essential part of flexible working hours in order to keep an accurate record of time actually spent in the office.

Flexible working hours have proved to be popular with office workers, especially women, who are able to fit in working time with looking after school-age children and shopping. They are also popular with office workers who travel long distances as they can fit in travelling time with less busy periods on rail or road.

FOR YOUR FOLDER

9. FLEXIBLE WORKING HOURS

Write these notes in your folder, filling in the missing words and phrases.

1) Flexible working hours is a system whereby office workers can _____ their starting and finishing times to suit their own convenience.

2) They have to work an agreed _____ per week.

3) The period of time when all workers have to be in the office is known as _____ time.

4) By working overtime, it is possible to _____ time which can then be taken in half-days off, by agreement with the firm.

5) An essential part of flexible working hours is _____ in and _____ out, in order to keep an accurate record of hours actually spent at work.

6) Flexible working hours are popular with married women who work in offices because they are able to fit in _____ with working time.

7) Flexible working hours are also popular with people who _____ long distances.

Trade Unions

THE TRADE UNION AND THE INDIVIDUAL

If you go to work for a large firm, where a particular trade union is represented, you may be asked to join that union by the union representative who also works for the firm — his wages are paid by his employer, not by the trade union. He (or she) is elected as a representative by the trade union members. The representative is known as a shop steward, and he is the link between the union and its members at that particular workplace. He will give you details of subscriptions and rights and privileges which you are entitled to. He is also the person to whom you should complain if you feel that your pay and/or conditions of work need to be improved. The shop steward will also keep you informed of union policy as it affects you.

As a union member you will be attached to a local 'branch' of the union. Here you may make your views known about any aspect of your local working conditions to the branch officials. A vote is taken on all issues and decisions discussed at the branch meeting, with the majority view being accepted.

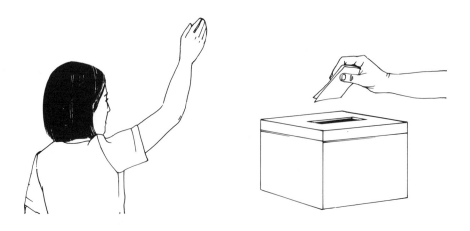

Two ways of voting

Many offices, particularly the small ones employing just a few people, may not have any union representative. In fact, none of the people who work in small offices may ever belong to a trade union. Whether you belong to a trade union is usually a matter of your choice, but there are a few exceptions.

In some companies the union to which most of the employees belong may negotiate an agreement with the employer that he will not engage anyone unless that person is prepared to join the union. This is known commonly as a 'closed shop' agreement. Usually such agreements are made by particular craft unions so that office workers (typists, shorthand-typists, receptionists) may not be affected by such a closed shop agreement. In any case, it is possible to refuse to join a union on religious or conscientious grounds, and if neither of these apply and you do not wish to join a union, you simply find a job elsewhere — whether to join a union or not is a matter for the individual to decide.

DISPUTES

If a dispute or disagreement arises between an employer and members of a union working at that particular place, the union members concerned may be called upon to 'strike' — that is, withdraw their labour from that particular employer. It sometimes happens that only members of a particular union withdraw their labour — other colleagues who may belong to a different union, but work at the same place, may continue to work. If the dispute is regarded as very serious by all the unions represented in a firm, then all the workers are called out on strike, irrespective of which union they may belong to. In all circumstances of strikes, any person who does not belong to a union has the right to go to work at his place of employment, even though some of his colleagues may try to persuade him not to work by means of 'picketing' which simply involves using 'peaceful persuasion' at the entrance to the firm.

In many cases disputes arise, and workers may be called upon to strike by a shop steward, which they are expected to do. Nevertheless, until the union's senior officials approve of strike action, the strike is 'unofficial'. Some strikes take place, are settled and never become officially recognised. Others may start as unofficial strikes and become official later on when senior officials of the union engage in 'negotiation' (discussions between union and management of the firm).

Usually strikes are settled by negotiation between the employer and trade union representatives, but in the occasional cases where a settlement cannot be reached, both sides may agree to refer the facts to the government's Advisory, Conciliation, and Arbitration Service (ACAS).

Officials of ACAS listen, separately, to each side and suggest some common grounds for discussion in order to end the strike.

If ACAS cannot end the dispute, the government may appoint an independent body to negotiate and to make recommendations for a settlement.

There are trade unions for professional people (doctors, lawyers, teachers), for particular trades (engineers, construction workers, plumbers, electricians) and for particular types of workers in industry and office work (railway workers, shop workers, miners, local government officers, civil servants, public employees and health service workers). There are also unions which cater for those whose work does not fall into a particular group but is of a more general nature – the Transport and General Workers Union and the Municipal and General Workers Union. These last two unions can look after the interests of clerical workers, secretaries and other office workers. The number of different unions is quite large.

Many trade unions include what is known as a 'political levy' as a separate part of the union subscription. This means that the political levy is sent to finance the funds of a political party that the union supports – usually the Labour Party. If you want to support union principles but do not agree with its politics, you may 'opt out' of paying the political levy. The trade union representative should make this clear to you before you join.

Types of Trade Unions

WHITE COLLAR AND BLUE COLLAR UNIONS

These are general descriptions of professional, supervisory and clerical workers' unions, in the case of white collar unions.

Blue collar unions cover the craftsmen and other manual workers' unions.

FOR YOUR FOLDER

10. TRADE UNIONS

Write these notes in your folder, filling in the missing words and phrases.

1) The trade union representative in a firm is known as the _____.

2) As a trade union member you will be attached to a local _____ of the union.

3) A 'closed shop' agreement means that the employer has agreed not to employ anyone except _____.

4) It is possible to decline to join a union on _____ or conscientious grounds.

5) Any person who does not belong to a union has the right to go to work at his place of employment even though some of his colleagues may try to persuade him not to work by means of _____ which simply means peaceful _____ at the firm's entrance.

6) Workers may be called upon to strike by a shop steward, but until the union's senior officials approve of the strike, it is _____.

7) When a strike cannot be settled by discussion between trade union representatives and management, the facts may be referred to a government body called _____.

8) Two unions which look after the interests of clerical workers are _____ and _____.

9) The separate part of a subscription to a trade union which is sent as a contribution to a political party's funds is known as a _____ _____.

10) It is not compulsory to pay this separate part if you want to support trade union _____ but do not agree with its politics.

Exercise 8

QUESTIONS ON TRADE UNIONS

1) Explain the meaning of a 'closed shop'.

2) What is the difference between an 'official strike' and an 'unofficial strike'?

3) What is the role of ACAS in connection with strikes?

4) What is the connection between trade unions and the Labour Party? Explain how it is possible to join a trade union and yet not wish to support the Labour Party.

5) When starting work in a firm where there is a trade union which looks after the interests of clerical workers, explain how you would make enquiries about joining.

SECTION B COMMUNICATIONS AND INFORMATION

CHAPTER 4

The Receptionist

Duties and Appearance

The receptionist's main job is to look after the visitors to a firm. She will, however, have time during the day when there are no callers, to do other work. She may:

- Type
- Operate a switchboard
- File
- Give out brochures and handbooks issued by her firm
- Open and arrange for distribution of mail; receive parcels, and registered or recorded delivery mail
- Help with making tea or coffee for visitors – as it is essential that the reception desk is never left unattended, many firms have vending machines so that callers are able to help themselves to refreshments.
- Be able to give simple first aid, when necessary.

Alternatively, there may be two receptionists – the head receptionist and her deputy – so that the reception desk is never left unmanned.

Visitors to a firm must never be kept waiting unnecessarily. They may go elsewhere if they are, and not return. Valuable business could be lost to the firm.

All large firms (and organisations such as universities, hospitals, colleges, local authorities) have receptionists. In addition, many small firms find their services very useful too – estate agents, accountants, solicitors, as well as doctors and dentists. In fact, almost any office where an appointments system makes the most efficient use of people's time.

A good receptionist should be:
- Polite
- Friendly
- Helpful
- Tactful
- Calm (above all, patient!)
- Neat
- Smart
- Well-groomed (hair, nails, make-up)

- Well-informed about her firm's products, layout and staff, so that she can direct visitors to the right offices, and answer any questions they may ask her.

The receptionist's voice is particularly important; it should be pleasant and clear. Some visitors may be foreigners and have difficulty understanding English.

Reception work is not suitable for shy people. A receptionist must be able to get on easily with strangers.

Generally speaking, an ideal receptionist should be aged 20 or over. She will have sufficient experience by then to be both confident and efficient at her job.

Types of Caller

CALLERS WHO HAVE MADE APPOINTMENTS might include:
- Applicants to be interviewed for vacant jobs
- Sales representatives
- Businessmen from other firms attending meetings
- Visitors from other firms, both in the UK and from overseas.

CALLERS WITHOUT APPOINTMENTS could be:
- People enquiring about vacancies for jobs
- Customers who have come to complain about the firm's goods
- Sales representatives hoping to see the chief buyer or a member of his staff.

REGULAR CALLERS NORMALLY WITHOUT APPOINTMENTS
- Postmen
- Security van drivers delivering cash for wages
- Delivery men from other firms
- Roadline delivery men
- British Rail (BR) delivery men
- Window cleaners, telephone disinfectant service staff, suppliers of pot plants
- People delivering letters and parcels from other firms by hand.

UNEXPECTED CALLERS WITHOUT APPOINTMENTS

These should be asked politely if they would like to write in for one. If they refuse to leave without making an appointment, the receptionist should telephone the secretary of the person the caller is hoping to see, and ask her when an appointment can be made.

Occasionally, callers insist on seeing the person they want without having made an appointment, and refuse to leave. This is where all the tact and patience of the receptionist is required. She should emphasise to the caller that the person he insists on seeing is at an important meeting and will not be available for several hours, or, alternatively, that he has gone to a meeting at another firm. Finally, if the caller still refuses to go, the receptionist should telephone the firm's security police, who will come and escort the caller out, but this is only as a last resort and, if the receptionist knows her job, should not be necessary.

Callers who have to wait because of an unavoidable delay should be looked after in the reception area, offered tea or coffee, and reassured from time to time that they have not been forgotten.

What to do if all else fails!

Greeting Callers and Dealing with Visiting Cards

Using a person's name is friendly and makes a caller feel welcome. The receptionist's name should be either on a brooch pinned to her dress or on a stand in front of her, so that callers can see her name at a glance and use it at once. The receptionist's first question to a caller should be to ask his or her name and then use it. Many businessmen have business visiting cards and will give one to the receptionist. Business visiting cards have the caller's name, his home address and telephone number, the caller's firm, firm's address and telephone number printed on them. Sometimes a card also gives information about the firm's products. The information on the business visiting card saves the receptionist asking the caller a great many questions. It also helps her to introduce the caller to anyone in the firm who may not know him.

Usually, business visiting cards (callers' cards) are left with the receptionist and she files them away in alphabetical order of the firms' names. Then, next time a caller comes whom the receptionist recognises, she is able to look up his business visiting card and refer to it for information.

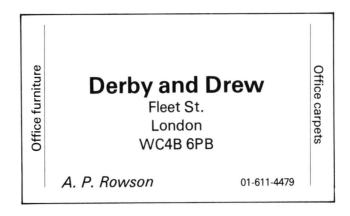

A business card

A card index box is useful for filing business visiting cards. They should be glued or taped to an index card, which makes them easier to handle and find. Business visiting cards form a useful record of callers and can be referred to for names and addresses for sending out advertising material.

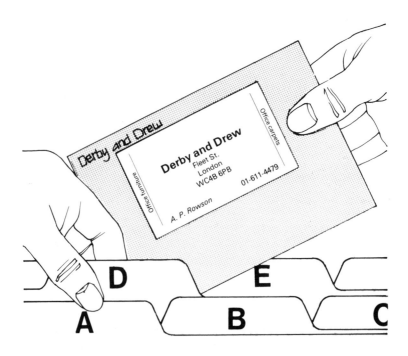

Filing a business card

Note that the above card is being filed under the name of the firm and not the name of the caller. This is because firms rarely change their names, whereas their employees frequently change their jobs, so it is easier for a receptionist to refer to a firm rather than to someone employed by a firm.

The Receptionist's Desk

In some firms, the receptionist may have a switchboard to look after. In all firms, she will have two telephones: one for internal calls; and the other for external calls. The latest telephones, however, incorporate external and internal lines in one instrument. She may also have a typewriter and a filing cabinet. She will also have her own records, consisting of:

● An index of callers' cards
● Records of callers (callers' register and appointments book)
● A staff 'in and out' book.

Her name may be on her desk in front of her (or on a brooch which she pins to her dress).

She will have a plan of the firm on the wall behind her.

She will also have an organisation chart on the wall. This gives the names of the directors and managers of her firm.

The receptionist's desk should be near to the main entrance of a firm, so that callers are able to find it easily. The picture below shows how an efficient, well-organised receptionist has planned her desk and office equipment.

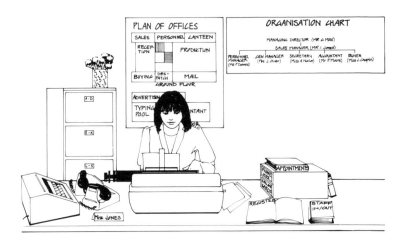

An efficient receptionist who is well-organised

FOR YOUR FOLDER

11. THE RECEPTIONIST AND HER DUTIES

Write these notes in your folder, filling in the missing words and phrases.

1) The receptionist's *main* job is to _____ after callers at a firm.

2) When there are no callers, the receptionist may have other duties such as:

    a _____.
    b _____.
    c _____.
    d _____.
    e _____.

3) The receptionist may be given a caller's card from which she can learn the _____.

4) Other information on a caller's card may be _____.

5) The receptionist will file caller's cards (business visiting cards) in alphabetical order of _____ names.

Exercise 9

QUESTIONS ON THE RECEPTIONIST AND HER DUTIES

1) Why is a receptionist important to a firm?

2) What effect might a 'couldn't-care-less' attitude have on callers?

3) Why is it important that a receptionist is well-informed about her firm's layout, products and staff?

4) What are the three different types of callers?

5) What sort of callers who call at a firm regularly would not normally have appointments?

6) Where should a receptionist have her name displayed?

7) Why is it important to use a person's name as soon as possible?

8) What is the correct procedure for dealing with a caller who arrives without an appointment?

9) What are the two important uses of business visiting cards?

10) What information does an organisation chart give?

11) Receptionists are employed by doctors, dentists, hotels, colleges, opticians and veterinaries. What is the ideal age for a receptionist and what type of person should she be?

12) Where should the receptionist's desk be situated?

13) What is the correct way to look after a caller who may have to wait in the reception area for a rather long time?

14) Look at the advertisement below and answer the questions about it.

WANTED: RECEPTIONIST/TELEPHONIST for large firm manufacturing domestic goods. Training will be given on a switchboard. Experience not essential but applicant must be able to type and have a pleasant personality and good telephone manner. Apply in writing to: Personnel Manager, Willis and Lever Ltd, 185 The Parade, Cricksville.

---

a Would this vacancy appeal to you if you were looking for a job?

b Do you think you would be suitable before having had some experience?

c What do you think is meant by a 'good telephone manner'?

d What sort of typing do you think the receptionist would do?

59

The Receptionist's Reference Books

The receptionist will often need to have reference books to help deal with visitors' enquiries. There is more about this in Chapter 8, especially on p. 158.

The Receptionist's Records

CALLERS' REGISTER

One of the other record books which the receptionist looks after is the *callers' register*. All callers to a firm sign this, with the exception of such callers as postmen and delivery men.

A callers' register shows the name of the caller, his firm or his home address, the time he arrived, who he saw in the firm, and whether he made a further appointment. Opposite is a page from a callers' register, showing the callers at a firm on the morning of 21 November 198—.

Under the heading 'Action Taken' are details about callers who arrived without appointments. This column shows that the usual way to deal with such callers is to ask them to write in for an appointment.

Occasionally, a caller refuses to leave without either seeing the person he wants, or having made an appointment. In either of these cases, the receptionist should telephone the secretary concerned and ask to make an appointment.

Exercise 10

CALLERS' REGISTER

Now rule up a copy of the callers' register page, leaving it blank except for headings, and fill in with the following information. Use today's date.

1) Mr James Brookes of S & J Electronics came at 1030 to see Mr J Ellis, managing director. He made another appointment on his way out for the same time and day next week.

2) Mr S Holmes, Mr A Simpson and Miss W Keene arrived at 1130. They all had appointments to see Mr H Long, the sales manager. All three callers were from Twist, Swindle & Dunnem, Chartered Accountants, Wordsworth Avenue, Champton.

3) Miss T Taplow, Office Equipment Supplies Ltd, Blacking, arrived to see Mr Jones the buyer at 1200, by appointment.

4) Mr C Vernon, Cast Iron Casting Co Ltd called at 1215 in the hope of seeing Mr G Kerr, production manager. He is writing in for an appointment.

CALLERS' REGISTER

DATE 198–	NAME OF CALLER	CALLER'S FIRM OR HOME ADDRESS	TIME OF ARRIVAL	SEEN BY	ACTION TAKEN
Nov. 21	L.M. Parkins	J. Mann + Co. Ltd.	09.00	K. Jones – Buyer	
	Mrs H. Simms	18 Hilary Ave. Worcester	09 45	No appointment	Writing to Personnel Officer with details.
	B.N. Yines	Carson Engineering	09 50	Personnel Manager	
	Miss A.B. Tomkins	44 Scott Cresc. Evesham	10.00	No appointment	Personnel Man's assistant seeing her on 28/11 at 10.00
	Miss K. Lyons	219 Lake Ave. Worcester	10 30	Personnel Manager	
	F. Parkins	Benson's Export Co.	10 35	Accounts Dept.	Made further appointment to see Chief Cashier 23/11
	Mrs A. Drew	Wilchester Technical College	11 00	Personnel Manager	
	P. Lester	Pejecta Paper Co.	11 05	No appointment	Appointment made to see K. Jones's assistant
	J.R. Smart	39 Market Place	11 20	No appointment	Writing to Production Manager with details
	Mrs W. Moxon	Office Equipment Supplies	11 30	Miss B. Burton Typing Pool Supervisor	
	Miss T. Baker	89 The Grove, Droitwich	12.00	No appointment	Writing to miss Burton with details
	B.M. Townsend	Bellevue Car Hire Co.	12 15	Transport officer	

61

APPOINTMENTS BOOK

This is used to record all future appointments and is used by the receptionist to see who is expected each day, and also to give future appointments to callers who arrive without one, or who have to make an additional appointment on leaving a firm.

A page from the appointments book for 21 November 198— would look like this.

Monday 21 November 198–			
NAME OF CALLER	**FIRM**	**TIME OF ARRIVAL**	**TO SEE**
Mr. L. M. Parkins	J. Mann + Co.	09 00	Mr K Jones
Mr. B. N. Vines	Carson Engineering	09 50	Personnel Manager
Miss K. Lyons	219 Lake Avenue	10 30	"
Mr. F. Perkins	Peterson's Export Co.	10 35	Accounts
Mrs. A. Drew	Wilchester Technical College	11 00	Personnel Manager
Mrs. W. Moxon	Office Equipment (Supplies)	11 30	Miss B. Burton Typing Pool
Mr B. M. Townsend	Bellevue Car Hire	12 30	Transport Officer

Rule up a copy of this page for an appointments book, leaving out the names and other details, and fill it in with the page from the callers' register which you have just completed.

STAFF 'IN AND OUT' BOOK

Another important record book which would be the receptionist's responsibility is a staff 'in and out' book. In this, all staff working in the firm write the reasons for going out of the firm during working hours, with their names, time of leaving and date. They also sign again when they return, writing down the time they returned. This book provides a record of staff absences, so that the receptionist can tell at a glance who has gone out of the firm. It is a much more efficient system than leaving notes or messages, which are easily lost. Where a firm operates flexible working hours, it may not be necessary although it is still useful to know *where* staff have gone, as well as *when*.

Exercise 11

STAFF 'IN AND OUT' BOOK

Following is a page from a staff 'in and out' book for 1 March 198—.

DATE	NAME	DEPT	TIME OUT	TIME IN	REASON

Rule up a similar page and complete it correctly from the following information:

1) Miss R Rhodes, wages, went out to the bank at 0930 and returned at 1000.

2) Miss V Marr went to the Post Office at 1100 and returned at 1120.

3) Mr L Moore, buying, left at 1430 to fly to Germany.

4) Mrs W Thompson went home ill at 1600.

5) Miss B Crowle left at 1635 for a doctor's appointment.

MESSAGES

The receptionist's duties include taking messages, and passing them on, verbally as well as in writing. It is very important that these messages are passed on immediately. A special message form is a help, as it reminds her not to forget to ask for any vital item of information before caller has gone.

MESSAGE FORM

Date. . . . . Time. . . . . For. . . . .
From. . . . .
Address. . . . .
Telephone No. . . . . Extension No. . . . .

Message (telephone/personal—cross out whichever does not apply)
. . . .
. . . .
. . . .
. . . .
. . . .

Taken by . . . .

Exercise 12

WRITING A MESSAGE

Use the form above to pass on the following details. Mrs D Knowles called to see Miss Burton, typing pool supervisor, on an important matter. Mrs Knowles would not make an appointment, but said she would like Miss Burton to telephone her at home after 7 pm today. Mrs Knowles' address is: 226 Ashtree Avenue, Boyston, and her telephone number is Boyston 886555. Sign the message form yourself, and date it for today, adding the time at which you are writing the message.

PASSING ON MESSAGES

Messages must be delivered as soon as possible. As the receptionist cannot leave her desk, she must ask her relief or her assistant to deliver the messages for her. Alternatively, she may be able to ask one of the firm's messengers to take her messages. Sometimes firms' messengers are young school-leavers, or they can be older, retired men or ex-service men. Their job is to take messages, letters, parcels, etc. around a firm.

If there are no firm's messengers, the receptionist would have to telephone through to the secretary of the manager concerned, and ask her to send someone to collect the message.

A copy of each message should be filed in date order, each day's messages then being arranged in alphabetical order of the *surname* of the person *to whom the message is addressed.* This is in case of a query later on. Carbon copies could be made (on a typewriter or by hand) or photocopies taken of any very important messages.

The Reception Area

GIVING A GOOD IMPRESSION

This is where visitors to a firm wait, either because they have arrived too early for an appointment, or the person they have called to see may be unexpectedly delayed.

It is important that the reception area gives visitors a good impression because it is quite often the first part of a firm they see, and if it is not welcoming and comfortable, they may decide to transfer their business to another firm.

KEEPING TIDY

The first things visitors notice on arrival may well be your own desk and equipment. The receptionist at the top of the page opposite is *not* likely to create a good impression. Can you see why?

How many things can you find wrong with this reception area?

A COMFORTABLE DESIGN FOR THE VISITOR

As well as being warm in winter, cool in summer, well lit and attractively decorated, the reception area should have comfortable chairs for the visitors, and it may also offer amenities such as vending machines for refreshments and cigarettes, toilets, payphone, coin changing machine, stamp machine and many other conveniences. Below is an assignment on designing a reception area, but first of all here is a picture of what the area near your desk should *not* look like. It is too small, visitors have nowhere to sit, and the receptionist has allowed a telephone conversation to go on for so long that a queue has formed.

'Shall be here for hours – shan't bother to wait.'

A badly organised reception area. How many things are wrong?

Exercise 13

DESIGNING A RECEPTION AREA

Trace the drawing of the reception area opposite, which is carpeted, heated, lighted, but is otherwise bare.

Then trace the items below which would help to make a reception area more comfortable and attractive to visitors who have to wait for a short time.

Cut out your tracings neatly and glue them into appropriate places on your drawing. When the glue has dried, colour your reception area suitably.

Then on a separate sheet of paper make a list of everything in your reception area, under the heading 'An Ideal Reception Area'.

The assignment will be graded according to the neatness of your design and how well you make your list. After you have finished this assignment compare your design with that on p. 70.

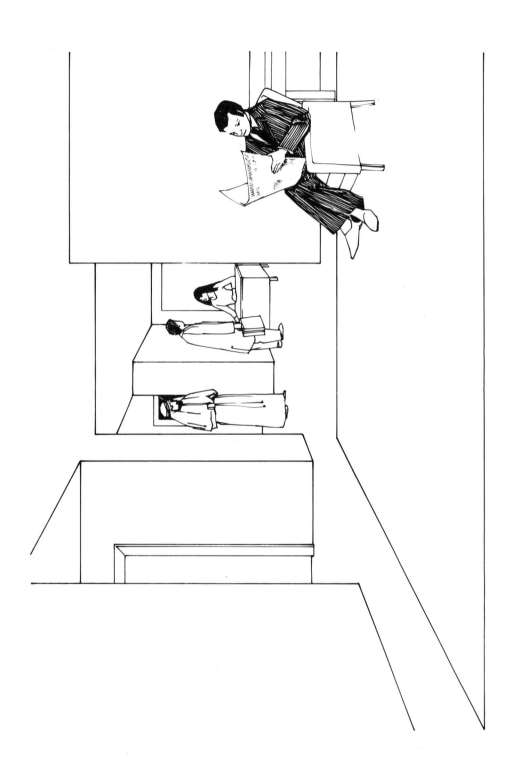

CHAPTER 5

Telecommunications

Answering the Telephone and Dealing with Messages

Always pick up the telephone receiver with the hand you do not normally write with. This will make it easier for you to write down a message if you have to!

Preparations for dealing with messages can be made before the telephone even rings.

By the side of every telephone should be:

- something to write *on*
- something to write *with*.

Better than a writing pad is a pad of telephone message forms, similar to the one opposite, so that the headings remind whoever is answering the phone of any questions they should ask the caller before he or she rings off.

It is always better to write messages down, at once, then read them back to the caller so that they can be checked, rather than to try and remember what was said.

After a message has been checked, it must then be taken to the person it is intended for without delay.

A caller may not be willing to leave a message. As an alternative, he could be asked:

- if he would like to phone back later;
- if he *would* like to be phoned back – he may suggest a suitable time.

In any case, he must be asked for his name, address (or his firm's name and address), telephone number and extension number, if he has one. The extension number is the number of his internal phone, and if it is known, the caller can ask for it and save the switchboard operator looking it up.

Never let a caller go without finding out who he is and his address.

If his name is a fairly common one, such as Smith or Jones, his address will be essential to identify him. There are a lot of Smiths in any telephone directory!

Exercise 14

TELEPHONE MESSAGES

```
┌─────────────────────────────────────────────────────────────┐
│                                                               │
│   TELEPHONE MESSAGE                                            │
│                                                               │
│   ┌─────────────────────┐  FROM ..Mrs. P. Barker..........   │
│   │ FOR.Mr. P.Jenkins... │  TEL NO ..436551.......EXTN..23.. │
│   │ DATE. Jan. 25th 198- │  COMPANY NAME..Barker and Lane.   │
│   │ TIME .1030 hours.... │  ADDRESS .Highfield Trading Estate│
│   │                      │  ...................Ruddstoke...   │
│   │ URGENT/NON-URGENT    │  ...............................   │
│   └─────────────────────┘  ...............................   │
│                                                               │
│   TAKEN BY.....P. Hill.....                                   │
│                                                               │
│   ___Mrs Barker regrets that she cannot call as___            │
│   ___arranged (at 1130 hours today) as she has___             │
│   ___been called away unexpectedly.___                        │
│                                                               │
│   ___She would be able to come on Friday 27___                │
│   ___January at the same time, Would you___                   │
│   ___please telephone her office to confirm?___               │
│                                                               │
│                                           P Hill               │
│                                                               │
└─────────────────────────────────────────────────────────────┘
```

Rule up three copies of the telephone message form, putting in the headings. Then complete them correctly, with the details in the following telephone messages. Sign the forms yourself.

1) The manager of the Swan Hotel, Oxbridge, telephone number 344567, rang up to say that arrangements for the staff dinner on 4 March at 1930 hours are now complete. A room has been booked for 30 people. Menus and prices are in the post. The message is for Mr C Bailey of personnel department.

2) Mr Vernon, of ABC Group Services Ltd, Milchester, telephone 733552 extension 8, telephoned to say he will be in the neighbourhood on 1 February and would like to see Mr Kendall, sales manager, at 1000 hours on that day, if it is convenient. Could Mr Kendall's secretary please confirm, or otherwise.

An example of a well planned reception area

3) Would Mrs J Grant, typing pool supervisor, please telephone Mrs G Hughes of J V White & Co Ltd, Blandwich, telephone 811356 extension 11, to let her know whether a demonstration of the offset-litho duplicator will be convenient on Monday 31 January at 1200 hours?

Inside and Outside Calls

Small firms may have one telephone for receiving *outside* (or *external*) calls only., Calls on an outside telephone in a firm should be answered by announcing the name of the firm, first, followed by 'good morning' or 'good afternoon'.

Larger firms will have two telephone systems – one for receiving and sending outside (external) calls and the other for offices to phone each other (internal calls).

Another type of telephone system will deal with both internal and outside calls. The type of call can be distinguished by the tone of the ring.

An *inside* or *internal* telephone should be answered by announcing the name of the office, followed by your own name: 'Sales department, Jane Jackson speaking'; or 'Mr Thompson's secretary speaking'.

In large firms where all outside calls are received by the switchboard operator, she will have given the name of the firm, so an incoming call would be taken by announcing name of department, office or manager. There is one important thing to remember with an outside call. It is that no caller must be left hanging on indefinitely while the person he wants to speak to is being found. He must be told frequently that he has not been forgotten, and can also be asked if he would like to be phoned back. This saves him wasting time and money.

Telephone Etiquette

WHAT TO DO IF YOU ARE CUT OFF

If you are cut off in the middle of a telephone conversation, replace the receiver, and wait for your caller to dial again, if it was an incoming call. If *you* made the call, you dial again, after replacing the receiver.

ENDING THE CALL

It is considered polite not to conclude a call if you are the person who was *called*. In other words, the person paying for the call should be the one to end it.

A Telephone Style

There are certain *slang expressions* which should never be used on the telephone:

'Hang on'

'Hello' – always name of firm, name of department, or name of boss.
'OK'
'Okey-doke'
'So long!'
'Cheerio!'
'See you!'
'Ta-ta!'
'Hang about a bit.'

Everyone uses some of these during normal conversation, but on the telephone they sound familiar and not very polite.

Neither should callers be addressed as 'dear', 'my dear', 'duck' or 'love' for the same reasons.

Some callers may be inclined to chat unnecessarily, especially if they ring up frequently. Chatting should not be encouraged – 'chatty' callers can be dealt with quite politely by being told that someone else is waiting to use the telephone.

Any telephone conversations which are overheard should never be repeated. They may not be confidential – but in any case should always be treated as if they are.

At the end of a telephone call, thank the caller for ringing and replace the receiver quietly. If you bang it down, it may reverberate in his ear – not pleasant.

When talking on the telephone, speak almost normally, but rather more slowly than usual, holding the receiver so that the mouthpiece is close to your mouth. Remember, it is a small microphone so you must speak directly into it. *Shouting* is no good at all – it merely distorts the sound.

Coping with Indistinct Callers

Sometimes your caller cannot hear you, even though you are speaking slowly and clearly. The line may be 'crackling' or your caller's English may not be very good. There is an internationally recognised way to spell out words, which all telephone operators use called the Standard Letter Analogy or Telephone Alphabet.

TELEPHONE ALPHABET

A	Alfred	J	Jack	S	Samuel
B	Benjamin	K	King	T	Tommy
C	Charlie	L	London	U	Uncle
D	David	M	Mary	V	Victor
E	Edward	N	Nellie	W	William
F	Frederick	O	Oliver	X	X-ray
G	George	P	Peter	Y	Yellow
H	Harry	Q	Queen	Z	Zebra
I	Isaac	R	Robert		

To use the telephone alphabet, you would spell out the word your caller couldn't hear like this:

The word she cannot hear is *parcel*

P – Peter, A – Alfred, R – Robert, C – Charlie, E – Edward, L – London and then repeat the word *parcel*.

Correct Dialling

According to British Telecom 1000 million calls fail each year, mostly because of misdialling. How often have you had to feel embarrassed and say, 'Sorry I must have the wrong number'? If you follow the following suggestions made by British Telecom you should make fewer mistakes!

Check the number first from your own records or the telephone directory for that area.

Write the number down if it is given to you orally.

Wait for the dialling tone before dialling.

Dial from a written record.

Dial with care. Pull the dial right round to the finger stop and let it return freely.

Don't pause too long between each figure.

Don't be a dozy dialler! But if you do make a mistake, replace the receiver and start again.

Wait up to 15 seconds for the equipment to connect you and, above all, *concentrate*.

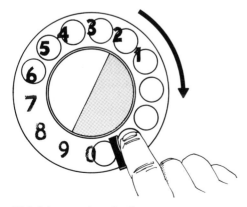

Dial right round to the finger stop

Dial the number very carefully

Telephone Charges

HOW TELEPHONE CALLS ARE CHARGED FOR

It is possible to dial most calls. Charges for these are recorded automatically on a meter at the telephone exchange. Charges are based on:

- Distance between caller and the person to whom he is speaking
- Time of day
- Day of the week
- Length of time the call takes (duration)

A Local Call is one made within the area around a town or city extending to about 900 square miles.

A Trunk Call is a call made outside this area. A trunk call can be dialled or made via the operator.

Most cities and large towns are now all-figure telephone numbers. This means that there is a number code which has to be dialled first, before the number of the person who is wanted on the telephone is dialled. All the codes now available in the Dialling Code Booklet. Before you dial it is very important to check that you have the right code.

On STD calls (Subscriber Trunk Dialling) there are no 'pips' to show how long the call has lasted. 'Pips' are only given on trunk calls (long-distance calls) connected by the operator. These 'pips' can be heard every three minutes.

Telephone calls are paid for every three months, when an account is sent to each subscriber (a subscriber is a person who rents a telephone from British Telecom). This account lists trunk calls, reversed charge calls separately but adds together STD (dialled) calls. VAT at the current rate is added to telephone bills. There is also an additional quarterly rental for the telephone.

Any subscriber who forgets to pay his or her bill is disconnected, after a warning has been given, and has to pay an extra charge, on top of the bill for the preceding quarter, before the telephone is reconnected.

Any faults in a telephone system will be repaired by British Telecom engineers usually without charge. They should be reported clearly and as accurately as possible from another telephone, giving the number of the faulty one, to the number given in the Dialling Code Booklet.

For full information about telephone charges, both inland and overseas, see the *British Telecom Guide*.

HOW TO KEEP TELEPHONE CHARGES TO A MINIMUM

It's not the number of calls that makes the bill high – it's the number of *units* recorded on the meter at the telephone exchange. A unit is measured by the length of the call, the distance between callers, the time of day and the day of the week.

Calls should be kept as short as possible.

Using the operator to make calls increases the cost – dial whenever possible.

Dial carefully – dialling a wrong number can cost a lot of money, when the wrong person answers, from a long distance.

Avoid 'person-to-person' calls and transferred charge calls unless absolutely necessary – the extra charge for these is now quite high.

The hour between 0800 and 0900 should be used as much as possible for telephoning. Now that many firms use flexitime, offices are open earlier and calls are cheaper at this time.

The afternoon is the next best time to make calls, especially long-distance ones. This is cheaper than making them in the morning.

The cheapest time for telephone calls at home is on Saturdays or Sundays, or after 1800 hours Monday to Friday.

Note that British Telecom *do not charge* if a caller is cut off or has to re-dial for a wrong number, where the person called answers *provided* that the operator is called and told. If not, the meter ticks up as usual and the charges go on the bill of the person making the call.

FOR YOUR FOLDER

12. HOW TELEPHONE CALLS ARE CHARGED FOR

Write these notes in your folder, filling in the missing words and phrases.

1) Charges for telephone calls are recorded automatically on a _____ at the telephone exchange.

2) STD means Subscriber _____.

3) On trunk calls connected by the operator _____ are heard every three minutes.

4) A _____ call is one made within the area around a town or city within about 900 square miles.

5) A trunk call can be _____ or made via the operator.

6) On STD calls there are no _____ to show how long the call is taking.

7) Telephone calls are cheapest on Saturdays and Sundays. On

weekdays, after working hours, they are cheapest between
_____ and _____.

8) On weekdays, during working hours, a telephone call is cheaper after
_____ and before _____.

9) Most cities and large towns are now on all-figure telephone numbers.
This means that there is a number code which has to be dialled first. All
the codes available are in the _____.

10) VAT is _____ to all telephone bills.

The Switchboard Operator

WHAT THE DIFFERENT TELEPHONE TONES MEAN

When you pick up a telephone receiver you should hear a low-pitched
'burr-burr'. This tells you that the telephone is working, and that you can
go ahead and dial the number you want. This is known as the *dialling
tone*.

After you have finished dialling, you should hear a repeated double ring
(the *ringing tone*) which tells you that the number you have dialled is
ringing.

If you hear a single, high-pitched note, repeated at intervals, you know
that the person whose number you dialled is already talking to someone
else on his telephone. What you can hear is the *engaged tone* – an
engagement ring in fact, but not the sort you can wear on the third finger
of your left hand!

If the number you dialled is out of order, you will hear a continuous,
high-pitched note. This is the *number unobtainable tone*.

THE PAY TONE

If you hear a series of rapid, high-pitched pips when you pick up your
receiver to *answer* the telephone, don't hang up – hang on. This is the
pay tone and it means that someone is calling you from a public
telephone box. You must announce your number as soon as the *pay
tone* stops and then give caller time to put his money in. Until he does
this, you cannot hear him, but he will be able to hear you.

TELEPHONE SYSTEMS IN A FIRM

The switchboard operator deals with all incoming calls (external)
telephone calls, re-routing (connecting) them to the person who has
been asked for. The switchboard operator also connects the employees
in the firm to the number they have asked her for. The exchange which
this type of operator uses is called a PMBX (Private Manual Branch
Exchange). A cordless PMBX is shown in the picture opposite. This one

has four exchange lines (one for each row) and twelve extensions (the number of switches in each row) but there are models of other sizes. The operator can either use a headset or a telephone.

An operator using a PMBX switchboard

HOW A SWITCHBOARD OPERATOR SHOULD DEAL WITH CALLS

Answering an external (outside) call. Give the name of the firm, followed by 'good morning' or 'good afternoon'.

The caller then states who he wants (giving the extension number if known). If he does not know the extension number, the operator will look it up from the alphabetical list she has near at hand, and dial it. If it is answered, the caller is connected. If no one answers, she tells the caller, and asks him whether he would like her to try again or prefer to phone back later. If the caller decides to wait while she tries again, and there is a delay of some minutes, the operator frequently comes back to the caller saying 'still trying to connect you' so that he does not think he has been forgotten, or cut off.

Answering an internal (inside) call. This will be someone working in the firm who wants an outside call. The operator will reply 'switchboard' and wait for the caller to tell her the number he or she wants. It is not fair to busy switchboard operators to expect them to look up telephone numbers, except on the rare occasions when it is impossible to find it – i.e. in a part of the country for which there is no directory available. Also, asking for the extension number saves a delay after the call has been answered at the other end. The firm's telephone operator there will be able to put the call straight through.

An automatic exchange is the type which allows employees to dial direct without the operator's help. This is known as a PABX (Private Automatic Branch Exchange). Incoming calls are still routed by the firm's operator. A disadvantage of PABX is that an extension number may be engaged on an internal call but the operator can break in and interrupt. The picture below shows an operator using a PABX system.

A modern PABX switchboard operator

FOR YOUR FOLDER

13. THE SWITCHBOARD OPERATOR

Write these notes in your folder, filling in the missing words and phrases.

1) The switchboard operator answers an external call by saying _____.

2) She answers an internal call by saying _____.

3) PMBX means _____.

4) Internal telephones in firms are _____; that is, employees are able to _____.

5) The most up-to-date types of telephone exchanges are _____.

6) When the operator is not able to connect a caller to the person he wants immediately, she will ask him if he would _____ or if he would _____.

Telephone Equipment

TELEPHONE ANSWERING MACHINE

A telephone answering machine can be connected to a telephone to answer calls when the office is closed, and there is no one to answer the telephone.

It makes use of a tape recorder. An incoming call starts the tape, which then plays a pre-recorded message. When the message ends, the set switches automatically to 'record' and the caller has a short time in which to give his name, address, and telephone number, followed by his message. The telephone answering machine then switches itself off until the next incoming call.

This equipment is particularly useful for doctors, veterinary surgeons, and dentists or any one-man businesses. People who wish to make appointments can telephone at any time.

Busy secretaries find a telephone answering machine useful, as it enables them to concentrate on urgent work without constantly being interrupted by the ringing of the telephone. The calls on the tape can be dealt with at a later, more convenient time.

Firms, such as travel agents, often give a telephone number in their advertisements (perhaps a Freefone number) to enable the public to telephone during the evening when their offices are closed, and give names and addresses for brochures advertising holidays to be sent to them.

Using a telephone answering machine

PUNCHED CARD CALLMAKER

With a punched card callmaker, the card can do the dialling for you. This can be done quickly and it eliminates the possibility of a wrong number. Each card can record up to 16 digits, and numbers are changed by punching a fresh card. An unlimited number of cards can be stored, each with one telephone number.

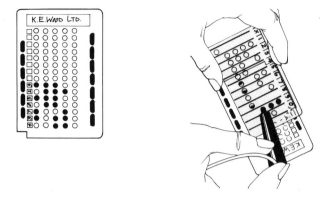

A punched card   Punching a card

The way to operate the callmaker is quite simple. You lift the handset and when you hear the dialling tone drop the appropriate card into the slot at the front of the callmaker unit. The number will be dialled automatically and the card drops through on to a tray. The pictures below show what the callmaker looks like.

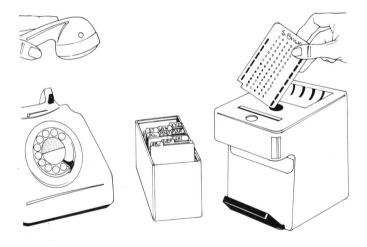

Using a callmaker

TAPE CALLMAKER

A tape callmaker is an alternative to the card callmaker. A magnetic tape stores 400 telephone numbers and each one can have up to 18 figures. Numbers can be altered, added, or removed when necessary. The magnetic tape has a writing surface with an index down the left-hand side. To make a call, the tape is moved until the required entry appears between the two guidelines on the window at the front.

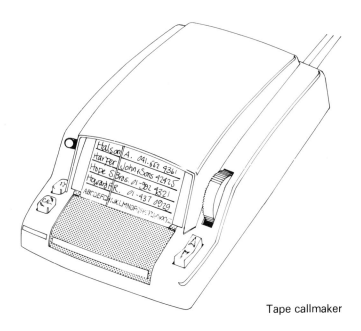

Tape callmaker

PICTURE SERVICES

It is possible to send pictures, photographs, drawings, printed, typed or written material by telegraph. British Telecom operates a service from London which sends exact copies (fascimiles) in black and white to many places in the world. The *British Telecom Guide* gives full details of charges, and the countries to which this service is available. The correct name for it is Intelpost.

A similar way of sending facsimiles of documents or drawings is by a transceiver, which can be attached to any telephone and will send the copies (also in black and white) to anyone anywhere in the world who has a transceiver and a telephone, in about five minutes. Documents sent by transceiver are received within minutes, on the desk of the recipient.

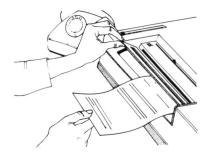

1) Place the document to be sent in the machine

2) Set the carriage levers to either side of the document

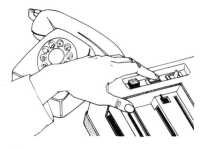

3) Switch to 'send'

4) Telephone to the recipient

Sending (above) and receiving (below) a document by facsimile transceiver

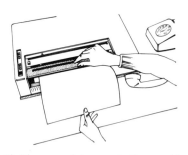

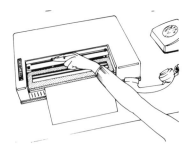

1) Place special paper in the machine

2) Switch the machine to 'receive'

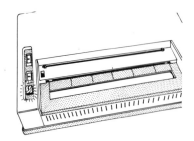

3) Switch machine to telephone line

4) After the machine has stopped the sender and recipient switch back to the telephone to confirm receipt of the document

Facsimile transceivers have a big advantage over teleprinters, because *anything* which can be put on paper can be sent. Teleprinters can only send letters and figures, not drawings and maps.

The other advantage of sending messages by facsimile transceiver is that it is cheaper than using Telex.

Special Telephones

LOUDSPEAKING TELEPHONE

A loudspeaking telephone has a loudspeaker incorporated into the normal telephone dialling arrangement, which can be switched on when a call is being made, so that both speakers in the telephone conversation can be heard by other people in the room. When the loudspeaker is switched off, the telephone conversation is carried on normally, i.e. only the two people speaking to each other can hear.

This telephone is quite different from an intercom, because it is part of an *external* telephone system. An intercom is part of an *internal* telephone system.

Loudspeaking telephone

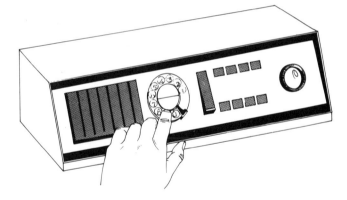

TRIMPHONE

A trimphone has a bleeper, the volume of which can be adjusted. It can be heard more easily in noisy areas than a bell. A trimphone sometimes has a dial which glows in the dark.

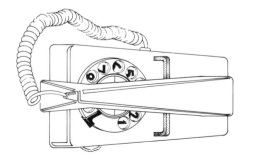

A Trimphone

PUSH-BUTTON TELEPHONE

There is another type of telephone: the push-button type. This is quicker to use than a dial, and there is less likelihood of making a mistake and getting a wrong number.

A push-button telephone

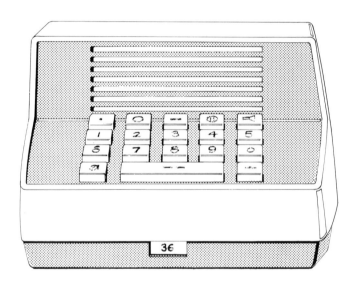

The intercom shown has a loudspeaker at the back and a push-button dialling system

INTERCOM

Communication from office to office (between the boss and his secretary for instance) is often done by an intercom. The message is relayed though a small loudspeaker so that all the secretary has to do is press a button and then she can hear.

On the top of the next page is the latest type of intercom, which can be left on a desk or picked up and used as a telephone receiver would be used.

TANNOY OR PUBLIC ADDRESS SYSTEM

Loudspeakers are necessary in noisy areas, such as factories, to call people to the telephone, which is situated in a quieter part of the building.

The picture shows some of the equipment for a public address system (left to right: a microphone for making a call; a telephone for answering a tannoy call; and two types of wall-mountable loudspeakers).

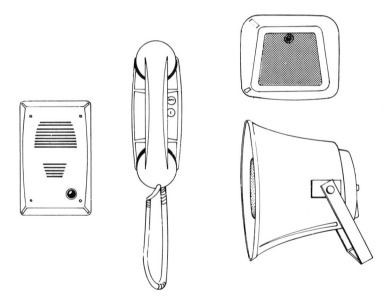

FLASHING LIGHTS

Where the ringing of a telephone disturbs people's concentration (where office workers may be spending most of their time on calculating figures, for example) different coloured lights which flash to indicate that someone is wanted on the telephone, are a noiseless alternative. Each member of staff will know which colour refers to him.

Other users of flashing lights are hospitals, where doctors are called from the wards for emergencies by this system, and in doctors' waiting rooms, where a different coloured light refers to a different doctor.

PAGING

People do move around – to meetings, to other parts of a large building, outside to other buildings, and it becomes very difficult for the telephonist to locate them either to give them a message which may be urgent, or to get them to speak to a telephone caller. One way to make sure that managers and other staff who are frequently away from their own telephones can be contacted is by using 'pocket paging'.

Pocket paging consists of a lightweight receiver, small enough to be carried in a pocket, or hooked over a belt, which 'bleeps' or vibrates when the telephone operator presses the button on the master control which she has close to her switchboard. When the pocket receiver 'bleeps', the person carrying it knows he or she has to go to the nearest telephone as quickly as possible.

FOR YOUR FOLDER

14. TELEPHONE EQUIPMENT

Write these notes in your folder, filling in the missing words and phrases.

1) The switchboard on which the operator deals with *incoming* and *outgoing* calls is a _____.

2) The switchboard on which the operator deals only with *incoming* calls is a _____.

3) Pushbuttons on a telephone in place of a dial provide a quicker method of dialling and are also _____.

4) A telephone answering machine is particularly useful for _____.

5) A punched card callmaker dials automatically when the punched card is dropped into a slot at the front of the callmaker. This is a quicker method than ordinary dialling and is also _____.

6) A magnetic tape callmaker stores up to _____ numbers.

7) A loudspeaking telephone can be switched on when a call is made so that _____.

8) A trimphone has a bleeper instead of a bell, the volume of which can be adjusted. The dial _____.

9) Communication from office to office (e.g. between a boss and his secretary) is often carried out by means of an _____.

10) In noisy areas a _____ is useful for calling people to the telephone.

11) Where the ringing of the telephone would disturb people's concentration, _____ are often used.

12) When someone moves around a factory a great deal and it is difficult to contact him by telephone _____ is useful.

13) What is a 'Payphone'?

14) Sending copies of documents in black and white by telephone is possible by a _____.

15) The machine connected to a telephone which records an incoming telephone message is a _____.

16) When the pre-recorded message has finished, the set switches automatically to record and the caller _____.

17) This equipment is especially useful for doctors, veterinary surgeons and _____.

18) People who wish to make _____ can telephone at any time.

19) Firms such as travel agents often give a _____ telephone number to encourage the public to telephone in for travel brochures.

20) _____ uses punched cards which dial telephone numbers automatically.

21) _____ uses magnetic tape which stores up to 400 telephone numbers and dials them automatically.

22) When several people want to hear a telephone conversation at the same time, a _____ is useful, as the caller's voice is amplified.

23) _____ are used on some telephones instead of dials. These have the advantage of _____.

24) They also avoid _____ when dialling.

Telephone Services

ALARM CALL

For a small charge, the telephone operator will ring at any time of the day or night, and go on ringing until the telephone is answered.

This is a useful arrangement when an early train or plane has to be caught, or for an urgent, early appointment.

PERSON-TO-PERSON CALL

A *person-to-person* call does not mean a friendly, chatty telephone call. It is one where there is no charge until the person asked for actually speaks on the telephone (apart from a small, additional charge by British Telecom). A person-to-person call avoids paying for the time wasted trying to find someone who may be out of his office frequently.

FIXED TIME CALL

A fixed time call is a way of making sure that the person called is by the telephone when caller rings. A fixed time call is especially useful for overseas calls, to countries where the time is different from the time in the British Isles.

ADC CALL

The caller may need to know how much a telephone call has cost, if for instance, she is telephoning from someone else's telephone. The call must be made through the operator (it cannot be dialled) the operator then asked to ring back at the end of the call and let the caller know the cost. This is known as Advice of Duration and Charge.

INFORMATION SERVICES

Information about gardening, weather, motoring, skiing, cricket scores, Stock Exchange prices, tourist facilities, the correct time, bed-time stories and even recipes and a hit record can all be obtained over the telephone by dialling the numbers given in your telephone directory.

The services are not free – the charges are the same as for ordinary calls, and the length of the call may be restricted.

TRANSFERRED CHARGE CALLS

Another name for a transferred charge call is a *reversed charge call*. This enables the caller to make a telephone call without payment, but first she must ask the operator to ring the person she wishes to speak to and ask if they are willing to pay for the call. Only when permission has been given will the operator connect the caller. This service is used in some firms by their representatives when they wish to telephone in whilst they are travelling around on firm's business. The switchboard operator would have a list of representatives and also keep a note of the transferred charge calls made.

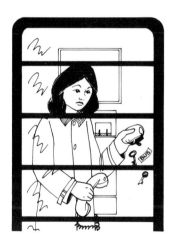

FREEFONE

Firms use this method to encourage customers to telephone them and ask for advertising material to be sent to them. A special Freefone number is published in their advertisements in newspapers and magazines, and all that the caller has to do is to ask the operator for the

Freefone number. The cost of the call is added to the account of the firm.

TELEPHONE CREDIT CARDS

These are used by businessmen travelling around, who may need to telephone their offices frequently from public call boxes.

Credit cards have a number on them, and it is this number which has to be given to the operator by the caller before he tells her what number he wants. The cost of the call goes on to the account corresponding to the credit card number. It is not necessary to use coins, but as all credit card calls have to go through the operator, they are more expensive.

EMERGENCY CALLS

There are three main emergency services:
- Fire
- Police
- Ambulance

and three other emergency services:
- Coastguard
- Cave or Mountain Rescue Services
- Lifeboat

To call any of the above services, dial 999. The operator will answer and ask which service you want. Then wait until the emergency service you have asked for speaks to you. They will want to know:
- The address of the person requiring help (not necessarily yourself)
- Directions to where they can be found (i.e. if they live in a very long road, it may be helpful to give a landmark such as a pub or church).

If you can keep cool and give helpful directions, this will save the emergency service wasting precious time looking for the house or area.

It is worthwhile practising making a 999 call in the dark – try it with your eyes closed. The figure 9 on the telephone dial is the last figure but one at the bottom of the dial. The last figure is 0. It is also important to remember to turn the dial carefully as far as it will go before dialling again, to make sure you do not dial the wrong number. Get a friend to watch you while you practise, *but leave the receiver on the hook during practice!*

It may one day be necessary to dial 999 in a darkened room and your practice will have been most useful.

One emergency which you do not dial 999 for is if there is a smell of gas. In this case, the Gas Board operate a 24-hour service and their number is in the telephone directory under Gas.

Make a note of it by the telephone, together with numbers for:
- Water Board (in case of leaking pipes)
- Plumber
- Electricity Board
- Nearest doctor

CONFRAVISION

Confravision is a British Telecom service which links individuals or groups of people in different cities by sound and vision. It is possible for people to see each other and talk to each other at the same time.

DATEL

Datel enables a computer installed in a firm to communicate with distant sites. Most Datel services can be used to much of Europe, the USA and a number of other countries. Datel (otherwise known as data transmission service) operates over the telephone network.

PRESTEL

This is a two-way computerised information service designed to give anyone who has a modified TV set and a telephone, immediate access to a store of useful information. Prestel supplies news, plus information from an enormous library to which a subscriber can refer at any time.

FOR YOUR FOLDER

15. TELEPHONE SERVICES

Write these notes in your folder, filling in the missing words and phrases.

1) If it is essential to be woken at any time of the night the British Telecom telephone operator will ring and continue to ring until the telephone is answered. This is known as an _____ call.

2) To avoid unnecessary expense when telephoning someone who may not always be near to his telephone, a _____ call cuts down the cost, as no charge is made (except a small surcharge) until the caller actually speaks to the person he wants.

3) It is possible to make a telephone call without payment, from a call-box, by asking the operator to ring the number required and obtaining the permission of the person called to paying for the call. This is known as a _____ call.

4) People who travel around and have to make frequent telephone calls to their head office will find a _____ _____ very useful, as this enables them to telephone from a call-box without using

coins – all they do is to give the British Telecom operator their _____ number.

5) Firms when advertising encourage the public to telephone them and ask for samples, catalogues etc. by using a special number which they can use free of charge. This is called _____.

6) Booking a telephone call for a certain time of day is known as a _____ call.

7) It may be necessary to know how much a telephone call has cost if it has been made from someone else's telephone. The British Telecom operator will ring back and tell caller if an _____ _____ _____ call is asked for beforehand.

8) There are many telephone information services and they cost the same as _____ telephone call. The length of an information call may be _____.

INTERNATIONAL TELEPHONE SERVICES

It is possible to dial direct by *ISD (International Subscriber Dialling)* to many overseas countries. These are all listed at the back of the Dialling Code Booklet.

If ISD is not available, an overseas call should be made by dialling 100 and asking for 'International Operator' or 'Continental Service' (depending on where the country is).

It is possible to dial direct from public callboxes or payphones to many overseas countries, but not all. This is because the calls to countries beyond a certain distance would be too expensive to be paid for by putting coins in.

International Dialling Codes are in the Dialling Code Booklet. It is possible to obtain up-to-date lists of International dialling codes by dialling 100 and asking for Freefone 2013, between 0900 and 1700.

There is also a free Phrasebook available with useful phrases for telephone operators who have many overseas calls to deal with. Copies of this can be obtained by dialling Freefone 2013.

British Telecom Guide also gives full details of charges for overseas telephone calls, as well as the time difference between the British Isles and other parts of the world.

It is possible to telephone ships at sea – details of this service are in the *British Telecom Guide*, too.

FOR YOUR FOLDER

16. INTERNATIONAL TELEPHONE SERVICES

Write these notes in your folder, filling in missing words and phrases.

1) International Dialling codes can be obtained by dialling _____ and asking for _____ between _____ and _____ .

2) Calls can be dialled direct from payphones to certain overseas countries, but not to those beyond a certain distance because _____ _____ .

3) A free phrasebook for telephone operators handling overseas calls is available by dialling _____ .

4) The _____ gives the time difference between the British Isles and other parts of the world.

Exercise 15

QUESTIONS ON INTERNATIONAL TELEPHONE SERVICES

1) What does ISD mean?

2) Where are the overseas countries listed to which it is possible to dial direct?

3) If it is not possible to dial direct, how would an overseas call be made?

4) Where are the International Dialling codes?

5) Where is other information about making overseas telephone calls?

6) Where is the information about making telephone calls to ships at sea?

Teleprinters and Telex

TELEX AND ITS ADVANTAGES

Telex enables someone to type a message to someone else without posting it. It is like sending a letter by telephone! The typist taps the keys in London for instance and the message can be printed out in Birmingham or a message from Manchester can be received in Milan.

Telex messages are quick – an expert operator is able to transmit at about 50 words a minute. Telex messages are less likely to be misunderstood if in foreign languages, as translations can be made carefully from a written message. Technical information is also received without errors.

Letters may take days, especially those from foreign countries.

FIFTEEN STAGES IN SENDING A LETTER AND GETTING A REPLY . . .

Taking dictation

Typing from notes

Checking letter

Signing letter

Taking it to Mail Room

Sticking stamp on

Posting

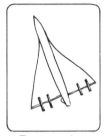
Transporting

Opening

Reading and dictating reply

Typing a reply

Letter handed back for re-typing because of errors

Signing reply

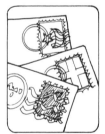
Posting it

Recipient reading reply

. . . BUT ONLY FOUR STAGES USING TELEX

Taking dictation

Transmitting

Receiving message

Sending a reply

94

Telex messages give a record both for the sender and for the person receiving the message. As the operator types out the message she is sending, it is automatically printed by the teleprinter receiving it. Up to six copies can be produced at once, if required. Red print indicates outgoing messages. Incoming messages (automatically received) are printed in black.

Incoming Telex messages can still be received even after the office is closed, at any time of the day or night, provided the power supply is left switched on and the teleprinter has a supply of paper left in it. This is especially useful for receiving messages from other parts of the world, where the time may be very different from the time in Britain.

Charges for Telex calls are based on distance between Telex subscribers and the length of the message (i.e. time taken to transmit a message). This is the way charges are calculated for telephone calls too.

The units which send and receive Telex messages are called *teleprinters*. They are available for rental from British Telecom. Rental charges include the maintenance of the teleprinter and there is an extra charge for the connection of each new Telex exchange line. Enquiries about the Telex service will be answered by your local Telephone Sales Office (see your telephone directory).

TELEPRINTER KEYBOARD AND DIALLING UNIT

The teleprinter keyboard is similar to that on a typewriter. What is printed by the operator on her machine is printed at the same time on another teleprinter at the other end of the line. Only capital letters are printed and there are certain special keys:

FIGURES or **FIGS.** After this key has been pressed the machine prints figures or symbols shown on the keys and allows WHO ARE YOU and BELL to be used.

WHO ARE YOU. When this key is depressed, the 'answer back' code, which identifies the other teleprinter operator is printed on both machines.

BELL. When this key is pressed an alarm bell rings on both machines.

LINE FEED. This key moves the paper upwards for the next line of type.

LETTERS or **LTRS.** When this key has been pressed the machine prints the letters shown on the keys as they are operated.

The dialling unit is similar to that of a telephone but there are four additional buttons:

DIAL   CLEAR   LOCAL   RESET

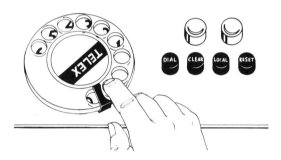

MAKING A TELEX CALL·

British Telecom will provide free training for office staff. Here are the basic stages for making a Telex call:

1) The operator presses the 'dial' button by the dial.

2) She dials the Telex number she wants (she has found this in the Telex Directory).

3) A green light on the teleprinter shines while it is sending or receiving a message.

4) After the operator has dialled the Telex number, she expects to receive the 'answerback code' of the number she has dialled, which tells her that she is connected to the right number. If a teleprinter is left switched on, it will automatically transmit its 'answerback code'.

5) The operator sends her own 'answerback code' to identify herself.

6) The operator types her message.

7) Identical messages appear on both teleprinters as the call progresses.

8) At the end of the call, the caller sends her 'answerback code' and presses the WHO ARE YOU key to obtain the code of the other machine.

9) The called teleprinter sends its 'answerback code'.

10) During the call, either teleprinter operator can press the BELL key, which lights a red lamp on both teleprinters, and also rings an alarm bell. This would be done to call the operator's attention to something in the message which was not clear. The bell would stop and the red light go out when the SPACE bar is pressed.

11) A call can be ended by either operator (either the one sending the message or the one on the machine receiving the message) pressing a button on the dialling unit.

While an operator is being trained, the teleprinter would be switched to local use, which would not prevent incoming calls from being received. The alarm bell and red light would warn that the teleprinter should be restored to normal use if a local call were received during training.

A teleprinter (Telex) operator

TELEX ABBREVIATIONS

The following abbreviations are recognised all over the world and are used by teleprinter operators sending Telex messages:

ABS   Absent or office closed.
CFM   Please confirm.
COL   Please collate, meaning please repeat. Used for figures in a message, or unusual words.

CRV Do you receive well or I receive well.
DER Out of order.
DF You are in communication with the called subscriber.
EEE Error.
NOM Waiting.
NCH Subscriber's number has been changed.
NR My call number is _____ *or* indicate your call number.
OCC Engaged.
OK Agreed or do you agree?
R Received.
RAP I shall call you back.
RPT Repeat.
SVP Please.
TAX What is the charge? or The charge is . . .
W Words.
WRU Who is there?
+ End of message.
+ + End of last message (i.e. there will be no further messages).

REFERENCE BOOKS

When you are operating a Telex you will need the following books:

British Telecom Guide
Telex Directory (UK)
International Telex Directory
Dictionary (Telex messages are *written,* not spoken, so check up on your spelling!)

Exercise 16

WORKING OUT A TELEX MESSAGE

Look at the Telex message on the opposite page.

1) What does EEE mean in the message?

2) What does CFM mean?

3) JAKVIN LPOOL is the 'answerback code' of the person to whom the Telex message is being sent. Who is JOHNVAL LDN?

4) What does LPOOL stand for?

5) What is LDN?

6) What does COL mean?

7) What do 1400 and 17.1.80 mean?

8) What does SVP mean?

9) Why are 1400 and 17.1.80 included?

10) What does + + mean?

JAKVIN LPOOL

JOHNVAL LDN

ATTENTION MRS K N NORMAN

MAY WE REMIND YOU AGAIN THAT WE HAVE NOT RECEIVED OUR ODRER EEE ORDER 8/543. SVP DELIVER IMMEDIATELY. CFM

1400

17.1.80

COL 8/543 1400 17.1.80 + +

JOHNVAL LDN

JAKVIN LPOOL

SENDING MESSAGES AUTOMATICALLY

Special equipment may be used on a teleprinter to speed up the sending of messages. This special equipment punches the messages on tape, in code, as the operator types them. This tape can then be fed through another machine called an automatic transmitter, which sends the message again at a speed of about 70 words a minute. There are some automatic transmitters capable of sending messages on punched tape at 120 words a minute.

While the teleprinter operator is not busy (during the first part of the morning, for instance) she would have an opportunity to pre-code messages on tape, which would be ready for sending. Sending pre-coded messages is a way of saving time, as they are transmitted more quickly than an operator is able to send them, so that pre-coded messages are cheaper to send.

Below is part of a message on punched tape. Messages can be understood from the punched tape, provided the code is known or is at hand.

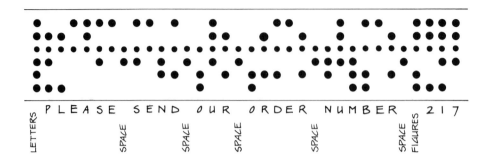

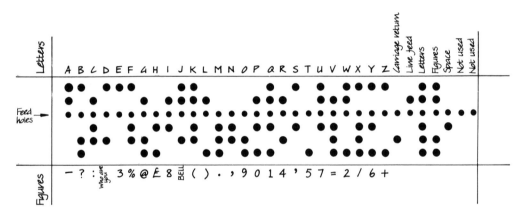

Punched tape code

Exercise 17

PUNCHED TAPE TELEX MESSAGES

1) Instead of the word 'please' what could the operator have used to shorten the message?

2) If the operator had not pressed the key for figures on the teleprinter what would have appeared on the message instead of '217'?

3) What would be punched at the beginning of this message, and at the end of it?

4) As the message contains figures, what does the operator do before ending the message?

5) Below is part of another pre-coded message. Using the master code, write down what it says.

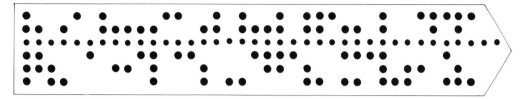

Punched tape

6) Try working out a coded message, perhaps in reply to the message above.

MULTELEX

Another way of reducing the cost of Telex messages is by using Multelex – this is for sending the *same message* to *four or more* people in the UK.

Telegrams may be sent by Telex both inland and overseas. The dialling codes are in the Telex directory. Telegrams may also be received on a teleprinter by arrangement with a Head Postmaster.

INTERNATIONAL TELEX CALLS

The Telex service is available to many countries throughout the world. It is possible to dial direct to New Zealand and to the United States of America, Canada and Europe.

Telex calls to other countries can be made through the London Telex switchboard operator.

International Telex Directories can be bought from the local Telephone Manager's office.

Details of charges for overseas Telex calls are in the *British Telecom Guide*.

FOR YOUR FOLDER

17. TELEX

Write these notes in your folder, filling in the missing words and phrases.

1) The machine used for the Telex service is called a _____.

2) Teleprinters have a keyboard similar to that of a _____.

3) A teleprinter is for _____ messages not _____ messages. In this way it is different from the telephone.

4) If a teleprinter is left switched on, messages can be received _____.

5) In order to receive messages when the office is closed, you must leave a supply of _____ in the teleprinter.

6) _____ copies can be printed at the same time on a teleprinter.

7) Answerback codes, Telex numbers and details of charges are all to be found in _____.

8) Telex messages can be pre-coded by _____.

9) On the normal teleprinters a message by punched tape can be sent at approximately _____ words a minute.

10) The same message repeated to four or more people in the United Kingdom will be cheaper through the _____ service.

11) The main advantage of a Telex message is that it reaches the person for whom it is intended _____ whereas a letter will take at least 24 hours, probably more if not sent first-class.

Exercise 18

CROSSWORD ON RECEPTION, TELEPHONE AND TELEPRINTER

Across

1 A receptionist should be polite and _____ (8)

3 She must not keep callers _____ unnecessarily (7)

7 Callers who have to wait must be _____ after by the receptionist (6)

12 The receptionist must _____ all messages to their destinations at once (4)

14 Callers' cameras, bags, etc. should be placed _____ the receptionist's desk for safety (5)

16 Callers should be escorted _____ and from the offices they are visiting (2)

17 As well as looking after callers, a receptionist may _____ as part of her duties (4)

22 _____ is a telephone service which firms use to encourage the public to telephone them (8)

24 The first impression _____ a firm is given by a receptionist (2)

26 This should be removed from the ashtrays several times during the day (3)

28 _____ of the regular callers, such as postmen or delivery men, signs the callers' register (4)

29 A receptionist's _____ and nails, as well as make-up, should be immaculate (4)

31 The Health and _____ at Work Act was passed in 1974 (6)

33 (and 21 down) A _____ _____ Call enables a telephone call to be made from a public call box without using coins (7, 6)

36 An _____ call will wake you early! (5)

37 A receptionist must never express _____ to a caller (5)

38 Speak more clearly (do not shout) to telephone callers who cannot _____ (4)

Down

1 Callers' cards must be _____ (5)
2 The staff 'in and out' book should be signed by staff *only* (yes or no?) (3)
4 The first _____ box in reception *must* be checked weekly (3)
5 As well as personal callers, a receptionist will have many callers on the _____ (9)
6 The British Telecom Guide _____ gives information about telephone services to countries all over the world (5)
8 Look _____ for callers who may need extra help (3)
9 A receptionist should _____ the answers to almost any questions about the firm she works in (4)
10 The abbreviation for 'editor' (2)
11 French for 'of' (2)
13 It is impolite to callers for a receptionist to _____ while on duty (3)
15 The colour of an outgoing Telex when typed is _____ (3)

18 Any _____ should be written on a specially printed form (7)
19 No one can _____ the importance of a good receptionist to a firm (4)
20 Answer the telephone as soon as it rings – do or don't? (2)
21 See 33 across
22 _____ drill should be practised regularly (4)
23 The Gas Board should be telephoned if there is a smell of gas – _____ 999 (3)
25 A _____ letter is useful for sending confirmation of appointments, or cancelling them (4)
27 Is a receptionist usually a 'he' or 'she'? (3)
30 Appearance _____ less important than a pleasant voice to a telephonist (2)
32 A person who has had an accident may be _____ful, and should be reassured (4)
34 _____ drivers do not sign the callers' register (3)
35 Girl's name (3)

103

Telegrams

SENDING A TELEGRAM

Because all business firms have telephones, and many have teleprinters too, telegrams are not much used in offices today, but they are still an important way of getting in touch with people who have no telephone and also of sending urgent messages to travellers by plane, train or ship. Telegrams can be sent almost anywhere but they must not contain bad language or threatening messages.

There are three ways of sending a telegram:

1) Printing in block capitals on a special form, or typing, and handing in at any Post Office which does telegraph business (not all Post Offices send telegrams).

2) Telephoning by dialling 'telegrams' and dictating the telegram to the operator. Instructions for obtaining the service for telegrams will be found in a telephone directory under 'Facilities and Services'. Before sending a telegram by telephone, the message should be written out: afterwards, a letter confirming the telegram should be sent, enclosing a copy of the telegram.

3) By Telex. Normal telegraph rates apply, but no charge is made for the Telex call.

Sending a telegram

When a telegram has been sent from an office, whether by telephone or by Telex, a letter confirming the message and containing a copy of it, is usually sent the same day. If a telegram is typed in an office, it is easy to take a carbon copy and file it with a copy of the letter confirming the telegram.

Business firms, or anyone who receives a large number of telegrams may register with the Post Office a specially shortened form of their address, to cut the cost of the telegram. The address is abbreviated to one word, plus the name of the town.

An example of such an address would be:

The Foxborough Engineering Co Ltd Halifax *abbreviated* to: FOXCO HALIFAX

This is known as a registered telegraphic address.

Below is a copy of a telegram form, with a message written on it, ready to be handed in at a Post Office.

Counter No.		POST ♔ OFFICE		Serial No.		
Office Stamp		**INLAND TELEGRAM** FOR POSTAGE STAMPS		Charge	Chargeable Words	Sent at/by
				Tariff £ excl RP		
				VAT £		
				RP £	Circulation	
	Prefix	Handed in	Service Instructions	Actual Words	TOTAL £	

If you wish to pay for a reply insert **RP** here

To BLOCK LETTERS THROUGHOUT PLEASE

CAROL BARNES

21. ARDEN AVENUE COVENTRY

CANNOT MEET YOU TOMORROW

NINETEENTH WRITING

BILL

The particulars on the back of this form should be completed.

A telegram form

It is much shorter than a letter, and includes no 'Dear' or 'Yours sincerely', or 'Kind regards' or 'How are you?' The message is as short as possible, without losing the sense.

Telegrams are charged for by the number of words in the message, plus the name and address of the addressee and the name of the sender. In addition to this there is an overall charge for each telegram, and VAT currently at 15 per cent. It is therefore important to keep telegrams as short as possible in order to cut down the cost.

Work out the cost of Bill Brown's telegram at current rates. The house number in the address counts as one word.

A telegram is still the cheapest way to send a message quickly to someone who is not on the telephone and to whom it is important to send information so that they receive it the same day.

Because Bill is sending a telegram to Carol, we know that she is not on the telephone.

Make a copy of the telegram form, omitting the message, and then fill it in with a message from Carol to Bill, asking him to telephone her at 325778. Bill's address is: 233 Sherbourne Avenue, Radborough.

Telegrams should be printed in block capitals, with the words well-spaced out, so that there is no possibility of a mistake by the Post Office clerk.

As messages on telegrams are so short, no punctuation is normally necessary but a full stop may have to be included to make the message quite clear to the person receiving it. The word STOP should be used between sentences; it is charged for as one word. No commas or other punctuation should be used.

- *Figures* in a telegram are charged for as under: up to five figures – as for one word; so 15000 – one word, 150000 – two words.

- *Figures in street numbers* are counted as one word: 123 Main Street – three words; 5 Earlsdon Road – three words.

- *Sums of money*, such as 25p or £25, where figures and letters or symbols are mixed, are counted as two words: 25p – two words; £25 – two words.

Work out the cost of Carol's telegram, and then add 15 per cent VAT.

Below is the part of the back of a telegram form. This is for the sender of a telegram to write his or her name and address on, including a telephone number, if they have one. This is not included in the telegraphed message and there is no charge for it. The name and address of the sender is for the information of the Post Office, in case the telegram cannot be delivered, for any reason. The sender will be told why the Post Office could not deliver his or her telegram.

---

*NAME AND ADDRESS OF SENDER. . . . .
    and telephone number (if any)

. . . .

. . . .

*NOTE: These particulars will not be telegraphed unless included in the message overleaf.

56-0832 5/74 RF/P Ltd.

The back of a telegram form

Make a copy of the back of a telegram form and complete it with Carol Barnes's name and address. There will be no telephone number. How do you know this?

Bill could have paid for a reply from Carol in advance. The box to the left of the space for the address on a telegram form is for the sender of a telegram to write 'RP' in if he wishes to pay in advance for a reply. RP is an *abbreviation for Reply Paid*. The cost of the telegram is then added to the amount the sender wishes to pay for a reply.

As each word on a telegram is charged for, it is important to leave anything off which is not absolutely essential. Very often titles such as Mr, Mrs, Miss, Dr can be omitted, as well as initials. A *group of initials*, as in A J K Clarke, counts as one word.

Hyphenated words (e.g. Southend-on-Sea, up-to-date) count as one word.

British Telecom will accept *abbreviations in common use* as one word, such as:

- c/o — Care of.
- ie — That is.
- eg — For example.
- MP — Member of Parliament.
- SAE — Stamped addressed envelope.

The *British Telecom Guide* gives full details of the cost of telegrams, and instructions for sending them. There is an extra charge for a greetings telegram.

FOR YOUR FOLDER

18. TELEGRAMS

Write these notes in your folder, filling in the missing words and phrases.

1) Telegrams may be sent in three different ways: by telephone, by Telex, and by _____.

2) Telegrams should be as short as possible in order to _____.

3) All punctuation should be left off telegrams, unless the word _____ is needed to make sense.

4) Figures are charged for on telegrams. The charge is based on _____ counting as one word.

5) Sums of money, such as £50, would count as _____ word(s).

6) The name Newcastle-upon-Tyne, would count as _____ word(s).

7) The abbreviation c/o counts as _____ word(s).

8) The back of a telegram form is for the _____ of the sender.

9) This is _____ included in the message and is not charged for by British Telecom.

10) A reply may be paid for in _____ to a telegram.

11) In order to save money by shortening the number of words in an address many firms register a special _____ address with the Post Office.

12) A cheaper way of sending a telegram is by the _____ service.

13) Greetings by telegram cost _____ than an ordinary telegram.

Exercise 19

TELEGRAMS

Below are some messages which are to be sent by telegram. Work out the cost of each one at current rates, not forgetting VAT.

1) Elaine Harrison 321 Strawberry Fields Newtonville
Cancel interview fourteenth January stop attend same time twenty-first January stop please confirm
Cartwright Spanmech Lambgrove

2) This is a Greetings Telegram: John Lane 2 High Street Freshley
Congratulations on passing your exam love grandad and gran

3) David Gartside c/o 88 Park Crescent Abberley Greatstone
Strike over report for work Monday ninth January 8 am
Jones Spanmech Anytown

Rewrite the following into messages suitable for sending by telegram so that they are as short as possible without losing the sense.

4) Elizabeth Styles 437 Bristol Road Bridgetown
Party planned for Thursday 5 January has been postponed because Tim has flu. Another party is planned for a later date but nothing certain has been arranged yet. Tim will be writing as soon as he is well enough. The message is from Tim's mother Mrs Warley.

5) John Wood 321 Stourbridge Road Catshill Hilldown
A message of best wishes from John's sister Karen on John's 18th birthday.

6) To Tiny Trees Football Pools to claim after scoring 24 points
   Telegraphic address is: Treepool Telex Liverpool
   Reference number is: 7 X 65
   The name and address of the claimant, which must be in the message,
   is: Robert Chatwin, 36 Highfield Road, Tyrwhit, Cardiff.

TELEGRAPH MONEY ORDERS

The Post Office is able to arrange for money to be sent quickly (i.e. the same day) to someone who may have lost his wallet or had it stolen, by a telegraph money order. This may be sent not only within the UK but to most countries overseas (see the list in the *Post Office Guide*).

Overleaf are the two sides of a telegraph money order form. These are available at Post Offices from which the telegrams are despatched.

A telegraph money order may be combined with a *greetings telegram* to make a present for a very special occasion. The charge for a greetings telegram is additional to the charges for the telegraph money order and for the transmission of the private message.

Registered telegraphic addresses may be used on telegraph money orders, both inland and overseas, but name of person receiving money must be added to the telegraphic address, e.g. John Spencer c/o Britsteel Cardiff.

Up to £100 may be sent by telegraph money order.

After the form has been completed by the sender, and the cost of sending a telegraph money order, plus the amount to be transferred to the addressee, has been paid to the Post Office, the following takes place:

A Girocheque is received by the addressee by special PO messenger from the Post Office.

The recipient takes the Girocheque to the Post Office, who will then cash it, after he has signed the Post Office form and also told the Post Office the correct name of the sender of the money. This is a check by the Post Office that the correct person is receiving the money.

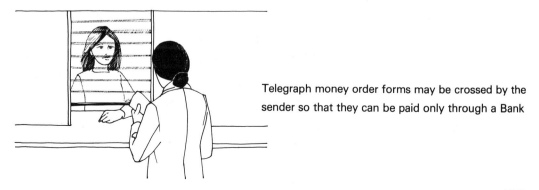

Telegraph money order forms may be crossed by the sender so that they can be paid only through a Bank

REQUEST FOR **INLAND MONEY ORDER** No.

Stamp of
Office

FOR

£`

PLEASE FILL IN THIS FORM

IN BLOCK CAPITAL LETTERS

PAYABLE TO

Mr., Mrs. or Miss	Christian Name (or initials) or forename	Surname

PAYABLE AT . . . . POST OFFICE

**NAME AND
ADDRESS OF
SENDER**

. . . .

. . . .

. . . .

P A Y M E N T
T H R O U G H
A   B A N K
BY
TELEGRAPH

Do you wish the Order to be crosssed for payment through a Bank? . . . .
(This is advisable if it will not inconvenience the Payee)

If you wish the Order to be telegraphed write "BY TELEGRAPH" across the front of this form
and fill in, overleaf, the address and other particulars in the appropriate space.

P.T.O.

SENDER — The name and address of the sender are required for official purposes.

PAYMENT — Payments will be subject to the possession by the Postmaster of sufficient funds.

DEFERRED
PAYMENT — Payment of an ordinary Money Order may be deferred for any period not exceeding 10 days, and no extra fee is charged. If deferred payment is desired the Sender must fill in and sign the following request and INFORM THE ISSUING OFFICER so that instructions may be given to the Paying Office. Payment of a Telegraph Money Order may not be deferred.

I request that the Money Order relative to this application may not be paid until . . . . days after the date of issue.

. . . .
Signature of Sender.

FOR **TELEGRAPH MONEY ORDERS ONLY**

If you wish the Order to be telegraphed write "BY TELEGRAPH" across the front of this form and fill in the particulars below. Telegraph Money Orders are made payable at the office nearest the recipient's address; but when the Telegraph Money Order is payable in Dublin, the name of the Post Office at which payment is required to be made should be stated in the appropriate space overleaf.

ADDRESS   TO
WHICH   THIS
T E L E G R A P H
ORDER   IS   TO
BE   SENT

. . . .

. . . .

P R I V A T E
M E S S A G E
(IF   ANY)

. . . .

. . . .

If the Payee is a woman the prefix "Mrs." or "Miss" should be given for inclusion in the telegram of advice.

If the Telegraph Order is to be called for at a Post Office the words "Post Office" should be entered in the address space and the Sender should inform the Payee where to apply for the Order.

The name (or name and address) of the Sender, if to be communicated to the Payee, must form part of the private message.

P803B

—McC—56-3096

The front and back of a Telegraph money order form

110

FOR YOUR FOLDER

19. TELEGRAPH MONEY ORDERS

Write these notes in your folder, filling in the missing words and phrases.

1) Up to _____ may be sent by telegraph money order.

2) The amount paid by the person sending a telegraph money order would be made up as follows: charge for telegraph money order, amount being sent and _____ (assuming no private message is being sent).

3) A person receiving money by telegraph money order receives a Girocheque. When he cashes the Girocheque he has to tell the Post Office clerk the _____.

4) If sender of money by telegraph money order wishes the addressee to collect the money through a bank, he will _____ the telegraph money order form.

5) A list of all overseas countries where telegraph money orders may be sent is in the _____.

6) Is it possible to combine a telegraph money order with a greetings telegram? _____

7) Registered telegraphic addresses _____ be used on telegraph money orders, but the name of person receiving the money _____.

8) The name or name and address of the sender of a telegraph money order must form part of a _____ message if it is to be sent to the recipient of a telegraph money order.

INTERNATIONAL TELEGRAMS

When urgent messages have to be sent abroad, telephone messages may not be the right method to use, especially if the office abroad is closed for the evening due to the time differences between the two countries.

The firm may also not be on Telex.

A simple answer would be to send a telegram. The Post Office will accept messages for any country overseas which handles international telegrams. It now has one of the most advanced and reliable international telegram services in the world based on a computerised switching system in London.

Telegrams can be sent by phone or, if the firm *is* on Telex, telegrams can be sent by this method.

(continued on p. 114)

Post Office International Telegram

Office Stamp	Cash	Account
	Charges	
	Tariff (excluding VAT) £	
Counter No.	VAT £	
	RP amount £	
	Total £	

Sent at	Forwarded No.		Acceptance No.	
To	Destination Ind.	Pty. Tar.	Orig Ind. **GB**	Ch. Words
By	Ch. Words /Act. Words	Date	Time	Service Instructions

This telegram will be charged at ordinary rate unless an indicator (URGENT, ELT, LT or GLT) is inserted between the double hyphens before the address.

BLOCK LETTERS THROUGHOUT PLEASE

= URGENT =

TO

JAMES WATKINS

KHANDI TEA ESTATE

KOTAGIRI

SOUTH INDIA

DOUBLE ORDER 443328 DATED FIFTH

MARCH STOP DELIVERY REQUIRED TO

LIVERPOOL DOCKS NOT SOUTHAMPTON

BARNES SUPERMART

SOUTHAMPTON

Name and Address of Sender (Not to be Telegraphed)

L W Barnes, Southern Supermarkets Ltd High Cross Southampton ....Telephone No. 445371 ....

The front of an international telegram

**Telegrams are accepted for all parts of the World
at Postal Telegraph Offices and at International Telegraph Offices**

If you want to send an international telegram by telephone or telex,
consult your telephone directory or telex dialling code card.
The charge for an international telegram depends upon the destination,
the number of words and its class.

Addressing a telegram for delivery by telephone or telex

It can be of advantage to the sender to have his telegram delivered by telephone
or telex and such delivery can be specified for telegrams to many countries.
The address should consist of the indicator TF, for telephone, or TLX, for telex,
followed by the telephone or telex number, the addressee's name and place of
destination.
The indicator, together with the telephone or telex number, is chargeable as one
word.

The Post Office Guide gives full information on international telegrams,
including tariffs and details of supplementary services.

Dd 362905 100M PADS S&K 12/74   T615(a)

The back of an international telegram

If your firm uses the international telegram service a great deal the Post Office International Telegraph Service has representatives around the UK, who will visit you and sort out any difficulties you may have. In the London area, telephone 836 1222 and ask for the Commerce and Press Division representative for your district. Otherwise, contact International Telegrams.

Charges. The charges for international telegrams are given in the *British Telecom Guide.* They are based on the number of words, the type of telegram and the distance the message has to be sent. The further it has to go, the more expensive it will be.

The international telegram on pp. 112–13 has been marked URGENT. The cost of an urgent international telegram is twice that of the ordinary type.

A cheaper rate for international telegrams is the Letter Rate. The letters LR must be written on the telegram form. Letter telegrams may be sent to most places outside Europe.

The Telephonist's Reference Books

Every telephonist needs at least a local telephone directory, but she is likely to need a number of other books as well. These are listed in Chapter 8 on p. 157.

CHAPTER 6

Written Communications

Business Letters

One of the most frequently used ways of passing on information between firms is by business letters. The secretary, shorthand-typist or audio-typist types a business letter from dictation (shorthand notes or on a cassette in a dictating machine see p. 127). Business letters are always typed on good-quality paper and have the firm's name, address and telephone number printed at the top. In addition, there may be a telegraphic address and a telex number. The names of the directors may appear at the foot of the letterheading.

As a business letter is to go from one firm to another, it is very important that the typing is neat and accurate, and that spelling and punctuation is excellent. A firm's first impression of another firm may be from a letter received from it.

SHAW & SHORT LTD
Wholesaler

Whitaker Street
MANCHESTER
M96 8TB

Tel:432888   Telex:990 111

Our Ref: PM/JK   25 November 198–

The Sales Manager
Office Equipment Supply Co Ltd
Knightley Road
Bromswood   Lancs
T45 7BC

Dear Sir

Thank you for your letter dated 20 November. I shall be pleased to see you when you call on 1 December in connection with your new model 6000 Word Processing machine and hope that it will be possible for you to arrange several demonstrations to our secretarial staff.

Yours faithfully
SHAW & SHORT LTD

Peter Mason

Peter Mason
Purchasing Officer

Envelopes

However carefully a letter is typed, all the effort is wasted if the envelope in which it is posted is wrongly addressed and it is delivered to the wrong place. The Post Office gives very clear directions about addressing envelopes in the *Post Office Guide,* together with a list of abbreviated county names which it will accept. Apart from the shortened names shown in this list, counties should be typed (or written) in full.

A correct postal address normally consists of:

- Name of addressee (the person to whom the letter is being sent)
- Number of house (or name of house if it has no number)
- Name of street, road, avenue or crescent
- District (where this applies)
- Post town
- County
- Postcode

The name of the POST TOWN should be in capitals, as this helps sorting at the Post Office.

```
Miss K. White
100 South Street
PURLEY
Surrey
CR2 4TJ
```

A correctly addressed envelope

POSTCODE

- Always show the Postcode as the *last* item of the address.
- Never use fullstops or other punctuation marks in the Postcode.
- Never underline the Postcode.
- If it is not possible to type (or write) a Postcode on a separate line, it is acceptable to the Post Office to show it on the same line as the county.

Postcodes are used in the mechanised sorting of mail. Every address in the United Kingdom has a Postcode.

Circular Letters

A circular letter is one of which many copies (sometimes hundreds of thousands) are sent out. Usually, circular letters are sent for advertising purposes, to inform possible customers about 'special offers' or new products to be introduced or new branches of a firm to be opened. The appearance of a circular letter must be of a high standard – it is possible by the use of a word processor (see pp. 131–2) to make each letter appear as if it had been individually typed. The other way of producing circular letters is by a duplicating process – preferably offset-litho which

---

**OFFICE EQUIPMENT
SUPPLY CO LTD.**

Knightley Road
BROMSWOOD
Lancs   Telephone : 859333
T45 7BC   Telex   : 674231

Date as postmark

Dear Customer

Word Processing Machines

We have pleasure in announcing that we are now in a position
to supply some of the latest range of word processing machines.
Prices and discounts will be sent to you by return, if you will
contact us either by telephone or letter, together with
descriptive leaflets.

This letter has been typed on a word processor, so that you can
judge for yourself the quality of the work produced by it.

Demonstrations of word processors can be arranged to suit your
convenience and, should you decide to buy one, a week's course
of instruction can be organised (which is all that is normally
needed) for any of your staff who may eventually be using the
machine.

We look forward to hearing further from you.

Yours faithfully
OFFICE EQUIPMENT SUPPLY CO LTD

Sales Manager

An example of a circular letter

produces good-quality copies. A circular letter does not contain an inside address and may have 'Date as postmark' printed where the date would normally be typed. This ensures that whenever the copies of a circular letter are prepared, they can still be used months later.

Form Letters

Form letters are business letters sent from one firm to another, or to members of the public (e.g. to someone who has applied for a vacancy, giving the time of an interview). Form letters are pre-printed (either by a duplicating process or a word processor—see Chapter 14 and pp. 131–2) on letter headings and are used in offices where a large number of similar letters are sent out and the only information which varies is the name, address and date. The variable information is added by the typist or clerk (it can be added in writing). Form letters save time and can be prepared beforehand during a slack period in an office. The appearance of form letters should be of a high standard as they are to be sent out of the firm. Departments in a firm sending form letters may be:

- Sales Department acknowledging orders (today this is done less frequently than it used to be, because of the cost of postage).
- Personnel Department arranging interviews and advising applicants about the outcome of interviews.

Postcards

These are sometimes sent in place of form letters; as they do not require envelopes, they save time and money. The name of the firm is printed at the top of the postcard, together with the address and telephone number, with a brief message underneath. All that has to be added is the date of sending the postcard and any other short, variable information (the illustration shows that the date of the letter which is being acknowledged has been written in). Postcards require the same stamps as letters, i.e. first or second class.

	Supershops Ltd
Customer Relations Department	Supershop House Paradise Lane Milchester, Devon Milchester 7619

Date / 2 June 198 –

Dear Sir/Madam
Thank you for your letter dated 1 June 198 –
which is receiving our attention.

A postcard message

HALL & GRIFFITH LIMITED

32 Lime Avenue
ELMSTOCK
Oakshire
Telephone Elmstock 36277

Our ref MS/

Date as postmark

Dear Sir/Madam

Thank you for your letter dated
asking for an appointment to see Mr/Mrs/Miss
                    of   Department.

Unfortunately Mr/Mrs/Miss
is away at present and is making no appointments for
several weeks.

Please write again next month if you wish to make
an appointment later.

Yours faithfully
HALL & GRIFFITH LIMITED

M Steele

M Steele
Personnel Manager

A form letter

Compliment slips

These contain the name and address of the firm, together with telephone numbers and telex number (if applicable). 'With compliments' is printed on, leaving just sufficient space for a brief message, or the sender's own name and title to be added. The size of compliment slips varies, but is usually about 4″ square. Compliment slips can be used for enclosing with catalogues, price lists – in fact, anything which is being sent by post where a letter is not necessary but where the recipient must know the name and address of the sender. They save typing letters and are used by many firms whose outgoing mail includes items for which the recipient is not expected to pay – the word 'complimentary' means 'given free'.

From
STANLEY THORNES (PUBLISHERS) LTD

Educa House, Old Station Drive,
off Leckhampton Road,
CHELTENHAM GL53 0DN. England.

WITH COMPLIMENTS

Mike Weaver

Telephone : Cheltenham (0242) 42127 and 42451
Telex : 43592

A compliment slip

Memoranda

It is usual to send written communications between offices on memoranda forms called 'memos'. One single 'memo' is a 'memorandum'. All that memos contain (besides the message) is the name of the sender, the name of the recipient, the date and, sometimes, a subject heading. There is no salutation ('Dear Sir'), no complimentary close ('Yours faithfully') and no inside address. It is usual for memos to be initialled, not signed in full, by the employees sending them.

```
MEMORANDUM

To:    Typing Pool Supervisor

From:  Peter Mason, Purchasing Officer      25 November 198-


Subject:   Demonstration of Word Processing Machine

The Sales Manager of Office Equipment Supply Co Ltd will be
visiting the firm on the 1 December to demonstrate a model
6000 Word Processing Machine. I am sure you will be interested
in this demonstration, and if you will telephone my secretary
sometime before the 1 December, she will let you know a
convenient time to see the machine. A later demonstration
can be arranged for members of your staff to see it.


                                          P.M
```

A memo

Circulation Slip or Distribution Slip

A 'circulation slip', or 'distribution slip' (sometimes also called a 'routing slip') is attached to a document that has to be read by a number of employees in turn. It consists of a list of names, and as each person passes on the document to the next on the list he ticks his own name. The document may be a letter which has been received in the incoming mail and has to be seen by more than one person (see p. 172).

Magazine on Word Processors Please read and pass on in order shown below:		
Name	Dept.	Initial/Date
G H Lamb	Buying	GHL, 10/10
Mrs K Potts	Sales	K.P. 11/10
D S Ames	Accounts	
Please return to: R Harris by: 13/10		

A circulation slip

Exercise 20

THE CIRCULATION SLIP

Make a copy of the circulation slip and complete it from the following details:

Miss K Lyons, secretary to the sales manager, has to see the letter *urgently*.

Mr K Samuels, personnel department, can see it at any time before the end of the week.

Mrs B Barton, typing pool, would like to see the letter tomorrow.

Mr V Smart, buying department, must see the letter some time today.

Mrs H English, accounts department, would like to see it the day after tomorrow.

Miss Lyons wants it when everyone else has finished with it.

Assume today is 20 October.

FOR YOUR FOLDER

20. WRITTEN COMMUNICATIONS

Write these notes in your folder, filling in the missing words and phrases.

1) Business letters are always typed on good quality paper and have the firm's name, address, telephone number, telegraphic address and _____ printed at the top.

2) When typing an envelope, the name of the _____ should be in capital letters.

3) The Postcode should be shown as the _____ of the address on a separate line if possible.

4) Postcodes are used in the _____ sorting of mail.

5) A circular letter is sent out for advertising purposes, to inform customers about special offers or _____ to be introduced.

6) 'Date as postmark' is sometimes printed on circular letters to ensure that whenever the copies of a circular letter are printed they can still be _____ months later.

7) Form letters are _____ and are used by firms when a great many similar letters are sent out.

8) Departments using form letters might be _____ for acknowledging orders or Personnel Department for arranging _____ and advising applicants about the _____.

9) Postcards are sometimes used for brief communications instead of form letters. As they do not need _____ they save time and money.

10) Compliment slips are often enclosed with items such as catalogues, price-lists where a letter is not necessary but recipient must know _____ .

11) Written communications between offices in a firm are _____ .

12) When a document is sent from one employee to another in a firm a _____ is often attached.

Meetings

TYPES OF MEETINGS

Business meetings in firms are usually informal and attended only by a few managers. A notice of a meeting may be sent out on a memo, which also sets out the purpose of the meeting. A manager's secretary may be present to take notes of what is discussed and decided at the meeting, which she later types out and distributes to those who attended the meeting.

A more formal type of meeting is one attended by the shareholders of a company. The chairman of the company often takes charge of this meeting ('chairs' it) and notes ('minutes') of the meeting may be taken by the company secretary (see pp. 4 – 5).

The topics for a committee to discuss are set out beforehand in the form of an agenda, which is sent round to committee members about a fortnight before each meeting, together with the date, time and place of the next meeting, by the secretary. The secretary and the chairman discuss the agenda beforehand and agree the items.

In many firms, the social club has a committee elected by the members of the club. This committee meets regularly to arrange functions for the members. The members of the social club also elect a chairman, secretary and treasurer to act as 'officers' of the club. At the committee meetings, the secretary takes notes for the 'minutes' (the minutes are a record of the proceedings of the committee meeting). The treasurer looks after the money spent by the club and also any money received. The job of the chairman is to make sure that the committee meetings are businesslike and orderly and that the topics to be discussed are dealt with sensibly.

Most clubs and societies (drama, cricket, sports, etc.) elect a committee to conduct their business for them. Every year there is a meeting which can be attended by all members, when the chairman, secretary and treasurer are elected. This is the AGM (annual general meeting).

The officers are usually elected by ballot – votes are marked on separate slips of paper by each voter and then placed in a ballot box. This is a 'secret' method – no one knows how anyone else has voted. At some meetings voting may be by a show of hands.

Below is an example of a combined agenda and notice of meeting for a Youth Club:

COMMITTEE MEETING OF THE MIDCHESTER
MANUFACTURING COMPANY SOCIAL CLUB

to be held in the Committee Room of the Midchester Works Canteen at 2000 on Thursday 20 November 198—.

AGENDA

1) Apologies for absence
2) Minutes of last Meeting
3) Matters arising out of the Minutes
4) Correspondence
5) Treasurer's report
6) Secretary's report
7) To discuss sports programme for summer 198—
8) To discuss raising of subscriptions
9) To discuss Christmas pantomine
10) Any other business
11) Date and time of next meeting.

Jane March
Secretary

An agenda is always set out in roughly the same order. In the agenda illustrated items 1, 2, 3, 4, 5, 6 would be dealt with before other matters for discussion. 'Any other business' allows committee members to raise questions on items not on the agenda. This is where the chairman's tact and firmness are needed so that the meeting does not go on too long. The date and time of the next meeting are always decided before the meeting is concluded. The only exception to this may be an Annual General Meeting, where it is not possible to decide as far as a year ahead.

MINUTES

'Minutes' are a record of what was decided at a meeting. They are usually kept in a Minute Book and signed by the chairman of the committee at the next meeting. Copies of Minutes are circulated to committee members after each meeting. It is the secretary's job to make notes of what has been decided during a meeting and then type (or write) them out as soon as possible after the meeting.

MINESTES of the Meeting of the Committee of the Midchester Manufacturing Company Social Club held on Thursday 20 November 198— in the Canteen at 2000.

Present: J Allan (Chairman)

P Carter   L Williams

H Jones   G Ziebarts

1)	APOLOGIES	There were no apologies for absence
2)	MINUTES	These were approved and signed by the Chairman
3)	MATTERS ARISING	There were none
4)	CORRESPONDENCE	The Secretary read a letter from Mr H Moore who has left the firm and regrets that he has to resign from the Committee. It was agreed that a letter should be sent to Mr Moore to thank him for all his help with the work of the Committee
5)	TREASURER'S REPORT	This had been circulated and was accepted
6)	SECRETARY'S REPORT	This had been circulated and was accepted
7)	SPORTS PROGRAMME FOR 198—	A sub-committee was formed who agreed to deal with the preliminary arrangements for this. The sub-committee consists of P Carter, H Jones and L Williams
8)	RAISING OF SUBSCRIPTIONS	It was agreed to defer discussion of this until the Annual General Meeting in February 198—
9)	CHRISTMAS PANTOMIME	As last year's Christmas pantomime had not been successful financially and in fact had made a loss it was agreed not to go ahead with one for 198—
10)	ANY OTHER BUSINESS	Concern was expressed by several members about the fall in membership of the Social Club and it was agreed to advertise in the Works Magazine as soon as possible to try and interest new employees in the Club
11)	DATE AND TIME OF NEXT MEETING	This was fixed for Thursday 18 December at 2000 in the Works Canteen.

Signed . . . .

Chairman

18/12/8—

FOR YOUR FOLDER

21. MEETINGS

Write these notes in your folder, filling in the missing words and phrases.

1) Officers of an organisation are usually the chairman, the treasurer and the _____.

2) The job of the chairman is to make sure that committee meetings are businesslike and _____.

3) Topics for a committee to discuss are set out beforehand in the form of an _____.

4) The meetings for all members of an organisation, when the chairman, secretary and treasurer are elected, is the _____, held once a year.

5) Officers are usually elected by _____ (slips of paper are marked by each voter and placed in a box).

6) Minutes are a record of what was _____ at a meeting.

7) It is the _____ job to take the minutes at a meeting.

8) Business meetings in a firm are usually _____ and attended by only a few _____.

9) A notice of a business meeting may be sent out on a _____.

10) A manager's secretary may be present to take notes of what is _____ and decided at a meeting.

11) A more formal type of meeting is one attended by the _____ of a company.

Exercise 21

ASSIGNMENTS FOR MEETINGS

1) Form a club and then hold an Annual General Meeting, electing by secret ballot a committee, treasurer, secretary and chairman.

2) Hold a committee meeting, after drawing up a suitable agenda.

3) Discuss what should be included in the minutes, after the meeting during which the secretary takes notes of what is discussed.

4) Make out an agenda for the next meeting.

CHAPTER 7

Office Machinery

There are lots of different machines in offices. The telephone is one which we have already looked at and later on in the book we will be looking at copiers and duplicators. What we are going to look at now are machines which help to put communications on to paper (typewriters and so on) and machines which process information (calculators and computers).

Audio-typing

One area in which the use of two pieces of equipment is combined is that of audio-typing. The typist listens through headphones to a pre-recorded cassette or tape and types what she hears. She can stop or start the recording by use of a pedal, thus leaving her hands free for typing. A competent audio-typist develops a technique which allows her to listen to quite long phrases, and type them back very quickly. She must also have a very good standard of English, as she has no 'copy' to look at. Her spelling and punctuation have to be very accurate indeed.

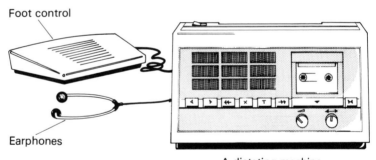

Foot control

Earphones

A dictating machine

Recording media used on dictating machines may be:
- belts or sleeves
- tapes
- cassettes
- sheets
- wire
- discs.

Magnetic media can be re-used. Non-magnetic media is used once only and then discarded. It is cheaper than magnetic to buy, but more expensive in the long term.

ADVANTAGES OF AUDIO-TYPING

The workload can be spread among several audio-typists

Cassettes, sleeves, tapes etc. can be posted

Time is saved while a secretary is typing from one audio machine and her boss is dictating on to another.

DISADVANTAGES OF AUDIO-TYPING

Audio-typing requires intense concentration and is tiring for long periods

The dictator's voice may be indistinct and difficult to hear

A great deal of background noise is often recorded also – many rooms in firms are far from sound-proof

Loss of personal contact between boss and typist or secretary

Recording media is difficult to keep entirely confidential – copies are easily 'dubbed'

Tapes are cleared when finished (if magnetic) and all records are lost – shorthand notes could be referred to later, long after the notes have been transcribed, if necessary.

CENTRALISED AUDIO-TYPING

With centralised audio-typing several dictating machines are in one room and the dictation is put on in offices in several parts of the firm. The tapes are then taken to the central audio-typing unit by messengers or direct tube. Centralised audio-typing often forms part of the typing pool (see p. 13).

BANK SYSTEM

In a bank system the manager has a microphone only in his office (sometimes like a telephone) and when he wants to dictate he dials a code and starts dictating after receiving a signal to say the machine is free. The tape is then taken to an audio-typist to be transcribed.

TANDEM SYSTEM

Yet another arrangement is the tandem system. Each typist has two dictating machines and can type from one while the other is available to record dictation. If she has any queries, she can telephone the person dictating to ask him what he said or even play back part of the tape to him, so that he can listen and explain. The 'tandem' system is used by many firms because it means the typist has some contact with the person dictating and feels the work is less impersonal.

A dictating machine cannot take over the role of the secretary, who is able to think for herself and use her own initiative. Ideally, a good secretary should be able to write shorthand *and* use audio-typing equipment.

Stenotyping

Stenotyping is a system of recording speech on a special machine. It is used as an alternative to writing shorthand – the machine prints the letters instead of the operator writing shorthand symbols with Biro or pencil. The notes still have to be typed back (transcribed) on a typewriter in the same way as shorthand notes have to be 'transcribed'.

The British stenotyping machine is called a Palantype.

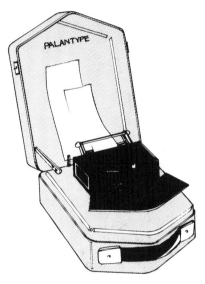

The operator of the Palantype uses phonetics instead of spelling the words in the ordinary way; that is, she writes down the words as they sound.

Stenotyping is used for court reporting where speakers are reported as they make their speeches – this is 'verbatim' reporting.

Stenotyping can also be used by secretaries and shorthand-typists in offices instead of shorthand.

It may soon be possible to combine stenotyping with computers (pp. 138—40) or word processors (see pp. 131—2) by using it as an 'input'.

Typewriters

There are two kinds of typewriters in general use in offices – electric and manual. In addition, there are what is known as 'special-purpose' typewriters which are used in offices where the work is highly specialised.

MANUAL TYPEWRITERS

There are three different kinds of manual typewriters:

- Standard length carriage used in most offices (14")
- Specially long carriage for typing wide documents
- Portable typewriters – extra light to carry so that they can be moved easily.

Manual typewriters are cheaper than electric typewriters, they need no power point, and are much less heavy than electric machines.

ELECTRIC TYPEWRITERS

These produce very good-quality work, when used by a well-trained typist, because of the evenness of touch. It is not possible to 'bang' too hard on electric typewriters. They are less tiring than manual typewriters for this reason, and also because of the 'repeater' keys on the machine – usually for underscore and fullstop. The carriage return is automatic, too, and helps to speed up the typist.

An electric typewriter

Some electric typewriters will produce more carbon copies than manual machines (a manual will produce about six). With very thin carbon and typing paper, an electric machine, with pressure adjusted to maximum, may produce up to 12 carbon copies. Some electric typewriters also 'justify' the right-hand margin – that is, they automatically space out the letters in the line of type so that the right-hand margin is exactly even, similar to right-hand margins in books. This greatly improves the appearance of the typing.

It is also possible to change the typeface on some electric machines – by means of a removable 'golfball' on which the characters are mounted or by means of a moulded segment. These interchangeable typefaces enable the typist to change the 'pitch' of her machine (i.e. the number of characters the machine produces per inch – pica is 10 and elite is 12) and also provide a different type-style for display work. In addition, some foreign languages (Russian for example) have different characters and an interchangeable typeface would have to be used for these.

Up to the present, electric typewriters which have been in general use have keyboards and carriage movements driven by an electric motor – the action is mechanical.

ELECTRONIC TYPEWRITERS

It is now possible to buy a truly electronic typewriter – the keyboard is controlled from an electric impulse through a circuit board (with silicon 'chips'). The weight of an electronic typewriter is about half that of an electric typewriter, and repairs are much easier and quicker to carry out, as it consists of only seven components, each of which can be replaced when necessary. The faulty part can be repaired and stored by the mechanic until required to repair another faulty machine.

The electronic typewriter is almost identical in operation to an electric typewriter except that it has a small 'memory' of eight characters which can be used to:

- backspace
- correct automatically
- adjust layout of headings.

The touch required on an electronic typewriter is feather light – even less than on the traditional electric typewriter.

The price of the two machines is almost the same.

The typing element is called a 'daisy wheel' because it is shaped like the petals on a daisy – there are no type bars or typeface. The 'daisy wheel' is interchangeable to give different pitch and characters.

MEMORY TYPEWRITER

This can store up to 200,000 characters (about 200 pages of A4 typing). The characters are not just the letters printed on the paper, but also include instructions to the machine regarding line spacing, headings, etc. A copy of each letter or document stored in the memory must be kept in a folder so that it is possible to refer to them for reference and retyping when required.

WORD PROCESSOR (OR TEXT PROCESSOR)

This is the more sophisticated development of the memory typewriter, where the storage of the typed material is outside the machine and may be on magnetic card or floppy disks (called 'floppy' because they are limp). A word processor also has a visual display unit (VDU) on which the typist can see what she is typing as she does it. It is printed out only when text and layout are satisfactory. Whole sections can be moved out, revised, added, deleted or enlarged. Only the new material will need to be retyped. On some word processors a high-speed independent 'printer' (a typewriter without a keyboard) prints out the work once it has been approved, from the memory, at 500 words per minute without possibility of errors – a perfect 'top' copy every time.

A word processor will produce all the repetitive work of a typist – circulars, reports, minutes, legal documents, much faster and with complete accuracy, and of a sufficiently high quality to be suitable for sending out to other firms or organisations.

FOR YOUR FOLDER

22. STENOTYPING, AUDIO-TYPING AND TYPEWRITERS

Write these notes in your folder, filling in the missing words and phrases.

1) Stenotyping is the system of taking down shorthand by _____.

2) Audio-typing is listening through headphones and _____ what has been recorded.

3) Audio-typists must have accurate typing with good speeds and excellent _____.

4) Audio-typing is useful because it spreads the work evenly among typists but has the disadvantage of _____.

5) Recording media may be tapes, cassettes or _____. Recording media are easily _____.

6) Manual typewriters may be standard, long-carriage or _____.

7) Electric typewriters produce good quality work and are less tiring for the typist to use than a manual typewriter because of the _____ on the electric machine and also because it is not possible to _____ on an electric machine.

8) Some electric typewriters have interchangeable typefaces which enable the typist to change the pitch of the machine and also provide a _____ _____ for display work.

9) An interchangeable typeface could also be useful for typing in a _____ language.

10) Keeping the right-hand margin absolutely straight is known as _____ it.

11) The latest electronic typewriter has a small memory of _____ characters and a 'daisy wheel' _____ element.

12) A memory typewriter can store up to 200,000 characters (about _____ pages of A4 typing).

13) A word processor has a visual display unit (VDU) and stores the material in its memory on magnetic card or _____.

14) A word processor will produce all the repetitive work of a typist – circulars, reports, minutes, _____ of a sufficiently high quality to be sent out to _____.

Supplies for the Typewriter

RIBBONS

Typewriter ribbons are made of nylon, silk, cotton, or carbon. Nylon and silk ribbons produce work of very good appearance but carbon ribbons produce the best imprint of all. The finer the fabric, the sharper the imprint. Unfortunately, carbon ribbons can be used once only and so are very expensive. Two-colour ribbons are available (called bichrome) usually red and black, and correcting ribbons, which switch from normal black to white, so that the error is typed over in white, made invisible and the correction typed over again in black.

COPYHOLDERS

Many typists are trained to stand their textbooks and notebooks upright on copyholders and prefer to continue to use them in the office. Complicated work is assisted by accurate line-by-line reading and some copyholders are electrically operated by means of a foot-controlled switch.

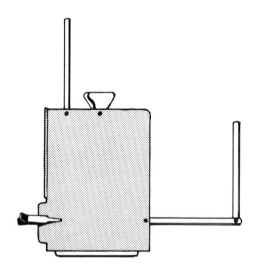

An electrically controlled copyholder

CONTINUOUS STATIONERY ATTACHMENT

This is fitted to the back of a typewriter (see p. 209) and enables the forms (which are in sets with interleaved carbon or NCR perforated between each set) to be fed into the machine and torn off as completed. A continuous stationery attachment saves the typist's time as each set of documents is ready in the typewriter when the previous one has been completed.

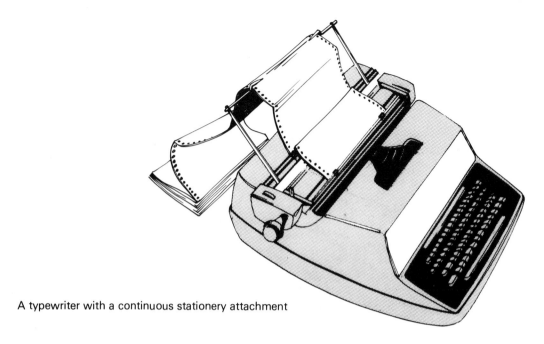

A typewriter with a continuous stationery attachment

Typist's Accessories

ERASERS

These are available in many shapes and sizes, from the pencil type, which can be sharpened to keep a fine erasing point, to the larger rectangular one which has a soft pencil rubber and a hard typewriter rubber combined.

ERASER SHIELDS

These are placed over the word to be corrected so that only the letters to be replaced are erased. Eraser shields are made of clear plastic.

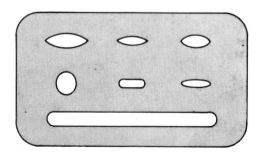

An eraser shield

LIQUID AND PAPER CORRECTIVE

These are available in many colours, including white, so that the colour of the letterheading and/or typing paper can be exactly matched. The error is 'painted' over, allowed to dry and then retyped.

The carbon copy must, of course, be erased in the normal way — if it is 'painted' out also, time must be allowed for it to dry. This way of correcting errors is very neat and effective *if* it is carried out carefully and gently.

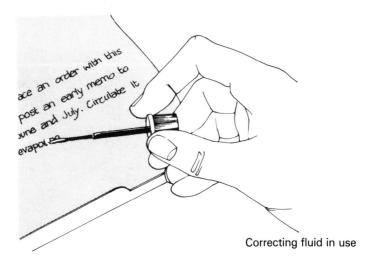

Correcting fluid in use

BACKING SHEETS

These can be supplied with scales showing the typing lines and inches along the top. They help to show the typist when she is nearing the bottom of her page. Backing sheets also protect the platen (roller) from wear and tear and improve the appearance of the work. The 'fold-over' top of a backing sheet helps to keep carbons and carbon copies level when the typist is feeding them into her machine.

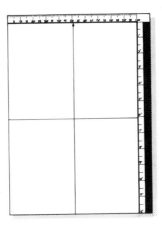

A scaled backing sheet

The Care of the Typewriter

A typewriter is an expensive and complex piece of machinery and should be looked after by the typist, whether it is her own portable, which she uses at home, or an electric typewriter she uses in an office.

1) Cover it *always* after use to keep out dust.

2) Remove dust daily (preferably first thing in the morning) especially underneath, because this rises into the machine and clogs it.

3) Rub out carefully, moving the carriage (using the margin release) so that the bits of rubber dust fall on to the desk and not into the type basket.

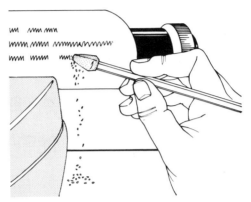

4) Use a backing sheet when single copies are being typed – this improves the look of the typing as well as protects the roller (platen) from wear and tear.

5) To move a typewriter, lift from *underneath*, not by the carriage and move both margins to the centre so that the carriage will not slide along.

6) Never leave a typewriter near the edge of a desk, where it could be accidentally knocked off by a passer-by.

7) Never leave a typewriter near a hot radiator – this will dry out the oil in the machine.

8) Each week, brush the typeface with a stiff brush and methylated spirits to remove surplus ink which eventually clogs the typeface. Clean finger-marks off the machine with spirit and dust with a soft brush where rubber dust has collected. Wipe the roller (platen) with a duster dampened with spirit.

9) Do not oil a typewriter – leave this to a trained mechanic. Surplus oil in a machine can ruin typing and is difficult to get rid of.

10) Always call in a trained mechanic to repair faults – don't try to mend them yourself.

FOR YOUR FOLDER

23. TYPEWRITER ACCESSORIES AND SUPPLIES

Write these notes in your folder, filling in the missing words and phrases.

1) Typewriter ribbons are made of nylon, silk, cotton or ＿＿＿＿＿＿＿.

2) Carbon ribbons produce the best imprint of all but can be used _____.

3) Apart from carbon ribbons, the best work is produced by _____ and _____.

4) Bi-chrome ribbons are _____ usually black and red.

5) Correcting ribbons can be switched from black to _____ so that the error is made _____ and can be retyped.

6) Copyholders are used to keep work upright and some are _____ operated by means of a foot-controlled switch.

7) A continuous stationery attachment enables sets of forms, perforated between sets, to be _____ and torn off when completed.

8) A useful accessory when correcting an error is an _____ which enables the typist to rub out only the incorrect letters she has mistyped.

9) Liquid and paper correctives are painted over errors, allowed to dry and then the correction is retyped. Carbon copies must be erased by rubbing out – if 'painted', time must be allowed for the corrective to _____.

10) Backing sheets are available with scales showing typing lines and inches along the top. They may also have a 'fold-over' top which helps to 'feed' _____ and _____ level into the typewriter.

Computers

WHAT DO THEY DO?

Computers are electronic machines which can:
- store information. This information is called *data*.
- sort out the data and, if required, perform calculations. This is called *data processing*.

In the office the computer may be used for:
- working out the payroll
- accountancy
- stock control
- market research
- production planning

HOW COMPUTERS WORK

Computers need instructions from trained people. These instructions are called *programs*, and the people who write them are called *programmers*. A programmer first of all has to produce a flow chart like the one shown below. Then this chart is translated into a special 'machine language' which the computer can respond to. After the instructions have been fed into the computer, a number of electrical circuits switch on and off using *binary arithmetic* to control them. (You may have learnt about binary arithmetic in your maths class.) The computer performs its operations very quickly. Unless the program is wrong, or has been wrongly inserted, or the computer has developed a fault, it should tell you what you want to know. Programming is sometimes called *software* and the computer equipment *hardware*.

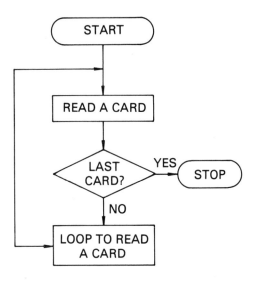

THE COMPUTER HARDWARE

A computer has five main parts:

- *the input.* Here information is put into the computer. This may be typed in at a keyboard or inserted in the form of printed cards, paper tape, magnetic tape or characters in magnetic ink. (This last type of input is used on cheques so that they can be sorted by banks' computers.)
- *the central processing unit.* This contains the parts of the computer which process the data.
- *the memory.* This is where information is stored in the computer.
- *the output.* This is where information comes out of the computer. It may appear on the screen of a *visual display unit (VDU)*, be printed out on paper by a *line printer*, or presented in a number of other ways (for example, on tape, microfilm or discs).
- *the backing store.* Information which is not actually being processed in the computer can be kept in a special backing store. Magnetic tapes can be kept in special cupboards, for example, which are kept at a constant temperature.

TYPES OF COMPUTER

There are three types of computer:

- *Mainframes* are large machines which would be used, for example, by banks.
- *Minicomputers* are much smaller and are now being used in many offices.
- *Microcomputers* are even smaller. They are used increasingly at home and on desk tops in the office. The sequence of operations in an automatic washing machine is programmed by a *microprocessor,* and this too can be thought of as a sort of microcomputer.

A computer 'terminal' consisting of 'input' (keyboard) and 'output' (VDU)

Calculators

Machines for adding have been used since the seventeenth century. One of the first machines capable of dealing with money columns was the Burroughs, produced in 1888. The cash registers largely in use until a few years ago were a development along the same lines. Modern calculators which carry out very complex mathematical calculations, as well as simple addition, subtraction and multiplication, have become smaller and cheaper due to the development of the 'silicon chip'. Pocket calculators are used everywhere today – in schools, colleges, offices, shops and home. The slimmest pocket calculator is no larger than a pocket diary, and there is even one with an alarm and a clock which prints a message when the alarm rings, to remind the person awoken where he has to go!

A pocket calculator

In offices, it is often useful to have a slightly larger, heavy-duty calculator to stand on a desk. It is also necessary when working with figures to have a record of the total, and some calculators print-out the calculation in addition to showing the answer in the display unit.

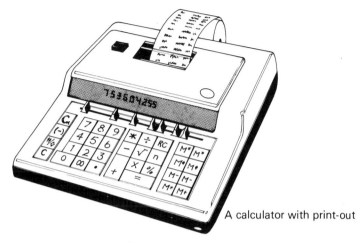

A calculator with print-out

The larger calculators can be plugged into the mains, or operated from batteries, some of which are rechargeable by being left plugged-in overnight.

A large desk-type calculator

The latest type of small calculator is 'solar-powered' − in other words, its battery is recharged by exposure to sunlight or artificial electric light.

Small pocket calculators may unfortunately be easily picked up and stolen, so they must be carefully stored away in locked cupboards in offices after use.

Calculators (the ones capable of the more complicated calculations) are sometimes described as 'pocket computers'. This is wrong − the essential difference between a computer and a calculator is that a calculator cannot work out sums by logic, i.e. produce an answer by selecting figures from a 'chain' whereas a computer is able to do so, from information stored in its 'memory'.

141

FOR YOUR FOLDER

24. COMPUTER AND CALCULATORS

Write these notes in your folder, filling in the missing words and phrases.

1) The sorting out of information in a computer is called _____ _____.

2) A computer may be used in the office for working out the payroll, accounting, stock control, market research and _____.

3) A set of instructions fed into a computer is called a _____. The person who writes this is called a _____ and his first task is to produce a _____ _____.

4) The arithmetic used in a computer is known as _____ arithmetic.

5) Programs are referred to as _____ and the computer equipment is called _____.

6) The five main parts of a computer are: the input, the central processing unit, the _____, the output and the backing store.

7) The input into a computer may consist of punched cards, paper tape, _____ tape or characters in _____ ink.

8) Information for the computer may appear on a screen called a _____ _____ _____ or printed on paper by a _____ _____.

9) The three types of computer are _____, _____ and _____.

10) Modern calculators carry out very complex mathematical calculations and have become smaller and cheaper due to the development of the _____.

11) The latest type of calculator is solar-powered – its battery is recharged by _____.

12) When it is necessary to have a record of figures used in a calculation a calculator with a _____ is essential.

13) Computers and calculators both work out sums, but only a computer can work out the _____ – this is the essential difference between them.

14) Calculators should not be called '_____ _____'.

Exercise 22

TYPEWRITERS, WORD PROCESSORS, COMPUTERS AND CALCULATORS

1) Compare the 'bank' system of audio-typing with the 'tandem' system and explain the disadvantages and advantages of each.

2) 'An audio-typist does not need such a high standard of English as a shorthand-typist.' Do you agree with this statement or not? Give your reasons.

3) Compare the work of a shorthand-typist with that of a stenotypist.

4) Electronic typewriters are the first of the typewriters to be controlled by silicon chips. Compare an electric typewriter with an electronic typewriter.

5) What are the advantages of a word processor?

6) Explain the advantages of copyholders and continuous stationery attachments.

7) List points to be observed in the care of a typewriter: (a) daily, (b) weekly, (c) when it is faulty.

8) What effect has the microprocessor (the silicon chip) had on computers?

9) How is information stored in a computer produced when required?

10) Compare pocket calculators with computers.

CHAPTER 8

Finding Out

Reference Books in General

'Finding out' is simple if you know which reference book to look in, and how to use reference books.

All public libraries have a good selection of reference books in a separate section. They are not to be taken out on loan because:

- They are usually large, heavy and awkward to carry
- They are expensive and librarians cannot afford to run the risk of losing them
- They have to be always available.

Reference books have to be replaced as soon as a new edition becomes available, because out-of-date facts are misleading and worse than useless.

HOW TO USE REFERENCE BOOKS

Check the contents list first, to verify that it is the right book for the information required. The contents list is at the beginning of a reference book, and is easy to find.

After you have found the topic you want in the contents list, turn to the index. This is at the back of a reference book, and is an alphabetical list of topics, very often divided by sub-headings in heavier type.

When using an index, remember that the item you are looking for may be under a different word with the same meaning (a 'synonym'):

'Car' may be under:
- Automobile
- Motor vehicle
- Motor car

so if you cannot find what you are looking for at once, try to think of another word with a similar meaning, and see if it is indexed under that.

While looking up information in a reference book, place slips of paper in between the pages which you want to go back to, as you work through the book. This makes it much easier to turn back later and recheck. Remember that many reference books have over a thousand pages!

OTHER WAYS OF HELPING THE USER

Some reference books have attached book marks in the form of ribbons or cards.

Others may have tabs on the edges of pages as 'signposts'.

Edge printing is often combined with different coloured pages.

There may also be a 'thumb' index.

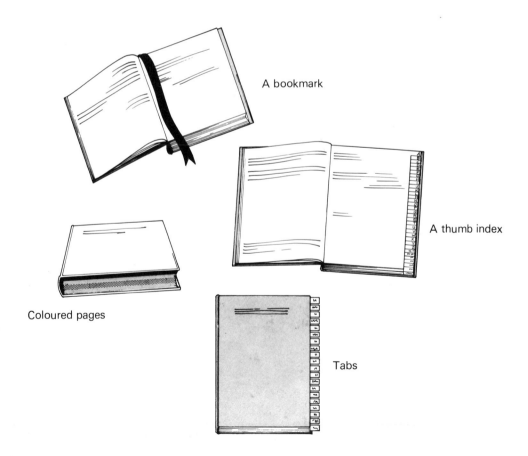

A bookmark

A thumb index

Coloured pages

Tabs

FOR YOUR FOLDER

25. HOW TO USE REFERENCE BOOKS

Write these notes in your folder, filling in the missing words and phrases.

1) Reference books are not lent to borrowers by public libraries because they are expensive and (mostly) very _____ and must always be _____.

2) Reference books need frequent replacement because the information *must* be _____.

3) At the front of all reference books is a _____ which lists the topics dealt with in the book.

4) At the back of all reference books is an _____ which is a detailed alphabetical list of all the facts in the book.

5) To help readers to find the information they need, some reference books have attached _____ in the form of _____.

6) While looking up information in a reference book, it is helpful to mark the pages with _____ as you go through the book.

7) Some reference books have different coloured pages with _____ to help the user.

8) _____ are given by tabs on the edges of the pages.

9) Another way of guiding the user of a reference book is by _____.

10) When using a reference book, remember that the item you are looking for may be under a different word with the same meaning – a _____.

General Knowledge

'General knowledge' means a knowledge of facts covering a wide range of topics. It is impossible for any one person to know everything, but a lot of information can be looked up in an encyclopaedia which consists of a book or series of books with topics arranged in alphabetical order.

Encyclopaedias contain information about people, events, places and modern technology. Because of their size, it is only possible to up-date them every few years, and so are soon out of date regarding facts concerning people, events and technology. Also, because encyclopaedias are so comprehensive, they cannot give detailed information on each subject – or they would be enormous!

It is necessary to use specialised reference books if detailed information is needed about one particular subject. These specialised reference books will be dealt with later.

The largest encyclopaedia is *Encyclopaedia Britannica*. It consists of about thirty separate books and is packed with all sorts of facts and figures. Although very good, it is probably too big and too expensive to keep handy in your office. You may, however, find the *Britannica* in your local library.

A small, compact one-book encyclopaedia which is published annually, and is therefore nearly always more up to date than the larger multi-volumed encyclopaedias, is *Pears Cyclopaedia*. *Pears* is divided under three main headings: Everyday information (dictionary, foreign phrases, commercial phrases and legal notes); Events, famous people, government and international organisations; Home and Personal (medical dictionary, gardening, sports, pets, and cookery).

Another general reference book published annually, is *Whitaker's Almanack*. This contains information about every country in the world, as well as statistics regarding imports and exports, revenue, population, production and industry in the United Kingdom. *Whitaker's* also contains information about the Royal family and members of the peerage, the House of Commons, the Law Courts, and the police and armed forces.

Pears and *Whitaker's Almanack* provide nearly all the information which may be needed on a general basis, in an easily portable up-to-date form. They have also another advantage – compared with the large encyclopaedias, they are relatively cheap. As well as reference books, general information can be obtained from the reference section of the central libraries in large cities by telephoning or writing. *The Daily Telegraph* maintains an information section at its library at 135 Fleet Street, London, where letters or telephone calls will be dealt with by expert staff.

Prestel

Prestel is British Telecom's two-way computerised service. It gives useful information on a television screen to anyone who has a modified set and a telephone. Users call their local Prestel Centre via their normal telephone line. Prestel supplies news and information from an enormous library, and one of the many useful information services Prestel utilises is in connection with vacancies for jobs. Eventually, Prestel will become international.

FOR YOUR FOLDER

26. GENERAL KNOWLEDGE

Write these notes in your folder, filling in the missing words and phrases.

1) Knowledge of facts covering a wide range of subjects is called _____ knowledge.

2) The most comprehensive encyclopaedia containing general knowledge is the _____.

3) General knowledge reference books are up-dated only every few years and are thus soon _____.

4) If detailed information is required on any subject a _____ is required.

5) A small single-volume encyclopaedia which is published annually is _____.

6) Another general reference book which is published annually is _____.

7) Information is obtainable from other sources than books. The British Telecom's two-way computerised information service is called _____.

8) One of the most useful information services the above supplies is in connection with _____.

9) The national newspaper which runs its own information section is the _____.

10) The _____ _____ of libraries in large cities will answer queries by letter or on the telephone.

Usage of English

A dictionary is essential both for the spelling and for the meanings of words.

A small dictionary is better than no dictionary at all, but, to be really useful, a dictionary should be as large and as comprehensive as possible. The smaller dictionaries do not give derivatives – that is, all the different words which come from one 'root' word – and are not so much help with the spelling or the meaning.

The *Concise Oxford Dictionary* (COD), *Chambers' Twentieth Century Dictionary,* and *Collins Dictionary of the English Language* are all excellent, comprehensive dictionaries. In addition to spelling and definitions, a dictionary may give the following information:

- Pronunciation
- Whether the word is slang, vulgar, or old-fashioned
- Abbreviations
- Foreign words and phrases
- Common English forenames
- Correct ways to address titled people.

As guides for spelling common words, three small books which can be very useful are: *The Little Oxford Dictionary, The Oxford Minidictionary* and the *Collins Gem Dictionary of Spelling and Word Division.*

A dictionary gives several words with the same meaning (synonyms) but a greater selection is given in *Roget's Thesaurus.* The word 'thesaurus' means a 'treasury'. *Roget's Thesaurus* is a 'treasury of words', which has words arranged in groups according to meaning. It is thus much more comprehensive than a dictionary. Using the *Thesaurus* gives you an idea of how rich the English language is.

566. STUDENT

.1 NOUNS student, pupil, scholar, learner, studier, educatee, trainee, *élève*[Fr]; inquirer; self-taught person, autodidact; auditor; monitor, prefect, praepostor [Brit]; — log *or* — logue.

.2 disciple, follower, apostle; convert, proselyte 145.7.

.3 self-taught man, autodidact.

.4 school child, school kid [informal]; schoolboy, school lad; schoolgirl; preschool child, preschooler, nursery school child, infant [Brit]; kindergartner, grade schooler, primary schooler, intermediate schooler; secondary schooler, prep schooler, preppie [informal], high schooler, schoolmate, schoolfellow, fellow student, classmate.

.5 college student, collegian, collegiate, varsity student [Brit informal], college boy or girl; co-ed [informal]; seminarian, seminarist; *bahur* [Heb], *yeshiva bocher* [Yid].

.6 undergraduate, undergrad [informal], cadet, midshipman; underclassman, freshman, freshie [informal], plebe, sophomore, soph [informal], upperclassman, junior, senior.

567. SCHOOL

.1 NOUNS school, educational institution, teaching institution, academic *or* scholastic institution, teaching and research institution, institute, academy, seminary, *Schule* [Ger], *école* [Fr], *escuela* [Sp].

.2 public school, common school, district school; union school, regional school, central school, consolidated school; private school; day school, country day school; boarding school, *pensionat* [Fr]; finishing school; dame school, blab school; special school, school for the handicapped; night school, evening school; summer school, vacation school; correspondence school; extension, university extension; school of continuing education, continuation school; platoon school; progressive school; free school, nongraded school, informal school, open classroom school; alternate *or* alternative school, street academy, storefront school, school without walls.

.3 [Brit terms] provided school, council school, board school; voluntary school, nonprovided school, national school, charity school.

.4 preschool, infant school [Brit], nursery,

A facsimile page from Roget's Thesaurus

To help with difficult points of grammar, *Fowler's Modern English Usage* is of great assistance. It helps to decide whether to put in an apostrophe or not, for instance, and whether to use 'principle' or 'principal' when the meaning is 'most important'.

Urdang's *Mispronounced, Misused and Misunderstood Words* gives guidance about spoken as well as written English.

A *Dictionary of Acronyms and Abbreviations* by Eric Pugh explains all those terms in common use such as NATO and SALT which are words in themselves — just in case you've forgotten what NATO and SALT stand for.

FOR YOUR FOLDER

27. USAGE OF ENGLISH

Write these notes in your folder, filling in the missing words and phrases.

1) For meanings of words a _____ is essential.

2) For another word with the same meaning (a synonym) a _____ is useful.

3) A _____ helps with pronunciation.

4) For assistance with awkward points of grammar, _____ would be useful.

5) If you were not sure you were using the word with the right meaning _____ would help.

6) The different words which come from one root word are called _____ .

7) Three good dictionaries are _____ , _____ and _____ .

8) The definition of a word is the _____ of a word.

9) The book to use to check whether a word is out of date is a _____ .

10) The book to use to check the spelling of the plural of a word is _____ .

11) A collection of first letters of words used as a word is an _____ .

12) The reference book to look up the above is _____ .

Exercise 23

USE OF *WHITAKER'S ALMANACK, PEARS' CYCLOPAEDIA* AND *ROGET'S THESAURUS*

You will find the answers to the following questions in Whitaker's Almanack.

1) What is the population of Nottingham?

2) When was the Union Jack first used (with the cross of St Patrick)?

3) What does it cost to visit the Stock Exchange in London?

4) Name the six states of Australia.

150

5) Where is the headquarters of the Waterways Board?

6) Where is the Bank of England?

7) To whom is the George Cross awarded?

8) Where is Hadrian's Wall?

9) When was the word 'Parliament' first used?

10) Where is the Foreign Office?

You will find the answers to the following questions in Pears' Cyclopaedia.

11) What is Lamaism?

12) Who were the Iceni?

13) What is a 'lace-wing'?

14) What is another name for 'aster'?

15) What took place in Caernarvon Castle on 1 July 1969?

16) Who lost his head in 1649?

17) When was President Kennedy assassinated?

18) What took place on 1 April 1973?

19) What time did the sun rise and set on 27 December 1970?

20) What is the capital of Massachusetts?

The answers to the following questions will be found in Roget's Thesaurus.

21) Find a synonym for 'angry'.

22) Find a synonym for 'lazy'.

23) Find a synonym for 'likable'.

24) Find a synonym for 'dress'.

25) Find a synonym for 'expert'.

26) Find a synonym for 'smelly'.

27) Find a synonym for 'impecunious'.

28) Find a synonym for 'well-behaved'.

29) Find a synonym for 'naughty'.

30) Find a synonym for 'kind'.

People

Information about famous people in this country is given in *Who's Who* (published annually).

International Who's Who lists famous people all over the world. There are several other *Who's Who's* giving specialised information – *Who's Who in Education* is an example.

Information about famous people who have died is given in *Who Was Who* and in the *Chambers' Biographical Dictionary* (prominent people all over the world).

People who have titles are listed in *Debrett's Peerage* and *Burke's Landed Gentry*.

Other specialised directories include:

Medical Register – doctors
Dentists' Register – dentists
Army List
Navy List } – lists of officers serving and retired
Air Force List
Crockford's Clerical Directory – clergy in the Church of England only
Directory of Directors – approximately 40 000 company directors with a list of their appointments
Black's Titles and Forms of Address – how to write and speak to titled people.

Exercise 24

USE OF *WHO'S WHO, INTERNATIONAL WHO'S WHO* AND *BLACK'S TITLES AND FORMS*

The answers to the following questions will be found in Who's Who.

1) What does Frank Muir list as his hobbies?

2) What are Mrs Thatcher's first names?

3) When did Sir Harold Wilson get married?

4) When was Arthur Askey made an OBE?

5) What does Denis Norden list as one of his hobbies?

6) What is the address of Patrick Moore, astronomer?

7) When did Sir Laurence Olivier marry Joan Plowright?

8) When did Dame Margot Fonteyn become President of the Royal Academy of Dancing?

9) Who is Brigid Brophy?

10) To which school did Lord Carrington go?

The answers to the following questions will be found in International Who's Who.

11) When was Dino de Laurentis born?

12) Who is Rosella Falk?

13) What did Naum Gabo publish in 1962?

14) When did Princess Grace marry Prince Rainier of Monaco?

15) Who is Edward Gierek?

16) When was Stefan Askenase born?

17) When was Charles Edward Barnes born?

18) What is Paul Clark's middle name?

19) Who is George Biddle?

20) When was the Hon. John Robert Nicholson born?

The answers to the following questions will be found in Black's Titles and Forms of Address.

21) If you spoke to the Queen, how would you address her?

22) How would you address an envelope to a retired Bishop?

23) What is the correct complimentary close on a letter to a Duchess?

24) Do the younger sons of a baronet have any form of title?

25) What does BAO stand for?

26) How would you address an envelope to an Archdeacon?

27) How would you speak to a Justice of the Peace when he is presiding on the Bench in Court?

28) What does 'Cantab' stand for?

29) What is the correct pronunciation of the name Knyvett?

30) If you were talking to Princess Anne, what would you call her?

Places and Travel

Books which could be useful for information on places and travel include:

- *a large atlas* – gives information about climate, products, population, terrain, rivers, oceans, lakes, boundaries, principal cities
- *road maps* – essential for car drivers
- *A – Z street maps* are available for most large cities in the British Isles
- *AA or RAC Handbooks* (free for members only) contain useful maps, information about hotels, ferries, distances between cities, population

Large street maps are available in many libraries and are useful for strangers visiting cities

ABC Railway Guide ABC World Airways Guide ABC Shipping Guide	They are essential for planning journeys. They contain detailed information about trains, ships, flights and are issued every month.
ABC Hotel Guide	This is a supplement to ABC World Airways Guide and is published twice-yearly, every January and June. It gives a comprehensive list of the main hotels all over the world.
ABC Travel Guide	This is issued quarterly and contains all the information necessary for travellers by air – about inoculations, vaccinations, visas, currency.
Hints to Businessmen	This is free, and is produced by the Department of Trade. It contains advice on consulates, hotels, customs and visas.
Statesman's Yearbook	Contains current information on countries of the world international organisations.

Exercise 25

USE OF TRAVEL REFERENCE BOOKS

The answers to the following questions will be found in the AA Book.

1) Which is the hotel in Worcester with the best food according to the AA?

2) Which is early closing day in Chichester?

3) Which day is market day in Ironbridge?

4) What is the distance from Keswick to London?

5) Which hotel in Spalding has rooms with private baths?

6) What are the licensing hours in Cambridge on weekdays?

7) What time is last post on Friday in Hereford?

8) Which county is Fleetwood in?

9) What is the population of Abberley?

10) Which restaurant in Buckingham meets the AA's Approved Standard?

The answers to the following questions will be found in the ABC Rail Guide.

11) What is the charge for sending luggage in advance from any British Rail Station in Great Britain (collection, conveyance and delivery)?

12) Is it possible for a passenger to insure himself or herself when travelling by rail?

13) Is it possible for a passenger to insure his or her luggage when travelling by rail?

14) What is the maximum age for a child to travel free on a train?

15) What is a 'Rover' rail ticket?

16) What are Motorail services?

17) Give one special facility for handicapped passengers.

18) What is the extra charge for reserving a seat on a train?

19) Is it possible to reserve a seat on a train by telephone?

20) If you were travelling by train to Bournemouth from London, at which station would you catch your train?

21) What is the telephone number for Passenger Service Information at Euston station?

22) What is the time of the first train from Charing Cross for Canterbury?

23) Is there a train on a Monday at 0427 from St Pancras to Barnsley?

24) What is the first train after 1200 from Coventry to London on a Saturday?

The answers to the following questions will be found in the ABC World Airways Guide.

25) What were the Bank Holidays in China last year?

26) What is the address of Air Tasmania?

27) Codes are used in the *ABC World Airways Guide* for cities. Which city has the code letters BRS?

28) Which city has the code letters BHX?

29) Flight Routing No 500 flies between which cities?

30) Flight Routing No 796 flies between which cities?

31) What is the name of the currency used in Poland?

32) What is the flying distance between Paris and Washington, DC?

33) What is the name of the Soviet airlines?

34) Air Nuigini is the national airline of which country?

35) What is the name of the currency used in Malaysia?

36) What were the Bank Holidays in Luxembourg last year?

37) What is the flying distance between Belgrade and Vienna?

38) Which city has the code letters COV?

39) Of which airline is 001 the code number?

The answers to the following questions will be found in the ABC Shipping Guide.

40) What is the Paris address of the CTC shipping line?

41) How many sailings are there on European Car Ferries between Great Britain and the Channel Islands?

42) How long does it take to sail between Folkestone and Calais by Sealink?

43) What is the address of Sealink UK Limited?

44) Which shipping line owns the *Chrissi Ammos*?

45) Has the ship *Adabelle Lykes* air-conditioned accommodation?

46) What is the address for the shipping office of Paquet Cruises?

47) Do Paquet Cruises carry cars?

48) Which countries do Paquet Cruises sail between?

49) What are the ports in Saudi Arabia?

50) Are there any shipping lines which operate in either of these ports?

51) What is the name of the shipping line which sails to Itea?

52) What type of ship is the *Bugel Eussa*?

53) What is the address of the Stena Line?

54) Which shipping line owns the *Queen Elizabeth 2*?

The answers to the following questions will be found in The Statesman's Yearbook.

55) What does USSR stand for?

56) What was the old name for Thailand?

57) Name the chief religion and currency in Chile.

58) When did India become a republic?

59) Which church in Sweden has the most members?

60) Who discovered the Fiji Islands?

61) Where are Andorra and Liechtenstein?

62) How many islands go to make up Japan?

63) When was the Declaration of Independence made by America?

64) When did the last Russian Emperor abdicate?

The Telephonist's Reference Books

The following would be needed by a competent telephonist and telex operator:

- *Local Telephone Directory.* This lists all the subscribers in the area, in alphabetical order of surnames.

  The green pages at the back of a telephone directory give useful details about information services, telephone equipment available from British Telecom, international telephone calls and telegrams.

- *Classified Trade Directory or Yellow Pages.* This lists people and organisations etc. in alphabetical order of their professions, occupations or trades, so that it is possible to find most florists, plumbers, hairdressers or poodle parlours in an area, when their individual names are not known.

- *Dialling Code Booklets.* These list all dialling codes – both overseas and inland.

- *British Telecom Guide.* This gives lots of information about overseas telephone services.

- *World Atlas.* This helps to locate foreign places.

- *Telex Directory.* Telex Directories for other parts of the world.

- *Alphabetical Index.* The most frequently used numbers, both internal and external, should be listed for quick reference under the name of the subscriber. An extension number in addition to the external number is useful, too, wherever possible.

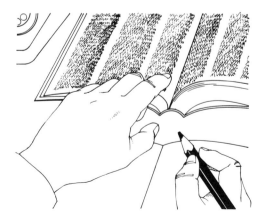

Record the numbers you often use

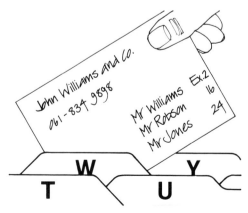

A card index for recording numbers

Exercise 26

THE TELEPHONIST'S REFERENCE BOOKS

The Classified Trade Directory (Yellow Pages) *and* British Telecom Guide *will be needed for questions 1−10.*

1) Give the name, address and telephone number of a car hire firm.

2) Give the name, address and telephone number of a watch repairer.

3) What is the minimum charge for an operator-assisted telephone call to Greece?

4) What is the time in Germany when it is 1000 hours in the British Isles?

5) What is the time in Canada when it is 1400 hours in the British Isles?

6) Is there a Telex service from this country to the USA?

7) Give the name, address and telephone number of a kennels.

8) What is the cost of a telegram to New Zealand (minimum charge)?

9) Give the name, address and telephone number of an estate agent.

10) Could a telephone credit card be used for a call to the Netherlands?

The Receptionist's Reference Books

Many of the books mentioned in this chapter will be useful for receptionists, but she may need additional books, pamphlets and magazines to help deal with visitor's enquiries. These may include:

- *Local guides to the area*
- *A map of the local area*
- *Local bus and train timetables*
- *A brochure on the firm's activities for visitors' information.*

Books in the Mail Room

The Post Office Guide is a 'must' in the mail room and several other books will be needed too. We shall deal with these in Chapter 9.

Miscellaneous Reference Books

Willings Press Guide	Contains a list of all British, and principal European periodicals and newspapers, together with the addresses and telephone numbers of the publishing offices.
Books in Print	Lists all books available with title, publisher, author and price.

Hansard	Is the official report of Parliamentary proceedings and contains a 'verbatim' (word for word) account of debates in Parliament.
Keesings Contemporary Archives	Contains information on current events, updated each week.
Ready Reckoner	Contains tables giving correct answers to many arithmetical problems.

Exercise 27

USE OF *WILLINGS PRESS GUIDE*

1) How many publications are there for chess players?

2) How many publications are there for people who keep horses, or are interested in them?

3) How many newspapers are published in Suffolk?

4) What are the names of the newspapers published in Cambridge?

5) What are the names of the newspapers published in Southall?

6) What is the address and telephone number of the head office of the *Kentish Times?*

7) What is the address and telephone number of the head office of the *Newcastle Journal?*

8) How often is *Kempe's Engineers' Yearbook* published?

9) How often is the *Police Gazette* published?

10) Is the general public able to buy the *Police Gazette?*

A final hint

If you cannot find the information in the book you think should contain it, try somewhere else. Not all dictionaries have the less usual words and not every encyclopaedia will tell you who Sweeney Todd was. Just keep trying different possibilities – and if you really do get stuck, your local library is there to help!

Exercise 28

CHOOSING THE RIGHT REFERENCE BOOK

In which reference book (or books) would you look to find the following information:

1) The meaning of an abbreviation you do not understand?

2) Regulations controlling the type of Christmas present to a friend in Kuwait?

3) How to address a letter to Lord Carrington?

4) The name and address of a manufacturer of squash racquets?

5) The number of votes the Labour Party were given in the last General Election?

6) The meaning of the word 'misrule'?

7) The actual name of Pope John Paul II?

8) At least four other words with the same meaning as 'calm'?

9) Which day is market day in Barnard Castle?

10) The population of Montevideo?

11) The telephone number and address of all the firms in Newcastle-upon-Tyne manufacturing rope?

12) The departure and arrival times of a train from Plymouth to London?

13) Whether Chile is mountainous or flat and its climate?

14) The telephone dialling code for Brussels?

15) Information about the growing of silk?

16) Whether to use 'further' or 'farther' in a piece of written English?

17) What UNESCO means?

18) Information about a large firm in your town?

19) The newspapers and magazines published in Carlisle?

20) Information about an event which took place last week and was the subject of much discussion on radio, television and in the national newspapers?

Exercise 29

GETTING INFORMATION FROM THE RIGHT REFERENCE BOOK

The answers to the following questions will be found in a dictionary, Who's Who, Black's Titles and Forms of Address, Post Office Guide, British Telecom Guide, Roget's Thesaurus, Willings Press Guide, the AA Handbook or the RAC Handbook.

1) Who is Roald Dahl?

2) How should the envelope be addressed which contains a letter to the Duchess of Kent?

3)   Is it possible to send saccharin to Albania?

4)   What day each week is there a cattle market in Loughborough?

5)   What is the correct pronunciation of the word 'mnemonic'?

6)   What is the meaning of 'mnemonic'?

7)   Find as many other words as you can with the same meaning as 'mnemonic'.

8)   Who are the publishers of *Woman's Weekly*?

9)   Where was Edward Heath born?

10) If you were speaking to the Dean of Westminster, what would you call him?

11) What would be the time in Greenland when it is 1400 in this country?

12) When did Glenda Jackson appear on TV as Elizabeth I?

13) How far from London is Paignton?

14) How much does *Sporting Life* cost?

15) *L'Express* is a Swiss newspaper. How often is it published?

16) What are the several different meanings of the word 'mite'?

17) Who is Peter de Polnay?

18) Is it possible to send a Telex message to Wake Island?

19) If you were speaking to Princess Anne, what would you call her?

20) Where would you write about advertising in *Honey*?

21) When did John le Carré write *Tinker Tailor Soldier Spy*?

22) What is the population of Lymm?

23) What does the abbreviation 'cdv' mean?

24) Which are the only football pools coupons which are allowed into Sarawak?

25) Who is Elisabeth Frink?

SECTION C **DEALING WITH PAPERWORK**

CHAPTER 9

The Mail Room

The Room Itself

Most firms large enough to be divided into departments have a mail room where letters and parcels are delivered by the postmen, and where all outgoing mail is stamped, or franked, before being taken to the post office or post box for collection. Staff working in a mail room are trained by a Supervisor and are efficient and (eventually) experienced, so that mail is dealt with promptly, both incoming and outgoing.

A well-organised mail room will contain scales (two types) for weighing both letters and parcels, franking machine, possibly other equipment for dealing with large quantities of outgoing mail, as well as mail room accessories and reference books for the staff to use to deal with any queries. Shelves and tables should be arranged to make it easier for the staff to carry out sorting incoming mail, and placing outgoing mail into the various categories ready for posting.

The illustration below shows one way in which a mail room could be arranged, and this is similar to a layout recommended by the Post Office for efficient handling of mail. The Post Office is extremely anxious that firms should organise their mail competently, as this makes the work of Post Office staff simpler.

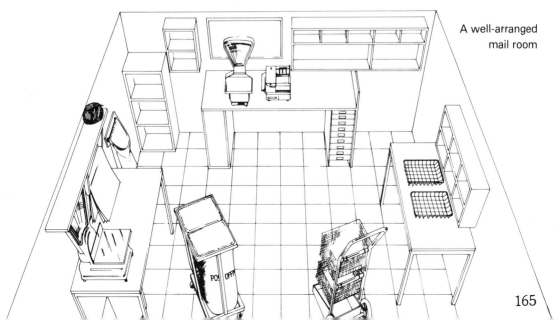

A well-arranged mail room

Incoming Mail

Mail arriving at a firm may include many different documents besides letters. There may be invoices, quotations, estimates, orders, applications for jobs and advertising material. It is very important to open and distribute the mail to the different departments without delay, so that the office staff and managers are able to make a start on their day's work. In a large firm, mail room staff may take it in turns to come in before other office workers in order to make sure that all the mail has been taken round to the departments by the time the office workers are ready to start. In a small office, the manager may open and deal with the letters himself.

One type of letter would never be opened except by the person to whom it is addressed. This is a letter marked 'Personal', 'Private' or 'Confidential', which would be placed on one side and handed over to the addressee unopened as soon as possible.

Styles of addressing a confidential letter

In order to be certain that mail is in an office early in the morning, some firms arrange with the Post Office to rent one of the Post Office Private Boxes at a Delivery Office. Letters and packets may be collected at any time from a private box, except on Sundays, or days when the Post Office does not deliver. Firms using this service are given a number by the Post Office to use as part of their address. The Post Office make a yearly charge for private boxes. A similar arrangement is possible for a private bag, into which a firm's mail is sorted at the Delivery Office, and which can be collected by the firm using it on normal Post Office delivery days. A charge is made by the Post Office for private bags, too.

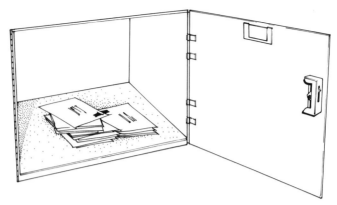

A Post Office Private Box

If a firm has no private box or bag at the Post Office's Delivery Office, mail will be delivered in the normal way by a postman to the reception desk of the firm, and mail room clerks will collect it from there using trolleys if there is a large quantity of letters and packets.

As it is so important to open and distribute the mail quickly, following a daily routine ensures that it is done efficiently:

1) 'Face' envelopes (i.e. turn envelopes so that address is the right side up and the right way round). While doing this, take out any envelopes marked 'Private' and place them on one side, unopened, for delivery with the opened mail.

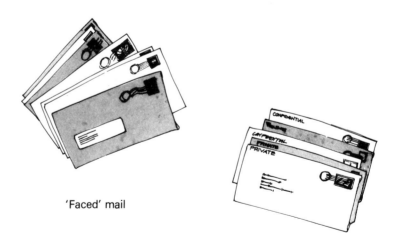

'Faced' mail

2) In some firms, it is usual to divide incoming mail into first and second-class, opening the first-class mail first, as it is (generally) more important. Second-class mail is a slower and cheaper service, normally taking two days to deliver. First- and second-class postal services are known as the 'two-tier' system.

3) Open envelopes by slitting *both* long edges. This can be done with a paper knife, or, more quickly, with an electrically operated letter opener.

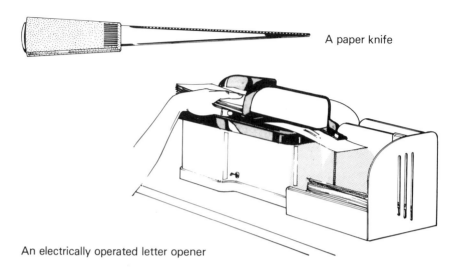

A paper knife

An electrically operated letter opener

The electric letter opener removes a very narrow strip or 'sliver' of paper from the edge of an envelope, so narrow that it is unlikely to damage the contents, but in order to make sure that this does not happen, the envelope must be tapped on the desk so that the contents drop to the bottom of the envelope. Slitting both long edges makes it easy to check very quickly that nothing has been left accidentally in the envelope. Some mail rooms keep opened envelopes for a few days in case of queries. The address or postmark on the envelope may be useful.

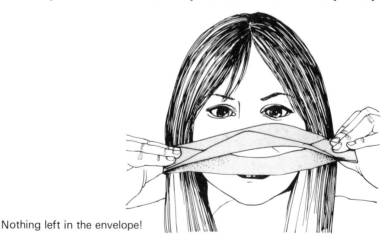

Nothing left in the envelope!

4) Unfold letters, or other documents, smoothing them out flat, and apply a date-stamp, taking care not to stamp over any of the typing or writing on the paper. Some firms use a stamp which automatically prints the time on the document as well as the date. Dating incoming mail is an

important check on when it was actually received in the mail room. An envelope marked 'Private' would be date stamped on the (unopened) envelope.

A date stamp

5) Some letters, or documents, may have enclosures attached to them, or folded with them. Enclosures may be: catalogues, price-lists, leaflets, samples, photographs, cheques, stamps or postal orders. If they have not been attached to the letter, they should be stapled to it at the top left-hand corner. Pins and paper clips are not suitable as they have a tendency to catch on to other papers by mistake. Paper clips would, of course, have to be used for photographs which could be damaged by staples.

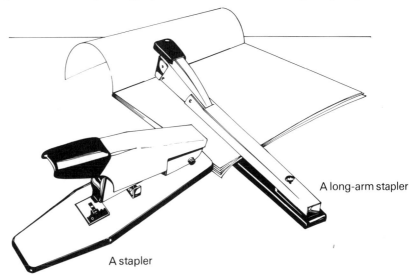

A long-arm stapler

A stapler

Letters containing money in any form should have the amount and the initials of the person opening the letter in pencil at the foot of the letter – this helps as a check in case of any later query. In some firms a remittances book is used into which all money received is entered before being taken to the cashier or the mail room supervisor. An entry in this book shows the date of receipt for each sum of money, the person or firm who sent it, and the amount. It also shows whether the money was received as a cheque, postal order or cash, and the signature of the person who recorded the information.

DATE	SENDER	REMITTANCE	AMOUNT	SIGNATURE
198—			£ p	
June 1st	M.L. Mann and Co. Ltd	Cheque	20—00	P. Fox
June 1st	Mrs F. Hopkins	P.O.	2—00	P. Fox
June 2	Messrs. Page & Vines	Chq.	49—75	S. Smith
June 4	Mr H.M. Harrison	Cash	10—00	S. Smith
June 4	Miss G. Manson	P.O.	5—00	J. Johnson
June 5	P.K. Engineering	Cheque	97.44	J. Johnson

A page from a remittances book

Exercise 30

THE REMITTANCES BOOK

Copy a remittances book page and rule it up.

Using today's date, enter the following remittances which have been received with this morning's mail. Initial the entries yourself.

Mrs O Marsh enclosed a postal order for £5.50
Miss K Neale enclosed a cheque for £10
Messrs Lang and Dunn enclosed a cheque for £50
Mr P Barnes enclosed £45 in notes
Mr F Pearce enclosed a cheque for £9
Miss M Knowles enclosed a postal order for 50p
Mrs R Frost enclosed 45p in stamps
Messrs Nash and Grimes enclosed a cheque for £34.75.

A register of incoming mail may be kept by a small firm; in most large firms this is no longer the practice.

Missing enclosures should be noted in pencil and initialled at the foot of the letter by the person opening it. It is easy to tell, in most cases, whether a letter should have an enclosure by a quick glance, as there are several ways in which a typist or secretary may indicate that something is attached to a letter:

a 'Enc.' (which is the abbreviation for 'Enclosure') typed at the bottom left-hand side of a letter.

b A small label with 'Enc.' or 'Enclosure' printed on it, affixed to the letter. Some firms instruct their typists and secretaries to stick a label on the envelope, too, as an extra check. Enclosure labels may be numbered, for reference when replying to the letter.

c The symbol / typed in the left-hand margin alongside the sentence which refers to the enclosure.

d Three dots (...) typed in the left-hand margin alongside the sentence which refers to the enclosure.

c and **d** are used less frequently than **a** or **b**.

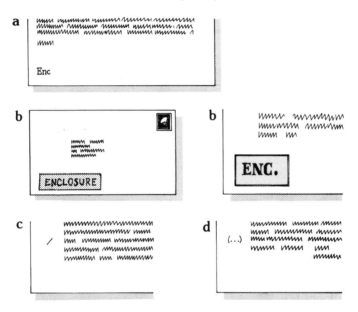

Different ways of indicating an enclosure

Distributing Mail to Different Departments

While sorting the mail, the mail room clerks will be looking for the following to help them to decide where to send it:

- 'For the attention of (followed by name)'. This would be typed under the inside address on a letter immediately *over* 'Dear Sir'.

- The letter may have a subject heading typed underneath 'Dear Sir'.

- There may be a reference at the top of the letter. This is usually the initials of the sender of the letter followed by the initials of his typist or secretary.

If the letter does not contain any of the above information, it may be helpful to read it through quickly.

Not all letters come by post. Some are delivered by firm's messengers and are inter-departmental. This is known as internal mail and, if confidential, may be enclosed in large envelopes which are printed with lines for the name of each recipient so that after opening the name is crossed out and the next name written underneath. Letters between offices, departments and even branches of the same firm, are known as 'memos' (see Chapter 6).

INTERNAL POST - Cross off last name: Use again. Do not seal flap

An envelope for internal mail (holes show whether it is empty or not)

Parcels may arrive later in the day, as may mail which has to be signed for in the presence of the postman. Into this latter category will come registered letters and recorded delivery. There is more information about these Post Office services in the next chapter.

It may be the responsibility of the mail room supervisor to arrange for a letter to be seen by more than one person, if the letter mentions several topics. She could arrange for this to be done by:

- asking a typist to type a copy with several carbon copies
- photocopying it
- sending the letter to each person or department accompanied by a routing slip (see pp. 121 – 2).

The choice of which method to adopt would depend on the urgency with which the letter had to be circulated. Photocopying is the quickest and most accurate, but it is also the most expensive. Carbon copies are the cheapest but the typist may make a mistake which could be serious. This method is slow, too. A routing slip also may take time as some people on the list could hold on to the letter thus delaying its progress round to the others on the list.

Equipment for dealing with incoming mail

A trolley

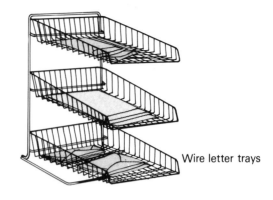

Wire letter trays

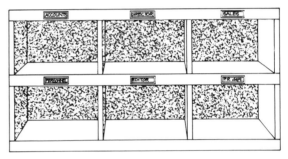

Pigeon holes

FOR YOUR FOLDER

28. INCOMING MAIL

Write these notes in your folder, filling in the missing words and phrases.

1) Mail arriving at a firm may include (besides letters) applications for jobs, orders, advertising material and _____.

2) It is very important to distribute the mail to the different departments without delay so that the _____ are able to make a start on _____.

3) In a large firm, mail room staff may _____ in order to make sure that all the mail has been distributed by the time the office workers are ready to start.

4) The type of letter which would *never* be opened in the mail room is marked _____ or _____ or _____.

5) In order to be certain that the mail arrives at offices early in the morning some firms arrange with the GPO to rent a _____ at a delivery office.

6) Sorting incoming mail starts with removing any marked 'Private' and _____ the envelopes containing the remainder of the mail.

7) Envelopes should be slit (either by paper knife or electric letter opener) along both _____ so that it is easy to check very quickly that _____.

8) When envelopes have been opened and contents removed, the letters or other documents should be _____ or _____ on a suitable blank space.

9) Enclosures should be _____ to the letters.

10) If the enclosure is money in any form (a remittance), the amount should be _____ and the initials of the person opening the letter in pencil at the foot of the letter.

11) In some firms a _____ book is used to enter all money received and is taken to the cashier or mail room supervisor.

12) Missing enclosures should be _____.

13) It is easy to tell whether there should be an enclosure with a letter by 'Enc.' typed at the foot of the letter, / in the left-hand margin, a small label with 'Enc.' or 'Enclosure' printed on or _____.

14) To help them sort the mail, mail room clerks will look for 'For the attention of _____, subject heading or _____.

15) Not all letters come by post. Some are from other departments and are known as _____ mail.

16) Parcels, registered mail and _____ may arrive later in the day.

17) Useful items for dealing with incoming mail are: stapler, trolley, wire letter trays, pigeon holes and _____.

Exercise 31

INCOMING MAIL

1) Describe the 'two-tier' system of mail delivery by the GPO.

2) Explain how you would deal with a letter which should have been accompanied by a cheque and the cheque was not in the envelope.

3) How can you quickly make sure that a letter does not have an enclosure?

4) Describe how you can decide where to deliver a letter.

5) How should all money be dealt with in incoming mail?

6) List some equipment for dealing with incoming mail.

7) Why is it necessary for staff dealing with incoming mail to arrive before other office staff?

8) There are several ways of arranging for more than one person to see a letter. Which is

   a quickest?
   b cheapest?
   c (in your opinion) most efficient (ignoring cost)?

9) Why are opened envelopes sometimes kept for a few days before being destroyed?

10) How could a mail room clerk make absolutely sure that she/he had left nothing in an envelope by accident?

Outgoing Mail

Mail for posting may arrive at any time during the day, but the afternoons are the busiest times in the mail room, and to avoid a sudden rush of mail, a system of regular collection from every department should be organised. Trays marked 'Outgoing Mail' placed where the messenger from the mail room can conveniently collect the mail at frequent intervals ensures that letters for posting are dealt with promptly. The mail room may also state a final collection time, after which no mail will be accepted for that day. This will avoid mail room staff having to stay late to deal with a last-minute rush and will ensure that Post Office collection times can be met.

In some firms, letters are sent to the mail room already folded and inserted into envelopes, with a pencilled '1' or '2' in the top right-hand corner, to show whether the letter has to go by first or second class post. It will still be necessary to weigh a letter if it is bulky or seems heavier than the maximum weight allowed by the GPO for minimum first class or second class postage. An addressee receiving a letter which has not enough stamps on it has to pay the postman *twice* the missing amount of postage, so the sender will not be popular!

Other letters which must be weighed are letters going abroad, whether by airmail or 'surface' mail. Airmail is expensive, and special thin paper and envelopes cut the cost down. There is also an airmail letter form (of A4 size) available at the Post Office which is the cheapest way to send letters by air. This is called an 'aerogramme' 'Surface' mail is carried by train, ship or van, and is cheaper than airmail but slower.

In many firms, letters and other documents are sent to the mail room accompanied by correctly typed envelopes, and the mail room clerk's job is to fold and insert the letters into the envelopes. While she is doing this, she should:

- check by looking at the letter to see if there should be an enclosure. If the enclosure is missing, the letter should be placed on one side and later returned to the sender.
- if there is an enclosure, attach it to the letter by stapling or, if not suitable, paper-clip. Pins should never be used as the person opening the envelope may receive a sharp jab.
- check that letter has been signed.
- check that inside address is the same as that on the accompanying envelope. If not, again put letter and envelope on one side for querying either with sender or mail room supervisor. 'Window' or 'aperture' envelopes are often used by firms to avoid the possibility of sending a letter to the wrong person or firm.

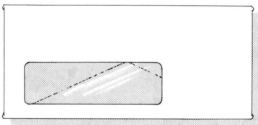

A window envelope. This envelope has a transparent panel

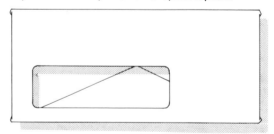

An aperture envelope. 'Aperture' is another word for 'space'. This envelope has space through which the address on the letter can be read

- fold the letter so that it fits the envelope with as few creases as possible. This is not as easy as it sounds, and most mail rooms have a special way of doing it. Some firms print their letterheading with small marks near the edges which indicate where the letter has to be folded.

- place the letter (with enclosure if there is one) into a suitably sized envelope and seal. The Post Office prefers envelopes to be within certain sizes (90 mm × 140 mm and 120 mm × 235 mm). These are known as POP envelopes (Post Office Preferred).
- weigh the letter if bulky (it may need extra postage) or if it is addressed to a country overseas
- affix correct stamps and place letter into one of the following three categories:
    (i) *Inland* – anywhere in the British Isles
    (ii) *Overseas* – both airmail and surface mail
    (iii) *Registered Post or Recorded Delivery* – for which a receipt has to be obtained from the Post Office. They cannot be posted in a letter-box.

A franking machine prints in red the value of a stamp on an envelope, postcard or label, as well as the date and time of posting, the place of posting, licence number of the machine, and an advertising slogan, if required. It saves the time spent on keeping a record of stamps used, as well as the trouble of sticking stamps on envelopes, parcels and packages.

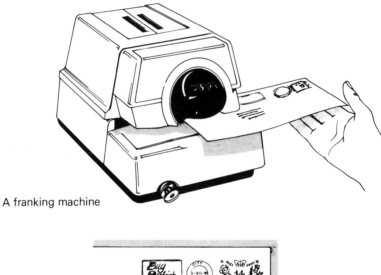

A franking machine

Franked envelopes, one with an advertising slogan and the other a franked label (no advertising slogan). Labels would be affixed to parcels or letters too bulky to go through a franking machine

Franking machines may be purchased or hired from the manufacturers. A licence to use the machine must first be obtained from the Post Office. There is no charge for this. The Post Office also sets a meter on a franking machine in accordance with the amount of money paid to them and then seals the meter. Each time an envelope, postcard or label is franked, this meter deducts the amount used – it is a 'descending' meter as the figures shown decrease. There is a second meter on a franking machine which increases or 'ascends' with each franked impression – this one is called an 'ascending' meter as the figures increase, showing the amount of postage used. A *franking meter control card* has to be sent to the Post Office every week, showing the reading of these two meters, even though no postage may have been used. Franking machines are lockable so that they cannot be used dishonestly. The mail room clerk whose responsibility it is to look after a franking machine has to reset the date each morning, and make sure the roller which holds the red ink making the impression does not need reinking. She also has to watch the 'descending' meter carefully, so that more money could be paid to the Post Office and the meter reset well before it is due to run out. A well-organised mail room will have a supply of postage stamps available in case the franking machine breaks down.

FRANKING MACHINE CONTROL CARD

Licensee ....
Meter Office
(as shown on Record Card) ....

Machine (or Meter) No ....

Setting or Recording Unit ....
   I certify that the following particulars in respect of the above described machine for

week-ended .... are correct:—

	ALL MACHINES	LOCKING MACHINES	ALL MACHINES
	Reading of Ascending Register (Totalisator)	Reading of Descending Register (Credit Meter)	Last entry in col. "Total Deposits" or "Total Settings" on Record Card
Mon.			
Tue.			
Wed.			
Thur.			
Fri.			
Sat.			

NOTE 1. Whether or not the machine has been used, this card must be posted on Saturday, or on Friday if no postings are made on Saturday.   Signed ....
NOTE 2. The daily entry must be made on completion of each day's postings.   .... 19 ....

Franked mail or 'metered mail' as it is also called, can by-pass Post Office facing and cancelling in the Post Office sorting office, often catching earlier trains and planes. Because such mail saves the Post Office time, it has to be posted in a special way – either handed in over the counter of a Post Office, tied in bundles and 'faced' or posted in a letter box in a special envelope for franked mail.

If an envelope or label has the wrong value franked on it by mistake, it should be kept and returned to the Post Office (when the franking machine meter is taken for resetting would be a suitable time). A refund will be given less five per cent of the value franked.

Some firms still like to keep a record of outgoing mail, even though there is a franking machine in use, and this record will just consist of names and addresses of recipients of letters and parcels.

Larger franking machines incorporate equipment for sealing envelopes as well as stacking them after they have been franked.

Exercise 32

THE FRANKING MACHINE CONTROL CARD

Complete a franking machine control card with the following details and state the balance of credit at the end of the week:

Name:		Excelsior Development Corporation
Meter office:		Plymouth Post Office
Unit:		$\frac{1}{2}$p
Machine number:		P.4962
Number of units purchased:		86,000 ⎫ at commencement of week
Number of units used:		80,015 ⎭
Monday:	used	1,115 units
Tuesday:	used	3,429 units
Wednesday:	used	1,009 units
Thursday:	purchased	10,000 units
	used	2,050 units
Friday:	used	1,760 units

Complete a franking machine control card with the following details and state the balance of credit at the end of the week:

Name:		Jones & Jenkins Bros
Meter Office:		Swansea Post Office
Unit:		$\frac{1}{2}$p
Machine number:		C.2314
Number of units purchased:		41,000 ⎫ at commencement of week
Number of units used:		35,000 ⎭
Monday:	used	3,050 units
Tuesday:	used	2,102 units
Wednesday:	purchased	5,000 units
	used	1,009 units
Thursday:	used	2,100 units
Friday:	used	1,562 units

Record Books

Some firms keep records of stamps used particularly if they do not have a franking machine.

THE POSTAGE BOOK

A postage book gives a detailed record of all letters, packets and parcels posted. An example is shown below.

STAMPS BOUGHT	NAME AND TOWN OF ADDRESSEE		STAMPS USED	DETAILS
£ P			£ P	
10 . 00	21 June 198–			
	F. Jones Ipswich		14	
	L. Naylor Cardiff		11½	
	P. Knight Coventry		29	Rec. delivery
	S. Singh Calcutta, India		30	Airmail
	K. Wilson & Sons Ltd	Reading	1 . 04	Reg. letter
	J. Ross and Co Ltd	Hove	11½	
	A. B. Rowe and Co	Rugby	2 . 20	Parcel
			4 . 20	
		Balance c/f	5 . 80	
10 . 00			10 . 00	
	22 June 198–			
5 . 80	Balance b/f			

Exercise 33

THE POSTAGE BOOK

Copy the postage book above and use it to make entries for the questions below. Using Postal Rates leaflets, work out the correct postage.

1) Stamps bought £10. Use today's date.
   First-class letter D Smythe, Canterbury
   First-class letter L Barnett, Coventry
   Second-class letter M Mole, Stoke-on-Trent
   Parcel weighing 2 kg (Rate) to V Scott
   Parcel weighing 3 kg (Rate) to M Mason
   Airmail letter to C Dunsford, Madras, India: 30 g
   Registered letter (value of contents £350)

   Total the stamps used, find the balance, and bring it forward to the next day.

2) Replace the stamps used in the exercise above. From an up-to-date Postal Rates leaflet, find the correct postal rates for the following and enter them in the Postage Book:

Recorded Delivery letter (second class) to P Tomkins, Hull
Recorded Delivery letter (first class) to Messrs T Price, Rugby
Registered packet to J K Brown & Co Ltd, Sutton – value £375
Airmail packet to Montreal, Canada – weighing 110 g
First class letter to Johnson, Bromsgrove
First class letter to Hill, Redditch
Second class letter (weighing 150 g) to Dawson, Cambridge.

THE RECORD OF STAMPS

A simple record of stamps is used in some firms as a check on the number of stamps used each day. Details of correspondents are omitted.

STAMPS BOUGHT	DATE	STAMPS USED	
£ P 15 . 00	21 June 198–	30 @ 14p 40 @ 11½p 10 @ 2½p Balance c/f	4 . 20 4 . 60 . 25 9 . 05 5 . 95
15 . 00 5 . 95	22 June 198–	Balance b/f	15 . 00

Other mail room equipment

- *Folding machine* — for folding letters and documents to be inserted into envelopes
- *Folding and inserting machine* — folds and inserts letters into the envelopes
- *Parcel scales*
 Letter balance } — essential for weighing letters and parcels to make sure they have the correct value stamps on them
- *Guillotine* — for cutting papers neatly
- *Addressing machine* — used in mail rooms where a great number of letters are sent out regularly to the same addressees.
- *Collators* — for sorting numbered papers into sets

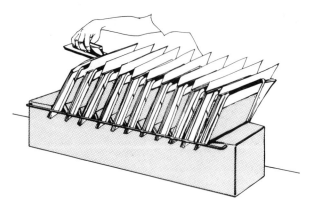

A horizontal collator

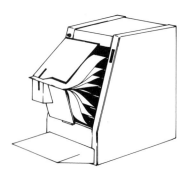

A vertical collator

● *A stamp affixing machine* — is fitted with a roll of postage stamps which can be bought at the Post Office. It avoids having loose stamps in a box which can be easily lost or 'borrowed' but it is still necessary to moisten the stamps and stick them on letters and parcels. A stamp affixing machine is not as efficient or useful as a franking machine.

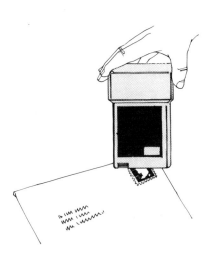

Small items used in a mail room are known as mail room sundries. A list of these sundries is as follows:

● Brown paper – for wrapping parcels
● Clear adhesive tape – to use instead of string
● Corrugated paper – for packing breakables
● Envelopes – POP sizes
● Gummed paper strip – also to use instead of string
● Paper knife – if there is no electric letter opener
● Scissors
● Sponge moistener – for moistening stamps and envelopes
● Roller moistener – does the same job
● Sealing wax – for sealing registered packets
● String

When you pack parcels, it is very important to make sure that they are strongly packed in suitable boxes. Every year the Post Office has to repack large numbers of parcels which become unfastened in the post and lose their contents. Parcels should be clearly addressed, with a stick-on label as well as a tie-on label, and should also have the name and address of the sender on the outside as well as the inside.

A parcel shedding its contents   A parcel correctly wrapped and labelled

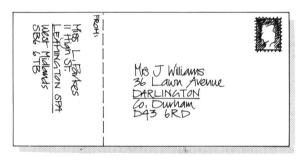

A parcel label

MAIL ROOM REFERENCE BOOKS

The *Post Office Guide,* issued (usually) each year by the Post Office, gives very clear and detailed instructions about parcelling everything, from musical instruments to umbrellas, and an up-to-date copy should be in every mail room for reference, not only in connection with parcels, but for information about postal rates and services to every country in the world. Separate leaflets (red for inland and blue for overseas) are issued by the Post Office after each change in postal rates. These give more detailed information than the *Post Office Guide. The Post Office Guide* may be bought from large post offices, the leaflets are free.

Other books useful in the mail room include:

- A large atlas
- A local *Classified Trade Directory (Yellow Pages)*
- Telephone Directories
- A-Z Street Maps

FOR YOUR FOLDER

29. OUTGOING MAIL

Write these notes in your folder, filling in the missing words and phrases.

1) The busiest time of the day in the mail room is the _____.

2) An instruction to the mail room about affixing a first-class or second-class stamp to a letter is by _____.

3) Letters which should be weighed to check if any extra postage is needed are airmail, surface mail and _____ letters.

4) Any letter which is under-stamped is penalised by the Post Office who ask twice the amount of the _____ from the unfortunate recipient.

5) Before placing a letter into an envelope and sealing it, the mail room clerk should check enclosures (if any), signature on letter and _____.

6) _____ envelopes are often used by firms to avoid the possibility of sending a letter to the wrong address.

7) POP (Post Office Preferred) envelopes are envelopes which the Post Office prefer to be within _____.

8) After envelopes are sealed, outgoing mail should be divided into three main categories – inland, overseas and _____.

9) To avoid sticking on stamps and keeping a postage book, many firms use a _____ machine which prints in red the value of a stamp as well as the _____.

10) Parcels can be stamped by this machine by using a _____.

11) Equipment essential for weighing letters is _____ and for weighing parcels _____.

12) For cutting papers neatly a _____ is necessary.

13) For sorting numbered papers into sets a _____ is useful.

14) In a very large mail room a folding and inserting machine folds and _____ into the envelopes.

15) Packing of parcels is very important. They should be clearly addressed with a _____ label as well as a _____ label and should have the name and address of the sender on the outside as well as the _____.

16) The most important mail room reference book, issued regularly by the Post Office is the *Post Office* _____.

Exercise 34

OUTGOING MAIL

1) Explain how the mail room clerks would know whether a sealed letter has to go by first-class or second-class mail.

2) What arrangements should be made by the mail room supervisor to try and avoid a 'rush' of mail in the afternoon, and also to make sure that collection times are met?

3) What are the four important steps to check before folding a letter and placing it in an envelope?

4) Which letters have to be taken to the Post Office and a receipt obtained for them?

5) A franking machine saves time and trouble in the mail room. What would be the duties of a mail room clerk, every day, if she were in charge of a franking machine?

6) How is the postage paid for when a franking machine is used?

7) How is franked mail posted?

8) Apart from saving time in the mail room, franked mail has another advantage. What is it?

9) What is the reference book in the mail room which lists trades and professions alphabetically?

10) Why is the *Post Office Guide* so important in the mail room?

CHAPTER 10

Mail, Parcels and Post Office Services

Information from the Post Office

It is most important for any office employee who has the responsibility of dealing with the despatch of mail to have a thorough knowledge of the Post Office mail service, and the regulations covering the despatch of mail.

The *Post Office Guide* and up-to-date Post Office leaflets giving the cost of stamps and the postage rates overseas are obtainable at most large Post Offices. The leaflets are free but you must pay for the *Post Office Guide*.

Inland Mail

'Inland mail' refers to letters, packets and parcels posted to destinations in the British Isles.

For letters and parcels there is a two-tier system, meaning that the sender may choose to send them first or second class. First-class post is dearer but arrives at its destination (usually) within 24 hours. Second-class post is cheaper, but slower, and it may take up to 4 days, depending upon when it is posted (e.g. a letter posted on Friday with a second class stamp may not arrive at the address of the recipient until the following Tuesday).

POSTCODES

This code is used by the Post Office to speed the sorting of mail in its sorting office. It is important that the correct postal code is written (or typed) on envelopes, parcels and packets or delivery may be delayed (see p. 175).

CERTIFICATE OF POSTING

This is a very cheap way of making sure that an important letter has actually been posted (and not still in someone's pocket!). The cost is 1p and the letter has to be handed in at a Post Office for the counter clerk to complete and stamp a receipt. (It must *not* be posted in a letterbox.)

This receipt, when taken back to the office, is proof that the letter has been posted, and when. Delivery of the letter is made by the postman in the ordinary way (through a letterbox) and no receipt form has to be signed by the recipient.

RECORDED DELIVERY

With this method, the Post Office issues a receipt on a yellow slip to the person posting the letter and also authorises the postman to collect a signature from the recipient, so that proof of posting and delivery is provided. Recorded Delivery is suitable only for letters and packets containing important papers – not valuables, because compensation is very limited. Papers suitable for sending by Recorded Delivery could be: passport, birth certificate, examination papers, legal documents – anything which could cause a great deal of inconvenience if lost.

REGISTERED POST

When anything valuable (up to a certain size and weight) has to be sent by post, it should be sent by Registered Post. Compensation is paid according to the amount of fee paid. Letters and packets sent by Registered Post are handled with special security measures by the Post Office and separately from ordinary mail. The counter clerk at the post office gives a receipt and the postman obtains one from the addressee. Registered post is for inland post only – valuables being sent abroad by post are sent by another Post Office service.

COMPENSATION FEE

This is the Post Office service which is for parcels over a certain weight containing valuables, for inland post only. The maximum amount of compensation paid is scaled according to the amount of fee paid.

Details of Registered Post, Recorded Delivery and Compensation Fee (CF Parcels) are in the Postal Rates (Inland) leaflets obtainable at all post offices free. These are updated after each change of postal rates.

Overseas Mail

PARCELS

The Post Office has a scheme of insurance for parcels going overseas which will provide compensation in the event of loss. The Postal Rates Overseas Compendium issued by the Post Office gives full details of rates for all overseas parcels.

LETTERS

The cheapest way to send a letter abroad by airmail is by using an airletter form, called an Aerogramme, obtainable at all post offices. The only disadvantage to these is that no enclosures are possible.

Other letters to be sent by airmail should be typed on very thin (airmail) paper and placed in a special airmail envelope as cost is calculated by weight – the rates are given in the Postal Rates (overseas) leaflet obtainable free at all post offices.

Letters can be sent surface mail, if there is no urgency, to any country outside Europe – all letters addressed to Europe go by airmail automatically, so there is no need to affix an airmail label to letters going there. (Because of this the airmail service to Europe is called the 'European All-up'.) Surface mail to countries outside Europe are carried by ship or train, or van, and is much slower than airmail. Surface mail rates are given in the post office leaflet on overseas postal rates.

CUSTOMS

All packets and parcels posted to an overseas destination require a declaration label describing the contents. This applies to both airmail and surface mail. A green label has to be completed where the value of the contents is *under* £50, and a white label where the value is over £50. The reason for this declaration is to inform the customs officers in the country to which the parcel is sent what it contains – on some articles a tax has to be paid by the recipient and this tax is known as 'duty'. Duty is imposed on some goods to discourage people from sending them, the idea being that if the goods are manufactured in that country, the inhabitants want to sell their own and prevent foreign goods of similar type competing with them. Gifts may be allowed in duty free in certain countries if described on the label as 'gifts'. The *Post Office Guide* gives full details of regulations to all the countries of the world.

INTERNATIONAL REPLY COUPONS

These are sold at the larger post offices in Great Britain and Northern Ireland, and are exchangeable in virtually all countries of the world for a stamp or stamps. The person to whom an international reply coupon is sent takes it to his nearest post office and exchanges it for a stamp issued by his own country – British stamps are not accepted in any foreign country. An international reply coupon is a convenient means of 'prepaying' the cost of a reply from abroad.

Services for sending mail quickly

DATAPOST

Datapost is a Post Office service which is for urgent parcels, packets and letters. It guarantees overnight delivery within the United Kingdom and very speedy delivery to many countries overseas. Datapost is now available on demand at Post Offices (previously it had to be arranged on

a contractual basis only). Datapost mail travels separately from ordinary mail and is accompanied throughout by post office staff (except when in transit on flights overseas). Items sent by Datapost overseas get fast Customs clearance, which is another advantage of the service.

Datapost is especially suitable for sending computer material, from firm to firm, who use hired computer time, but it can be used for any items where a guaranteed delivery is important – laboratory specimens from hospitals or samples to prospective customers.

A receipt is given for all Datapost items, so that firms using the service have proof of delivery.

EXPRESSPOST

This is a special same-day messenger service. Expresspost collects and delivers and is ideal for urgent documents and small packages, or last-minute birthday cards and presents. Within-city delivery time is normally 2 hours or less; it also operates between an increasing number of major cities. Charges are based on distance.

RAILWAY LETTERS

This is a service for first-class letters only for transmission by train from one railway station to another, either to be called for at the station, or to be transferred to the post. It is only available provided stations are staffed and have facilities for dealing with mail.

SPECIAL DELIVERY

Under this service, the sender of a postal packet may arrange for its special delivery by a messenger *after* its arrival at the office of delivery, provided that this will ensure earlier delivery than by normal postal treatment. Special Delivery is for first-class mail only, and can be used for letters or parcels. It is also suitable for Recorded Delivery, Registered and Compensation Fee services. There is a special delivery fee in addition to the full ordinary postage, for one mile of delivery distance; beyond one mile additional charges are collected from the addressee.

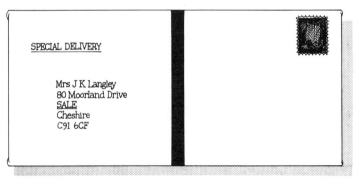

SPECIAL DELIVERY

Mrs J K Langley
80 Moorland Drive
SALE
Cheshire
C91 6CF

A letter addressed for Special Delivery

MARKING FOR SPECIAL DELIVERY

The words 'Special Delivery' must be marked above the address on the left-hand side of the letter or parcel. A broad blue or black perpendicular line must also be drawn from top to bottom on both the front and the back of a letter and completely round a parcel.

Parcels Services – inland

RAILWAY PARCELS

This is a service operated in a similar way to Railway Letters (see opposite). A parcel may be handed in at an express delivery post office, and it is possible to ask for a Post Office messenger to collect it at the station of destination.

SPECIAL DELIVERY

Parcels may also be sent quickly by this service (see opposite).

CASH ON DELIVERY (COD)

Under this service the cost of the article delivered can be collected by the postman from the recipient. This sum is then sent to the sender of the parcel by means of a special order. All parcels must be registered. It is a service often used by mail order firms and mentioned in their advertisements in newspapers and magazines. Anyone sending an order does not enclose a remittance, but pays the cost of the goods received to the postman delivering the parcel.

BRITISH RAIL PARCELS SERVICES

The two services operated by British Rail for parcels are Station-to-Station and Red Star. With both these services a recipient must collect his parcel from a station. Red Star is the faster service of the two.

ROADLINE

Roadline (formerly British Road Services) is a national carrier service carrying parcels by road rather than rail.

Poste Restante

This is a Post Office service which enables people on holiday or businessmen travelling around to collect their letters even when they are not sure where they will be staying. Letters must be addressed as follows:

Mr K Matthews		Mrs E Holder
Poste Restante		(to be called for)
Post Office		Post Office
TUNBRIDGE WELLS	or	TUNBRIDGE WELLS
Kent		Kent
TW9 1AJ		TW9 1AJ

Callers for letters have to produce proof of identity – a driving licence, rent book, cheque card or bank book would be suitable.

Letters are kept by the Post Office for 2 weeks (4 weeks if from abroad).

Post Restante cannot be used for more than 3 months by the same person – it is a service for the use of travellers only.

Licences

Licences are obtainable at most main post offices for:

- Television sets
- Dogs
- Franking machines
- Motor vehicles

Miscellaneous Post Office Services

These include:

- 'One-year British visitors' passports
- Application forms for 10-year passports – the standard type of passport.
- Application forms for driving licences and MOT tests and driving tests.
- National insurance stamps for the self-employed.

Pensions

The following are some of the pensions and benefits payable by post offices on behalf of the government:

- Widows' pensions
- Forces' pensions
- Supplementary pensions
- Invalidity benefits
- Family income supplements
- Child benefits
- Maternity benefits

FOR YOUR FOLDER

30. POST OFFICE SERVICES

Write these notes in your folder, filling in the missing words and phrases.

1) An inexpensive way of obtaining proof of posting of an important letter is by _____.

2) If proof of delivery as well as proof of posting is required for a package containing important papers, a _____ is the correct service.

3) Registered Post is the post office service to use for anything _____ (up to a certain weight) which is being posted inland.

4) Compensation is paid for lost articles according to the amount of _____.

5) The Post Office service for parcels (inland only) containing valuables is _____.

6) Full details of parcels to be sent overseas is in the _____.

7) The cheapest way to send an airmail letter abroad is by _____.

8) All letters go to _____ by airmail, so there is no need to affix an airmail label. The service is known as _____.

9) Letters and parcels sent surface mail are cheaper but _____.

10) Surface mail is transported by ship, van or _____.

11) Surface mail rates are given in _____.

12) All packets and parcels posted abroad require a _____.

13) Where the value of the contents is under £50 a _____ label is required.

14) Where the value of the contents is over £50 a _____ label is required.

15) Parcels which may be allowed in duty free are _____ parcels.

16) Duty is imposed on some goods entering a foreign country to _____.

17) Full details of regulations about parcels overseas is in the _____.

18) For sending the equivalent of a stamp abroad an _____ is necessary.

19) There are several services for sending mail to ensure its arrival on the same day – Expresspost, Railway Letters and _____.

Exercise 35

POST OFFICE MAIL SERVICES

What Post Office services would you use for the following?

1) A parcel containing a valuable piece of china, weighing 3½ kg?

2) A packet containing gold earrings valued at £50?

3) An envelope containing birth and marriage certificates?

4) Regular daily, weekly or monthly deliveries of computer or other urgent material?

5) The equivalent of a stamp to a pen friend in Holland?

Answer the following questions.

6) What must you ask for at the post office if the firm you are working for requires proof that an unregistered or unrecorded letter has been posted?

7) Paying the postman for goods ordered from a mail order firm is called what?

8) Name one Post Office service for speedy delivery of letters and packets.

9) A green adhesive customs label has to go on a parcel being sent abroad if the value is how much?

10) A white non-adhesive label is necessary for a parcel going abroad if the value is how much?

11) Is it correct that letters going by airmail to Europe do not need an airmail label?

12) Postal rates for inland and overseas mail are in the latest Post Office leaflets or up-to-date _____.

Exercise 36

MAIL SERVICES

1) You want to send a parcel weighing 1 kg overseas by air mail to Wellington, New Zealand.
   a What will this cost?
   b How frequent is the service?
   c How long will it take from London to New Zealand?
   d What, if any, are the Customs requirements?
   (Use the *Post Office Guide*.)

2) Under what conditions are letters and postcards sent to Europe by air mail as the means of transmission without extra charge?
   (Use the *Post Office Guide*.)

   Under what conditions does this service include printed papers, samples etc.?

3) Mr Wood wants several extra 13-amp sockets fitted throughout the office. He asks you to obtain the names and addresses of three nearby electricians in order to obtain estimates. Provide these from your local Yellow Pages.

4) Mr Wood is considering the installation of a franking machine and asks you to provide information in answer to the following questions:

  a Is a licence necessary? If so, where can it be obtained?

  b When are payments for postage made?

  c How is franked correspondence posted?

  d What record, if any, has to be kept of the use made of the franking machine?

  e How often, and by whom, must the machine be inspected? Why is this necessary?

  f Which companies are licensed by the Postmaster General to supply franking machines?

5) Complete the blanks from the alternatives listed:

  The Recorded Delivery Service provides a record of _____

  ● posting only;

  ● delivery only;

  ● posting and delivery as well as compensation if the packet is lost or damaged in the post.

  A fee per packet is charged for this service _____

  ● in addition to postage;

  ● in place of postage;

  ● in lieu of postage.

  Recorded delivery packets must be _____

  ● put in a letter-box;

  ● handed in at a post office;

  ● retained by the sender after completion of a special receipt form.

  The detachable gummed label at the end of this form must be removed and _____ .

6) What service does the Post Office offer enabling a firm to collect mail early in the morning before normal delivery by the postman?

7) State the overnight service available for sending computer material through the mail.

8) What Post Office service enables me to cover the value of a parcel against loss?

9) If I am in doubt about a postal service where can I find details of it?

Exercise 37

POSTAL ASSIGNMENTS

Obtain the current postal rates leaflet issued by the Post Office and calculate the cost of each of the following:

(i) a second-class letter, weight 40 g to Glasgow,

(ii) a first-class letter, weight 310 g to Jersey,

(iii) a first-class letter, weight 200 g to Dublin,

(iv) a registered letter, £450 value, weight 45 g to London,

(v) a second-class recorded delivery letter, weight 70 g to Leeds (advice of delivery requested at time of posting),

(vi) a parcel weighting 6 kg addressed to Bradford,

(vii) a compensation fee parcel to Birmingham weighing 8 kg, value £70.

Exercise 38

CALCULATING POSTAGE

By referring to the *Post Office Guide* calculate the amount of postage due on the following items, state the total expenditure and list the documents or labels which would have to be completed for dispatch from a Post Office:

1)	Catalogue by second-class mail	84 g
2)	Letter by second-class mail	112 g
3)	Letter by Recorded Delivery first-class	28 g
4)	Second-class letter by Recorded Delivery	14 g
5)	Letter to Belgium	42 g
6)	Airmail letter to New Zealand	56 g
7)	Parcel (surface mail) to India	908 g
8)	Parcel (value £50) – local	1½ kg
9)	Reply coupon for USA	
10)	Redirection of a parcel to another address in the same postal district	3 kg

Exercise 39

USE OF THE *POST OFFICE GUIDE*

1) If a number of tiles had to be sent by post, how should they be packed?

2) What is the cost of an envelope pre-printed with a first-class stamp?

3) What is the weight limit for second-class letters?

4) What is the special postage rate for the blind?

5) What is the Business Reply Service?

6) How would a parcel containing a salmon posted in Scotland be marked?

7) What are the names and addresses of the three firms manufacturing franking machines?

8) How should fresh flowers be packed for posting?

9) How should live bees be packed?

10) How should umbrellas be packed for posting?

11) Is it possible to send *boxes* of matches by post?

12) Is red a colour approved by the Post Office for packets or envelopes?

13) What is an aperture envelope?

14) What is 'selectapost'?

15) What does the Post Office charge for redirecting letters after moving house?

16) How is an envelope marked when being despatched by Special Delivery?

17) What is Datapost?

18) What is Freepost?

19) Is the Compensation Fee service suitable for sending banknotes and coins?

20) How must a registered packet be packed?

21) What is the maximum weight for letter post?

22) Do printed papers posted abroad require customs declaration labels?

23) Where is the blue airmail label affixed on a parcel being despatched abroad by airmail?

24) Is it possible to send silkworms abroad?

25) Is it possible to send chewing gum to Moscow?

26) Is it possible to send a pigskin handbag to Saudi Arabia?

27) Is it possible to send cigarettes to the Vatican?

28) Is it possible to send raffle tickets to Israel?

29) Is it possible to send imitation pearls to Qatar?

30) Is it allowed to send chewing gum to Russia? (Look this up under 'Union of Soviet Socialist Republics'.)

CHAPTER 11

Stationery Store

What 'stationery' is

Stationery forms only a small part of the stock held in a firm, but it is becoming more and more expensive, and issues of stationery should be carefully controlled, for economy reasons.

Items which come into the category of 'stationery' include not only paper but:

- staplers and staples
- hole punches
- adhesive tape
- paper clips and pins
- rubber bands
- bulldog clips
- treasury tags
- folders – all types (see p. 250)
- labels
- rubber thimbles
- string and brown paper
- rubber stamps and pads
- wire baskets.

There are, of course, lots of different types of paper such as:

- typing paper – bond and bank, A4 and A5, white and coloured
- letterheading, A4 and A5 sizes
- memoranda, A4 and A5 sizes
- envelopes – all sizes
- carbon paper.

And there are also:

- typewriter ribbons
- duplicating paper – ink and spirit (see Chapter 12)
- duplicating ink
- ink stencils

In a small firm, the secretary (or her assistant) may be responsible for issuing stationery. As stock costs money and storage space in cupboards is always valuable in an office, it is important that no unnecessary 'stockpiling' of paper etc. takes place. A method of avoiding 'stockpiling'

Stationery Stock Card

Item _Treasury Tags_
(boxes of 50) mixed colours

Maximum Stock _40 boxes_
Minimum Stock: _10 boxes_

Date 198—	Receipts			Issues			Balance in Stock
	Quantity Received	Invoice No.	Supplier	Quantity Issued	Requisition No.	Department	
January 1							30 boxes
" 8				1 box	153	Reception	29 "
" 11				10 boxes	401	Filing dept.	19 "
March 1				8 boxes	477	Personnel dept.	11 "
" 3	25 boxes	450	Office Equipment Supplies Ltd				36 "

A filled-in stationery stock card

is to keep a careful record of everything in the stationery store on a stationery stock card, as illustrated above.

The stationery stock card shows the minimum amount below which the stock should not fall, and the maximum amount likely to be required. This should not be exceeded, otherwise money is tied up and storage space is being used unnecessarily. Maximum/minimum levels enable the secretary or clerk in charge of stationery stock to see at a glance from the stock card whether issues of certain items are increasing and to whom. Stock cards also enable the reordering to be done well before stock falls too low. In the card illustrated the person in charge should never allow the number of boxes of treasury tags to fall below 10, but she should never stock up to give a total of more than 40. The right-hand column keeps a record of the number in stock and when these fell to 11, she decided to reorder.

Reordering Stationery

Reordering of stationery stock is often done by the buying department and an order from the stationery supervisor is sent to this department at regular intervals — perhaps once a month — or when shortage causes an emergency.

Issuing Stationery to Staff

Stationery is ordered by staff on a stores requisition form (see overleaf). It is useful to have a checklist of all the items in the stationery store attached to the outside of the door, and circulated round to all staff likely

Stationery Requisition	Job No. _____
From	
To	

QUANTITY	DESCRIPTION

Signed _____ Date _____

Stationery Requisition	Job No. _____
From	Department entered here
To	Stationery store

QUANTITY	DESCRIPTION
Amount required	Item required

Signed _Signature of person collecting stationery_ Date _Today's_

to be ordering the stationery, so that the requisition forms for ordering stationery can be completed from it.

Shelves in cupboards containing stationery should be labelled. The cupboards must be kept locked, with keys in the possession of at least two people in case one is absent for any reason. Unlocked cupboards encourage the indiscriminate and haphazard issuing of stationery and also enable people to help themselves, with no records of who has taken which item.

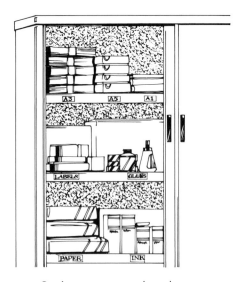

Stationery store cupboard

Issuing of stationery must be carried out at certain times on pre-arranged days. No busy office worker can afford to be interrupted constantly and unexpectedly during a working day by requests for ballpoint pens or a typewriter ribbon. A notice stating times of issuing stationery should be clearly displayed on the door of the stationery cupboard and could also be circulated with the list of stationery available:

STATIONERY will be issued ONLY on Mondays, Wednesdays and Fridays between 0930 and 1030.

REQUISITIONS may be left in the basket marked "Stationery Requisitions" on the desk in my office; please state requirements clearly, to avoid any misunderstandings.

Stationery will be left ready for collection (if ordered in advance) in Room 601 which will be unlocked on Mondays, Wednesdays and Fridays between 0930 and 1030.

It is important for the clerk in charge to be very firm about not making exceptions to the rules about when stationery is issued – or very soon *everyone* will expect to be treated as special cases!

Stocktaking

Checking of stock in the stationery store must be done at regular intervals – about twice a year is normal – to make sure that the stock card balances are accurate and agree with the quantity on the cupboard shelves. It also gives a good opportunity for the stationery stock to be tidied and shelves relabelled if necessary. Counting sheets of paper one by one takes far too long, and a quick way to check is to make a two-inch notch in a piece of cardboard and measure the piles of paper, allowing approximately 400 sheets for every two inches. Most paper for duplicating and typing is delivered from the manufacturers in boxes containing one ream, and there are 500 sheets in each ream.

Empty boxes are worth keeping for placing 'orders' in readiness for collection.

Requisitions can be placed on top so that it is clear whose orders they are.

FOR YOUR FOLDER

31. STATIONERY STOCK CONTROL

Write these notes in your folder, filling in the missing words and phrases.

1) Issues of stationery in a firm must be carefully controlled because it is becoming more and more _____.

2) It is important that no unnecessary stocking of stationery takes place in a firm because _____ is always valuable in offices.

3) Maximum/minimum levels of stock enable the clerk or secretary in charge of stationery to _____ whether issues of stationery are _____ or _____ and to whom they have been issued.

4) It is useful to have a checklist of _____ so that people in a firm know what is kept in the stationery store.

5) Stationery required *for* the stationery store is ordered from the _____ department.

6) Cupboards containing stationery should have _____ shelves and be kept _____.

7) Issuing of stationery should be done at times and on days _____.

8) _____ should be carried out regularly to make sure that the balance on each stock card agrees with the quantity on the shelves.

9) A ream of paper contains _____ sheets.

10) It takes a long time to count individual sheets of paper (e.g. letterheading) and a quick way to check the number of sheets is to measure with a 2″ notch in a piece of cardboard. Two inches = _____ sheets.

Exercise 40

STATIONERY STOCK CONTROL

1) Why is it important to keep accurate records of all stationery issued in a firm?

2) What is meant by 'minimum' stock?

3) What is meant by 'maximum' stock?

4) What are the two documents used in the issuing of stock?

5) What does the figure in the 'balance' column mean?

6) What is 'stock-taking' and why is it necessary?

7) Why is it important to issue stock only on certain days and at certain times?

8) Why is the locking of the stationery cupboard so important?

9) Which department reorders stock *for* the stationery cupboard?

10) What is 'stockpiling' and why is it important to avoid it?

Exercise 41

ASSIGNMENTS ON STOCK CARDS

1) *Stock card no 1 and requisition no 389* (see p. 203)
   a Stationery stock card no 1 is for wallet folders. What are these shaped like?

Stationery Stock Card — No. 1

Item: Folders - wallet A4

Maximum Stock: 1000
Minimum Stock: 100

Date 198-	Receipts			Issues			Balance in Stock
	Quantity Received	Invoice No.	Supplier	Quantity Issued	Requisition No.	Department	
Jan. 5							900
" 8				200	389	Filing	700
" 14				50	398	Reception	650
Feb. 1				100	453	Sales	550
" 10				400	468	Filing	150
" 15	800	130	H W Smug & Co.				950

Stationery Requisition — Job No. 389

From: Filing Dept.
To: Stationery Store

QUANTITY	DESCRIPTION
200	A4 Wallet Folders

Signed: W. Walker   Date: 8 January 198-

Stationery Requisition — Job No. 471

From: Sales Dept.
To: Stationery Store

QUANTITY	DESCRIPTION
2 reams	Typing paper, A4 Bank, yellow

Signed: B. Barnes   Date: 10 February 198-

Stationery Stock Card — No. 2

Item: Typing paper A4 Bank, yellow

Maximum Stock: 25 reams
Minimum Stock: 5 reams

Date 198-	Receipts			Issues			Balance in Stock
	Quantity Received	Invoice No.	Supplier	Quantity Issued	Requisition No.	Department	
							15
Jan. 31	10	8310	Potts paper Co.				25
Feb. 10				2	471	Sales	23
" 15				15	490	Typing pool	8
" 24				3	511	Buying	5
" 25	20	10014	Potts paper Co.				25
March 1				5	529	Typing pool	20

b Which department used most of these folders?

c On which date was the stock of wallet folders lowest?

d On which date was the stock of wallet folders highest?

e Requisition no 389 gives quantity, description and size – what else *might* be important to the filing department?

2) *Stock card no 2* (see p. 203)

Make out the other three requisitions which are shown on the stock card and number them 490, 511 and 529. Sign them yourself for the typing pool and exchange with someone else in your class for the buying department.

Stationery Requisition   Job No. ___910___

From ___Personnel Dept.___

To ___Stationery Store___

QUANTITY	DESCRIPTION
2 reams	Letterheading A4

Signed ___F·Simms___   Date ___9 May 198-___

Stationery Requisition   Job No. ___923___

From ___Sales Dept___

To ___Stationery store___

QUANTITY	DESCRIPTION
5 reams	Letterheading A4

Signed ___T Tonks___   Date ___11 May 198-___

Requisition   Job No. ___970___

From ___Buying Dept.___

To ___Stationery Store___

QUANTITY	DESCRIPTION
10 reams	Letterheading A4

Signed ___L. Martin___   Date ___23 May 198-___

Requisition   Job No. ___980___

From ___General Manager's Office___

To ___Stationery Store___

QUANTITY	DESCRIPTION
3 reams	Letterheading A4

Signed ___Jean Page___   Date ___28 May 198-___

---

3) *Requisition nos 910, 923, 970 and 980* (see above)

Make out a stationery stock card for these requisitions. Details of stock are as follows:

● maximum stock is 200 reams

● minimum stock is 50 reams

● supplier: Perfecta Printing Co

● balance in stock is 70 reams on 8 May 198—

● 50 reams are received on 31 May against Invoice 09439.

Complete by entering the balance in stock on 31 May 198—.

4) Below is an unfinished stock card. Copy the details on to another stock card and fill in the missing details.

Stationery Stock Card

Item: Ink Duplicating Paper – green
Maximum Stock: 500 reams
Minimum Stock: 150 reams

Date	Receipts			Issues			Balance in Stock
198–	Quantity Received	Invoice No.	Supplier	Quantity Issued	Requisition No.	Department	
Jan 31							300
Feb 17					471	Typing pool	150
" 27				10	519	Production	
March 4					531	Sales	100
" 12				75	588	Reprography	
" 15	250	3201	Potts Paper Co.				

5) The stock card below is wrong. Can you find the mistakes? Copy out the details on another stock card and correct the mistakes.

Stationery Stock Card

Item: Wire basket 3" x 11" x 15"
Maximum Stock: 50
Minimum Stock: 10

Date	Receipts			Issues			Balance in Stock
198–	Quantity Received	Invoice No.	Supplier	Quantity Issued	Requisition No.	Department	
1 Sept							40
21 "				3	1521	Reception	36
1 Oct				1	1602	Accounts	35
7 "				5	1621	Wages	20
3 Nov				10	1778	Filing	10
8 "	40	0553	Office Equipment Supplies Ltd.				50
15 "				5	1810	Personnel	55
3 Dec				6	2001	Sales	47

6) Make out a stationery stock card for ball-point pens, black. Maximum stock is 120, minimum stock is 50. Balance in stock on 31 May 198— is 70. Then make out requisitions for each person overleaf who orders ball-point pens and get different people in your class to sign them. Enter each of them on your stock card. Number the requisitions 200 to 206. New stock arrives on 3 June 198—. If your stock card is correct, the balance in stock on 5 June 198— should be *103*.

Betty Bloggs of reception rushes into the stationery store on Monday 1 June 198— at 0925 with a requisition for 6 black ball-point pens. (She is only just in time!) On Wednesday 3 June there is a delivery of stationery from H W Smug & Co, Barnsley, which includes 60 ball-point pens. The invoice number is 677891. Mrs L Timms from the typing pool brings a requisition for 3 black ball-point pens on 3 June as also does Fred Finch from the advertising department. On Friday 5 June there is a real rush for black ball-point pens – Sally Smart from the sales department wants 4; Ian Johnson from the personnel office wants 2; Martin Sparrow from the purchasing office wants 3; and Tracey Twitter from 'wages' wants 6.

7) Make out requisitions for the following (in each exercise) and then enter them up on a stationery stock card, first adding maximum and minimum stock and 'Item' at the top of the stock card:

a Item: HB Pencils   Max Stock: 300
                     Min Stock: 100
Supplier: H W Smug & Co, Barnsley

1 April 198—	Balance in stock was 110
2 April 198—	against Requisition No 745, 10 were issued to the sales dept
4 April 198—	against Requisition No 777, 30 were issued to the drawing office
7 April 198—	against Requisition No 824, 10 were issued to the buying dept
8 April 198—	against Invoice No 99926, 100 were received.

b Item: Boxes of staples No 19 ⅜″   Max Stock: 100 boxes
                                         Min stock: 10 boxes
Supplier: H W Smug & Co, Barnsley

6 May 198—	Balance in stock was 100 boxes
7 May 198—	against Requisition No 901, 5 boxes were issued to personnel dept.
15 May 198—	against Requisition No 947, 10 boxes were issued to advertising dept
22 May 198—	against Requisition No 961, 35 boxes were issued to typing pool
29 May 198—	against Invoice No 7361, 50 boxes were received.

c Item: Staplers F 19   Max Stock: 100
                     Min Stock: 25
Supplier; H W Smug & Co, Barnsley

1 June 198—	Balance in stock 30
4 June 198—	against Requisition No 1007, 2 were issued to the mail room
4 June 198—	against Invoice No 7441, 70 were received

10 June 198—	against Requisition No 1117, 3 were issued to the production dept
17 June 198—	against Requisition No 1138, 3 were issued to the sales dept

---

d Item: Typewriter ribbons, all black, for Adler/Olympia machines

Max Stock: 250

Min Stock: 10

Supplier: Office Equipment Supplies Ltd, Manchester

1 July 198—	against Invoice No 2472, 100 were received (balance: 150)
3 July 198—	against Requisition No 1243, 5 were issued to the general manager's office
10 July 198—	against Requisition No 1276, 3 were issued to the typing pool
17 July 198—	against Requisition No 1305, 10 were issued to personnel dept
18 July 198—	against Requisition No 1309, 12 were issued to the buying dept
20 July 198—	against Invoice No 2779, 30 were received.

CHAPTER 12

Copying and Duplicating

Carbon Copies

There are two main types of carbon paper – 'single' is coated on one side and double on both sides. Single carbon paper is the one most widely used and is available in various 'weights', i.e. thicknesses. 'Heavyweight' produces one or two clear copies but lasts a long time; 'medium-weight' produces up to five copies at a time; and 'lightweight' gives more than five copies but can be used only a few times before the copies are no longer clear.

Most firms today use what is known as 'long-life' carbon paper which is plastic-coated and is clean, easy to handle and less likely to curl or crease. It is this type of carbon paper which will be referred to from now on. Carbon paper is available in a variety of strong colours – red, black, blue, purple and green. It is often useful for identification purposes to send a certain colour to a particular department, or person.

Each sheet of medium-weight or heavyweight carbon paper can be used about 200 times. When the centre of A4 sized carbon paper is no longer producing good, clear copies, it should be cut in half (to give two sheets of A5). This will redistribute the wear.

CARE OF CARBON PAPER

Carbon paper should be stored flat, preferably in a box, away from radiators in a cool place.

Creased carbon paper produces 'trees' on the carbon copies. A 'treed' carbon copy is the sign of a careless typist.

A carbon copy with trees

Careful erasing prolongs the life of carbon paper. Rubber dust should be brushed off the carbon paper after erasing, away from the type basket on to the desk. The typewriter carriage should be moved as far as possible to left or right before rubbing out (see p. 137).

HANDLING CARBON PAPER

Some typists use carbon paper with the top left- or right-hand corner cut away. This enables the carbon paper to be shaken out while the carbon copies are held between thumb and first finger.

 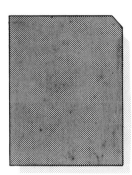

A carbon paper with the corner cut away

ONE-TIME CARBONS

These are a thin, inexpensive type of carbon paper, often used for interleaving documents supplied in sets – teleprinter rolls, computer stationery, invoices, statements, etc. and after removal from the documents are scrapped. One-time carbon saves the typist inserting carbons, although she still has to take them out. Another use for 'one-time' carbons is with ink stencils (see pp. 217–22).

CONTINUOUS STATIONERY

This consists of sets of documents which are fed in from a continuous roll attached to a typewriter by a special attachment (see p. 135). After each document has been typed, it can be torn off the roll by means of perforations, and the next document is brought into the machine, ready for typing. Continuous stationery increases the speed with which the typist produces the documents – inserting carbons, placing the 'set' in the typewriter and removing the carbons often takes far more time than actually typing the information on the documents.

Continuous stationery may be interleaved with 'one-time' carbons or NCR paper (see p. 210).

A backing sheet with folded end helps to keep carbon and typewriting paper straight and level (see also pp. 134–5).

NUMBERS OF COPIES OBTAINABLE BY CARBON PAPER

The maximum number of copies is obtainable by using lightweight carbon paper and thin ('flimsy') typing paper – this will be about 8 or 9 readable copies on a manual typewriter.

Using the same lightweight carbon paper and 'flimsy' typing paper, an electric typewriter may possibly produce about 12 copies, with pressure control set at maximum.

Using medium-weight carbon paper (which is the most generally used weight in offices) and 'bank' typing paper ('bank' is slightly thicker than 'flimsy') a manual typewriter will produce about 6 readable copies.

Several copies produced by carbon paper from one typing are often referred to as 'manifolds', and typing a document with several carbon copies is known as 'manifolding'.

NCR

NCR when used in connection with making copies means 'no carbon required'. NCR paper produces copies by the use of chemicals, either on the back of the paper, or on the back and the front. NCR paper is supplied in sets, lightly attached at the top and thus saves the typist inserting and removing carbons. NCR paper will produce about five clear, readable copies. It is used for invoices, orders, statements, Telex messages, computer print-outs.

NCR paper is clean to handle, quicker for the typist, and less storage space is required in the stationery store cupboard for boxes of carbon paper. NCR is, however, more expensive than ordinary paper plus carbon paper. It is also difficult to make corrections on the copies – erasing is almost impossible, and it is necessary to use a special corrective which has to be painted on. The final disadvantage is that it is very easy to mark NCR copies accidentally as people often do not realise that documents are NCR-coated. Even franking envelopes in the post can mark NCR copies occasionally.

FOR YOUR FOLDER

32. CARBONS AND CARBON COPYING

Write these notes in your folder, filling in the missing words and phrases.

1) The thickness of carbon paper is referred to as its _____.

2) Different coloured carbon copies may be sent to _____.

3) To make the maximum use of carbon, A4 size should be cut in _____ and reused as _____. This will _____ _____.

4) 'Trees' on carbon copies are caused by _____ in carbon paper.

5) Carbon paper should be stored _____ away from _____.

6) Careful _____ prolongs the life of carbon paper.

7) Cutting away the _____ or _____ of carbon paper enables the typist to shake out the carbons without handling them.

8) A _____ with folded end helps to keep carbon and typing paper _____.

9) A manual typewriter will produce about _____ copies, using 'bank' typing paper and _____ carbon paper.

10) To produce the maximum number of carbon copies it is necessary to use _____ paper and _____ carbon paper on a manual typewriter.

11) NCR means _____.

12) NCR paper produces copies by means of _____.

13) NCR saves the typist's _____ is _____ to handle and less _____ is required in the stationery store cupboard.

14) It is, however, difficult to make _____ on NCR copies.

15) NCR copies can also be _____ marked.

16) NCR paper is more _____ than ordinary typing paper and carbons.

17) Inexpensive, thin carbon which is used once and then scrapped is called _____.

18) Sets of documents which are fed into a typewriter from a roll at the back of a typewriter on a special attachment are called _____.

19) Carbon used in this type of stationery may be _____ or _____.

Exercise 42

CARBON AND CARBON COPYING

1) Explain the term 'manifolding'.

2) Compare NCR with 'one-time' carbons, and give the disadvantages and advantages of each.

3) How does continuous stationery save a typist's time?

4) Explain the term 'weight' when used in connection with carbon paper.

5) Paper is available in different thicknesses. 'Flimsy' is known in the papermaking trade as airmail. 'Bond' is good quality paper used for top copies, letterheading, etc. Explain how 'bank' paper is used and what its quality is.

Office Copiers

Using carbon paper means that copies are made at the same time that the original is typed. Systems which exactly copy an original *after* it has been typed (or written) are:

- photocopiers
- heat transfer machines
- dual spectrum copiers
- dyeline (diazo) copiers
- electrostatic copiers.

PHOTOCOPYING

Photocopying is a photographic process which uses light and chemicals. The copy produced is slightly damp – this method is used infrequently for this reason.

The word 'photocopying' is also used to describe 'electrostatic copying' —but that is a different process (see p. 213).

HEAT TRANSFER COPYING

Heat transfer copying (also known as 'thermography') will not copy ball-point ink – only inks which have a carbon content (fibre-tipped pens, typewriter ribbon, indian ink) or lead pencil. Copies tend to fade after a time and are, therefore, useful for internal work only. A heat (thermal) copier will also make a master for a spirit duplicator or dyeline copier, an ink stencil for an ink duplicator and transparency for an overhead projector. Special paper is needed for heat transfer copies, which is expensive. A thermal copier will also 'laminate', that is, coat sheets with a thin film of plastic to protect from dust.

DYELINE (DIAZO)

This is a system mainly used in drawing offices. It involves the use of light and chemicals plus special paper. It is the cheapest form of photocopying but the copy is likely to fade.

DUAL SPECTRUM

This system uses light and heat and produces a 'dry' copy on specially treated paper, from a negative of the original which is then processed through heat to produce a dry copy. Paper for the copies is expensive and because each one has to go through two processes, it is slow. 'Dual' means 'two'.

The 'dry' process of copying is very popular in offices today because of the delay caused by waiting for damp copies to dry. Where only a few, exact copies (facsimiles) are required, the dual spectrum or heat transfer (thermal) copier are the most convenient.

ELECTROSTATIC COPYING

When hundreds, or perhaps thousands, of exact copies are needed urgently, the electrostatic system of copying is the most efficient. It produces a dry copy every half-second at the touch of a button on plain (bond) paper without the use of chemicals. Instead it operates by using static electricity. (You can demonstrate static electricity by combing your hair and then using the comb to pick up a small piece of paper.) Electrostatic copiers use a special powdered ink combined with this force to produce copies. Because no specially treated paper is used, the copies are cheaper than those produced by other types of copiers. Plates for offset-litho duplicators (see p. 226) can also be made on an electrostatic copier.

Some electrostatic copiers will reduce the copies in size thus saving paper. The name Xerox is widely used for dry-copying and means (in Greek) dry. It is, however, a trade mark, and there are other electrostatic copiers available (e.g. Mitsubishi, Canon).

Copiers which require special paper produce more expensive copies than electrostatic copiers which use plain paper, but the latter are much more expensive to buy and do not justify this extra cost unless large numbers of copies are needed frequently.

There is a type of copier that can reproduce coloured copies, but it is still very expensive and unlikely to become widely used in offices except for specialised uses.

FOR YOUR FOLDER

33. OFFICE COPIERS

Write these notes in your folder, filling in the missing words and phrases.

1) Exact (facsimile) copies produced by all office copiers have the advantage of being completely _____.

2) These copies are therefore especially suitable when speed is vital, and when the original document being copied contains diagrams, technical

data or is in a foreign language, and the typist could easily make a _____.

3) The copying system widely used in drawing offices is _____.

4) Special paper required for the dual spectrum system is _____ to buy.

5) The dual spectrum system produces a _____ copy but is slow because the process involves both light and heat.

6) A thermal copier (heat transfer copier) uses _____ to produce copies.

7) A thermal copier also produces overhead projector transparencies and _____ in addition to masters for dyeline copiers.

8) Some thermal copiers also produce _____ stencils.

9) Thermal copiers will not reproduce _____.

10) When large numbers of copies are required, the most efficient, cheapest and quickest method of dry copying on to plain paper is _____.

11) Copiers which copy on to plain paper are expensive to buy (or lease) and are only necessary if _____ of copies are to be made regularly.

12) There are copiers available which will reproduce _____ but they are very expensive.

Duplicating

The word 'duplicating' refers to the production of a large number of copies whereas 'copying' refers to a small number (about six) or a single copy.

Electrostatic copiers both duplicate and copy, because they produce, very quickly, as many or as few copies as required.

SPIRIT DUPLICATING

A method which produces many copies from a master sheet, cheaply and quickly, is spirit duplicating. It gets its name from the spirit which is fed into the duplicator and which washes off a little of the carbon at the back of the master sheet to print each copy. It is not suitable for documents which are intended to be sent out of a firm (external use) because the copies are not 'crisp' and of sufficiently high quality. In fact, they are 'carbon' copies, although the carbon which produces them is of a different type to that used in typewriters. It is called *hectograph* carbon.

214

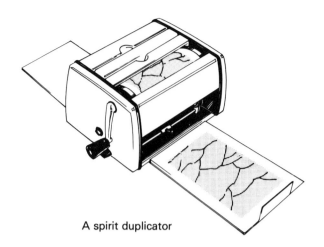

A spirit duplicator

Spirit duplicating has the great advantage of being the only method where colour can be introduced easily and effectively in one 'run'.

The master sheet for spirit duplicating can be written on by (ball-point, pencil or any sharp-pointed instrument) or a mixture of all three and typed on or drawn on; one side of the master sheet is coated with china clay, and it is this side which is placed downwards on the carbon paper, with the carbonised surface upwards. Thus when writing or typing on the master sheet, a 'mirror' image is transferred to the china clay side by the carbon.

Typing is carried out in the normal way, but with a slightly firmer touch. A backing sheet is essential so that the maximum amount of carbon is transferred to the master sheet. There is no necessity to switch the typewriter ribbon off by means of the 'stencil' switch. After use, the special carbon is scrapped, although small, unused pieces can be kept for the purpose of correcting errors. Any errors should either be scraped off the back of the master sheet (it is this side which does the printing) or erased with a special eraser, or painted over with correcting fluid and allowed to dry. If scraped off with a penknife or razor blade, care should be taken not to make a hole in the master sheet. After the mistake has been removed, by whatever method, a small piece of unused carbon (from the small unused pieces rescued from larger sheets) should be placed behind the error, and the correction typed very firmly over the top, or written over, as the case may be.

Colour is changed easily by changing the sheet of carbon behind the master sheet. There are seven different coloured carbons available: green, red, blue, yellow, brown, black and purple.

Each master sheet will produce about 300 copies. If more are required, a second master sheet is needed.

Spirit-duplicated copies fade if left in daylight for any length of time. Spirit masters can be stored and re-used, if kept flat, in protective paper folders, away from daylight. It is essential to label and date them clearly so that they can be identified when required.

Masters for a spirit duplicator can also be made very quickly by a thermal copier (see p. 212).

Paper used for spirit duplicating is non-absorbent and is suitable for writing on with ball-point pen. It is therefore useful for duplicating forms with blanks to be completed for internal use in a firm.

Spirit duplicating is particularly suitable for diagrams, maps and job cards where colour is essential. It is cheaper than other forms of duplicating when about 200 copies are required, but the quality of the work is not good enough to be used for external work.

FOR YOUR FOLDER

34. SPIRIT DUPLICATING

Write these notes in your folder, filling in the missing words and phrases.

1) A spirit 'master' will produce approximately _____ copies.

2) Spirit masters can be typed on, written on or drawn on. When you are typing, the typewriter is not switched to _____.

3) The special carbon is placed carbonised side upwards behind the _____.

4) Errors on a spirit master can be removed by a special eraser, penknife or razor blade or _____.

5) Retyping after removing an error must be done over _____.

6) Colour is quickly and easily changed by _____.

7) Spirit duplicating is the only method of duplicating where colour can be produced effectively and easily in one _____.

8) Spirit masters can be reused if stored _____ and interleaved to prevent the carbonised surface from coming into contact with other spirit masters.

9) Copies made by a spirit duplicator _____ if left in daylight.

10) Spirit duplicating is especially suitable for maps, diagrams, forms for internal use and _____.

Ink duplicating

This is sometimes referred to as 'stencil' duplicating, because the ink in the duplicator goes through the spaces made on the 'stencil' by the typewriter keys.

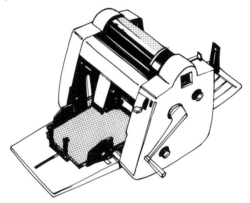

An ink duplicator

Stencils are thin, tough, fibrous sheets, coated with a wax-like composition. They can be typed on, written on, or drawn on, although writing and drawing needs a special tool called a stylus, with a special steel tip. A steel plate under the stencil gives a firm surface to write or draw on.

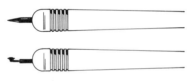

Stylus pens

A stencil 'set' supplied by the manufacturers consists of a backing sheet, and a stencil, in between which is a piece of carbon, usually 'one-time' carbon coated on both sides. This gives a copy on the backing sheet which is easier to read for checking than the typing on the stencil, and also an impression on the back of the stencil which enables the typist to see her work as she types it. Also, the carbon paper checks the 'chopping out' of o's, p's, b's if her touch is too heavy.

While a stencil is being typed, the ribbon on the typewriter is switched off by using the stencil switch and the typeface strikes the stencil direct, over the ribbon, making the impressions through which the ink in the duplicator will pass.

Capital letters, figures, and fractions should be typed a little more heavily than normal, o's, c's, e's, b's, p's, full stops, commas and hyphens, as well as the underscore more gently, otherwise holes will be made in the stencil which will then print blobs of ink instead of letters.

If a mistake is made, liquid corrective (it is usually pink or white in colour) is painted over the error, a pencil inserted behind the stencil and over the backing sheet and carbon. When dry (after about 45 seconds) the correction can be typed with a firm (but not too hard) touch.

A liquid stencil corrective applied to a stencil

It is most important to remember to type in the corrections after painting on corrective, because if it has been applied and forgotten, the copies duplicated will contain blank spaces which will then have to be filled in on each sheet, separately – very time-consuming especially if thousands of sheets have been run off!

The completed stencil should be read through *before* it is taken out of the typewriter, as it is easier to make corrections then. Replacing it into the typewriter and realigning is always more difficult.

The copy on the backing sheet should be used for the final check and the safest method is for the typist to read to a colleague – it is always difficult for someone to spot their own errors.

The typeface should always be cleaned after typing a stencil, because the stencil tissue will clog letters such as a's, o's, p's and b's especially. Cleaning the typeface before typing a stencil is good practice too, to ensure a good clear stencil.

A thin sheet of clear plastic film placed over a stencil before starting to type helps to avoid clogging the typeface and also prevents cutting out o's, p's, b's, etc. if the typist has a heavy touch.

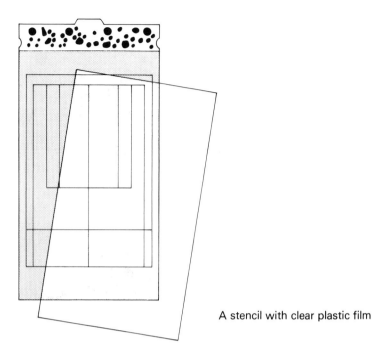

A stencil with clear plastic film

If a signature is needed on the duplicated copies, this should be done after the final checking of the stencil, with a stylus. Remember, if this is overlooked someone may be faced with the prospect of signing his or her name 5,000 times!

I should have signed the stencil!

After typing, checking and signing (if required) the 'one-time' carbon is discarded, but the backing sheet remains on – it is used to smooth the stencil on to the drum of the duplicator and also to help to store the stencil if it is to be reused.

The paper used for ink-duplicating is semi-absorbent (so that the ink does not smudge) and is available in many pastel colours as well as white. Because it is slightly absorbent, it is not as suitable for writing on as spirit duplicating paper, which has a smooth surface.

Ink-duplicated copies are of good quality and suitable for external use as well as internal. About 5000 good clear copies can be obtained from one stencil if it is handled carefully and expertly.

When more than about a dozen good-quality copies of a document are required, ink duplicating is the cheapest way of producing them.

Colour can be introduced by changing the tube of ink on the duplicator, and by typing a stencil for each colour change. The duplicator drum has to be changed too, and the work on each stencil carefully aligned so that the various colours fit where required.

Ink stencils can be stored and reused; suspending in a cabinet or placing flat in an absorbent folder are the best methods. It is important to label stencils if they are to be reused, otherwise it will be difficult to identify them. One copy of the stencilled sheet should be attached, for reference.

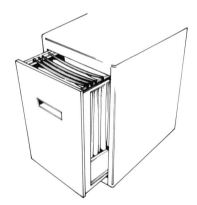

Stencils suspended in storage cabinet

Some work to be typed on a stencil is complicated and involves columns and careful layout. In this case, it is better to type it out on plain paper first, to check spacing across and lines down, before starting a stencil. Stencils are not cheap and it is wasteful to scrap them unnecessarily.

'Grafting' on a stencil consists of cutting out the word, phrase or even a complete paragraph and replacing it with a fresh piece of correctly-typed stencil – this replacement piece is called the 'graft'.

It requires a lot of patience and practice, and spoiled stencils should be kept for this purpose. The 'graft' should be slightly larger than the piece which has been removed and is affixed to the stencil with corrective, which must be allowed to dry thoroughly before the stencil is placed on the duplicator. If the graft is a fairly large one, turn the stencil over and reinforce the corrective from the back, all around the edge of the join.

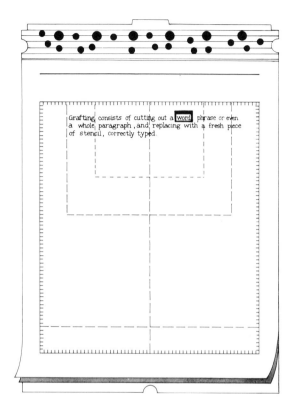

Grafting consists of cutting out a word phrase or even a whole paragraph, and replacing with a fresh piece of stencil, correctly typed.

Grafting

An electronic scanner will make stencils for an ink duplicator speedily and accurately, as also will a thermal copier (see p. 212).

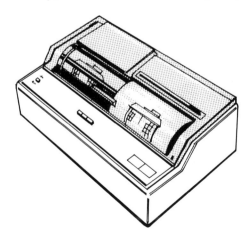

An electronic scanner for making ink duplicator stencils

It is frequently said that 'anyone who can type can type a stencil'. So they can, after a fashion, but there is rather more to it than that. The finest quality stencil work depends upon the skill used in typing and operating the duplicator. Here is a checklist for typing an ink stencil:

221

Before starting to type have you:

- Cleaned the typeface on your machine? thoroughly? One clogged character will, by its repetition ruin the appearance of the whole page.
- Switched the typewriter to stencil *(most important)*?
- Put correction fluid close at hand?
- Placed plastic film over stencil?
- Made sure the stencil is absolutely flat and smooth on the typewriter roller? (Any bulging will cause creases and cracks.)
- Typed a draft of any complicated work?

While typing have you:

- Remembered about typing capitals etc. more firmly and o's, p's etc. more lightly?
- Started to type well below printed 'safety-line' on stencil at top? (If too near it will smudge on the copies.)
- Retyped over all 'blanked-out' errors? (Hold up to light to make sure.)
- Checked *again* for errors?

After typing have you:

- Had someone else to check from the backing sheet while you read to them?
- Had the stencil signed (if required)?
- Found out how many copies required and on what colour paper?
- Found out whether the stencil is to be stored for reuse?

FOR YOUR FOLDER

35. INK DUPLICATING

Write these notes in your folder, filling in the missing words and phrases.

1) An ink stencil will produce several _____ copies if handled with care.

2) An ink stencil can be stored and reused by _____ or _____.

3) Paper used for ink duplicating is _____ and not suitable for writing on with ball-point.

4) Before starting to type on ink stencil, the typeface of a typewriter should be cleaned and the typewriter ribbon switched _____.

5) Complicated stencils should be _____ first on plain paper.

6) The special tool for writing on an ink stencil is called a _____.

7) While writing or drawing on an ink stencil, it is necessary to place a _____ underneath the stencil to give a firm surface.

8) Capital letters, figures and fractions should be typed _____ than normal.

9) Full stops, underscore, hyphen, comma, o's, p's, b's, c's should be typed more _____ than normal.

10) If a mistake is made, _____ is painted over the error, allowed to dry and the correction _____.

11) If stencils are to be stored for reuse, it is important to _____.

12) Colour can be introduced on an ink stencil by changing the tube of ink, changing the drum on the duplicator and _____.

13) Ink-duplicated copies are of sufficiently high standard to be used for _____ work.

14) Plastic film placed over stencil before typing prevents _____ and also _____.

15) Ink stencils can be produced by a thermal copier and an _____.

Exercise 43

INK AND SPIRIT DUPLICATING

1) What would be the better method of duplicating to use in the following circumstances (assuming that your office had both a spirit and an ink duplicator):

   a sending 100 memos around to branch managers?
   b sending 1500 circular letters to customers?
   c duplicating 500 programmes for the firm's annual pantomime?
   d producing diagrams of a new process to be used in a workshop for 30 employees?
   e producing about 250 forms to be completed by employees in connection with a pension fund?
   f producing about 3500 price-lists to send out to other firms?
   g producing 50 copies of a sales chart with several colours?
   h producing 30 copies of the minutes of a meeting held by the sales manager?
   i producing 30 copies of an agenda for the next sales meeting?
   j producing 500 copies of the works magazine?

2) You have been asked by your employer to help to decide whether to purchase a spirit or an ink duplicator. Set out the various advantages and disadvantages of each.

3) Spirit duplicating is the system which enables colour to be changed easily. How is this done?

4) If you make a mistake on a spirit master, how do you put it right?

5) How many copies would a spirit master give (maximum)?

6) Could you store a spirit master and reuse it?

7) Name three different documents which a spirit master would be especially useful for.

8) What happens to spirit master copies if they are left in daylight?

9) Do you switch your typewriter to 'stencil' when typing a spirit master?

10) Is it possible to write on a spirit master?

11) When typing an *ink* stencil, what do you type twice (or harder than normal)?

12) What do you type more *lightly* on an ink stencil?

13) How do you correct an error on an ink stencil?

14) Can you reuse an ink stencil after it has been on the duplicator?

15) What do you write with on an ink stencil?

16) How many copies would you hope to get from an ink stencil (maximum)?

17) What do you use if your typewriter cuts letters out of an ink stencil?

18) What is *grafting*?

19) What special attention does a typewriter need before and after typing an ink stencil?

20) Which produces the best typed copies, ink or spirit?

One use of spirit duplicating

Exercise 44

DUPLICATING ASSIGNMENTS

(If you are unable to type your teacher could type these for you, ready for you to run off.)

Spirit

1) Draw a simple sketch map of the area around your school/college showing the railway stations and bus stations and any landmarks which would be helpful to a visitor who is a stranger to the area. Indicate the scale. The top of the sketch map must be north.

2) Draft a notice giving the date, time and place of a meeting to be held in your firm for the sales representatives of five areas – Midlands, West, North, South, East. Each area will have a meeting on each of five different dates – vary the colour for each meeting on the same sheet.

3) Draw up a programme for a works outing to London to go to the theatre by coach at Christmas. There will be a meal on the way to the theatre.

Ink

4) Type an ink stencil for the minutes of the meeting of the works social club at which the outing to a London theatre was agreed. Run off 12 specimen copies (or, alternatively, one for each member of your class). An ink stencil would in fact be needed for these minutes because there are 500 members of your works social club!

5) Type an ink stencil for a circular letter to customers of your firm telling them about an exhibition of your products which will be held in a large hotel in your area in about a month's time. Include a tear-off slip which can be returned to your firm, indicating whether they are likely to attend or not. Run off 12 specimen copies.

6) Type an ink stencil of a programme for a school play – run off sufficient copies for one copy each for your class.

Offset-litho Duplicating

Offset duplicating (or simply 'offset') involves taking an impression first on a rubber cylinder and from the rubber cylinder printing on to paper. This gives a clearer, smudge-free impression and produces high-quality work which is like printing. 'Litho' is the abbreviated form of 'lithography' which means literally 'printing by stone'. Printing by stone is a process using grease and water that was discovered about 200 years ago This principle of oil and water not mixing is still used in offset-lithography, but today thin metal or paper plates are used instead of stone for the master copy.

The old-fashioned way of lithographic printing

If you mop up some spilt liquid with a tissue and then press the tissue against a piece of paper, the resultant damp patch is 'offset'.

Different colours can be introduced into offset-litho duplicating, but a separate master and 'run' through the duplicator is needed for each colour.

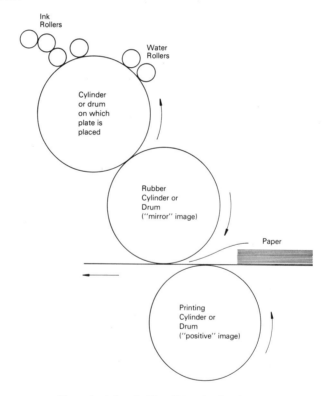

Ink
Rollers

Water
Rollers

Cylinder
or drum
on which
plate is
placed

Rubber
Cylinder or
Drum
("mirror" image)

Paper

Printing
Cylinder or
Drum
("positive" image)

The principle of offset-litho duplicating

There are many different kinds of plates, and it is important to choose the appropriate plate for the number of copies required.

Metal plates can produce tens of thousands of copies. If only several hundred are needed, a paper plate is more economical. Both paper and metal plates can be reused if stored carefully in labelled and dated folders. Plates must be handled only at each end, as any finger prints will cause smudges on the copies.

Erasing on a paper plate can be done with a special offset-litho eraser. Erasing on a metal plate can be done with a glass brush or pumice block.

Paper used for the copies produced by an offset-litho duplicator is often of very high quality, and the copies are therefore not cheap; but the work is suitable for any printing work needed by a firm — letter headings, catalogues, price lists, order forms and invoices.

Offset-litho duplicators are expensive to buy (or lease) and the outlay is only justified if very large numbers (hundreds of thousands) of documents are to be run off regularly. Otherwise the cost will not be recovered — forms, letter headings, etc. are more economically produced by an outside printer.

The modern, desk-top offset-litho duplicator is clean and easy to use, after initial instruction by a skilled operator.

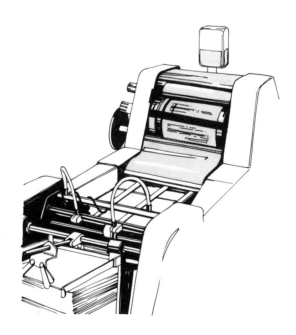

An offset-litho duplicator

Master plates can be written on with ball-point or pencil, and typed on.

Typing requires a special offset-litho typewriter ribbon.

Master plates can also be produced by an electrostatic copier (see p. 213) or an electronic scanner (see p. 221).

REPROGRAPHY COMPARISONS

Process	Approximate No. of Copies	Speed	Cost	Quality	Colour	Master Storage	Disadvantages	Advantages
Offset-litho	Dependent upon type of plate used – metal: tens of thousands; paper several hundred	Excellent	Paper is often more expensive than that used for ink or spirit duplicating	Excellent	Yes	Yes	Operation of equipment needs special training	Plates for offset-litho can be made by electro-static photo-copier from any copy.
Office copiers (excluding heat transfer copiers) (see pp. 212 – 3)	Unlimited	Excellent	High – paper is expensive	Excellent	Is possible but copies and equipment are expensive	Yes	Cost of paper and, sometimes, cost of equipment	Ease of operation
Facsimile-transceiver	One at a time	Excellent	Paper and equipment expensive	Excellent	No – see above	Yes	Only possible to send copies to recipients who have transceivers	Speed and accuracy
Word processing(see pp. 131–2)	Unlimited	Excellent	High cost of equipment, although silicone chips are reducing the cost rapidly	Excellent	No	Yes, in a 'memory'		Corrects errors, inserts para-grahs, re-arranges material auto-matically. Stores material in a 'memory' and re-types if required

REPROGRAPHY COMPARISONS

Process	Approximate No. of Copies	Speed	Cost	Quality	Colour	Master Storage	Disadvantages	Advantages
Carbon copies	10/12 max (6 on a manual type-writer)	Erasing slows down production in time	Low in material high in time	Top copy only is good quality. Carbon copies suitable for internal distribution	Yes, with different coloured carbons or paper	—	Time is wasted by handling carbons	Any competent typist can produce carbon copies
NCR		Regulated by speed of typist	Special chemically treated paper is expensive	As above	No	—	Easily marked accidentally. Erasing is not possible.	Clean—no carbons to handle
Spirit duplicating	200/300	Good – on an electric duplicator	Low – paper and master sheets inexpensive	Suitable for internal distribution only	Yes – very effectively and easily	Yes, with care. Can be reused	Copies fade in daylight	Master sheets can be written on or typed on. Master sheets can also be made by a thermal copier.
Ink (stencil duplicating)	Several thousand	Excellent	Low – paper and stencil inexpensive	Excellent, suitable for external distribution	Is possible only by typing a separate stencil for each	Yes – in an absorbent folder or susp-ended	The best results are achieved by typing, but it is possible to draw or write on an ink stencil with a special stylus	Stencils for ink duplicating can be made by a thermal copier or an electronic stencil cutter (scanner)

FOR YOUR FOLDER

36. OFFSET-LITHO DUPLICATING

Write these notes in your folder, filling in the missing words and phrases.

1) Colour can be introduced in offset-litho duplicating, but each colour requires a _____ plate and a _____ run.

2) Tens of thousands of copies can be produced by _____ plates.

3) Several hundred copies can be produced by _____ plates.

4) Offset-litho master plates can be reused if _____.

5) They must be held at the ends as finger-prints cause _____.

6) The work produced by an offset-litho duplicator is of a very high standard, suitable for catalogues, letter headings and _____.

7) The copies are not cheap and not economical unless _____ quantities are required regularly.

8) Master plates for an offset-litho duplicator can be produced by an electronic scanner and _____.

9) They can also be written on with _____ or _____.

10) Typing on an offset-duplicator plate requires a special _____.

CHAPTER 13

Filing and Indexing

A filing spike

What is wrong with this way of filing papers?

Write down all the disadvantages you can think of, and then turn over the page and check your answers.

Why filing on a 'spike' is not very efficient

1) All the papers have holes in them.

2) The papers will get dusty.

3) If the bottom papers are wanted, all the others have to be taken off first.

4) The papers will get very creased around the edges.

Why file?

Filing means putting away papers so that they can be found when they are wanted.

Everyone has papers of some sort – a birth certificate, a school report, examination certificates. These papers have to be kept because of the information on them, which may be needed at a later date.

Firms keep papers for the same reason, and they have large quantities of papers, because all their records are stored on them.

We have seen that a spike is not a very good way of filing but it is better than leaving papers in heaps, in no particular order.

It takes a long time to find one particular document if it is in a large stack of filing waiting to be put away.

Filing should be done several times a day if possible, so that the files are up-to-date.

The reason for filing!

There are several different systems of filing, but whichever system is used in a firm, dealing with filing should be done in the same way.

The first step to be taken when preparing to file is to collect all the papers together.

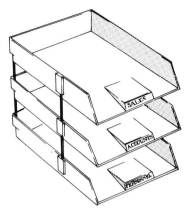

Trays for collecting filing

Some offices have labelled trays or wire baskets into which all the papers ready for filing are placed during the day.

These trays should be emptied frequently by the filing clerk.

While she is sorting, it is important for her to check that the papers have been attended to and may be filed. How does she know this?

Special marks or 'release symbols' are used in firms to indicate that a document has been dealt with, and may be filed. There are some examples of 'release symbols' above. These are:

- a line across the paper
- a large 'F' for 'File'
- an instruction (stamped on the paper with a rubber stamp) to file the paper.

Examples of 'release symbols'

Any documents which do not have the firm's release symbol on them should be put on one side into a tray labelled 'queries' so that the filing clerk can return them to the department they came from for confirmation that they can be filed, and for the release symbols to be added.

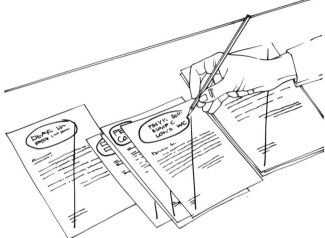

A filing clerk circling 'filing point' while pre-sorting the filing

While looking for release symbols, the filing clerk would be able to check the 'filing point' at the same time. The 'filing point' is the name under which the paper will be filed. It is a help if the filing point is circled or underlined on the paper with a coloured felt pen while pre-sorting.

Papers are often fastened together with paper clips or pins. These should be taken out before filing, and replaced by staples. Paper clips catch on to other papers accidentally, and pins can cause painful pricks.

After pre-sorting, checking for release symbols and marking the filing points, the next step when dealing with filing is:

PLACING THE PAPERS IN THE RIGHT FILE

This is the most important part of the whole of the filing process. A paper placed in the wrong file will be very difficult to find and could well be lost for ever.

The most recent paper is always placed on top of all the other papers in a file. These papers will have been filed in date order, too, so that the oldest paper is at the bottom, or back of the file.

Papers should be flat and square in the file so that they remain uncreased.

The other reason for placing papers carefully in a file is to keep them clean and free from dust, but mainly:

Filing is done in order to find documents when needed.

More annoyance, frustration and waste of time is caused in firms by not being able to find a paper that is needed quickly than almost anything else.

A trolley with wire trays is useful for the collection of filing

After collecting the filing, the next step is to sort it into the order in which is will be filed. This is called 'pre-sorting'.

Pre-sorting saves time, as the papers are in the right order before they are taken to the filing cabinet, and there is no need to make frequent journeys to and from the filing cabinet.

A desk-top sorter is divided into sections each labelled with a letter of the alphabet, and papers are placed behind the flaps in their right section.

A desk-top sorter

What sort of papers are filed?

Much filing consists of letters which have come into a firm.

These incoming letters have the name of the firm printed in large type at the top of the paper, with the address, telephone number, telegraphic address and telex number – if they have one – printed underneath. Incoming business letters from firms are easily recognisable by a filing clerk. They are filed under the names of the firms who have sent them – this would be the 'filing point' which the filing clerk would circle or underline while pre-sorting.

HEATWELLS LTD

Received
13 Feb 198-
0900

Filing point

Pilgrim Street
WOLVERHAMPTON
WH33 5BQ

Tel: 532 666
Telegrams: Heatwells Wolverhampton
Telex: 356774

Our Ref JK/DC   12 February 198-

Messrs Grant and Binns Ltd
Fairfield Works
Lincroft Trading Estate
MARSTON   M85 4TB

Dear Sirs

Our engineer, Mr G K Adams, will be calling at your works on Monday, 20 February, to discuss with your Chief Engineer the possibility of installing a new heating system in your canteen.

This has already been discussed with Mr Stephens, your Canteen Manager. Perhaps he could be present when Mr Adams calls. He hopes to be at your firm by 10 am on 20 February.

Yours faithfully
HEATWELLS LTD

Release symbol

FILE

John Kemp
Sales Manager

A business letter, with release symbol, ready for filing

Replies to letters

When replies to letters are typed, a carbon copy is typed at the same time, and this is sent, with the letter which has been answered, to the filing clerk. They are filed in the same file.

Carbon copies do not need release symbols, as they are copies of outgoing letters.

A filing clerk would soon learn to recognise carbon copies because they are often on coloured paper, but also there is no printed name of firm at the top of the letter.

CS/KP

12 February 198–

Heatwells Ltd — *Filing point*
Pilgrim Street
WOLVERHAMPTON
WH33 5BQ

For the attention of Mr J Kemp, Sales Manager

Dear Sirs

Your letter dated 12 February has been passed on to me, and I look forward to meeting your engineer, Mr G K Adams, when he calls on the 20 February at 10 am, to discuss the proposed new heating system in the canteen here.

Yours faithfully
GRANT AND BINNS LTD

C Stephens
Canteen Manager

A carbon copy of the reply sent to Heatwells Ltd. Note that there is no firm's name at the top of the letter.

There is another type of business letter, besides business letters from firms. This is a personal business letter – one sent from a private individual to a firm.

There would be no printed name at the top of a personal business letter. Instead, there would be a private address, either typed or written. Some people do have their own printed notepaper, but this would still consist of address and telephone number, if they had one. There would be no name at the top of the paper.

---

25 Avoncroft Avenue
St Andrews
MARSTON
M96 6TB

Received
14 Feb 198-
0915

13 February 198-

Messrs Grant and Binns Ltd
Fairfield Works
Lincroft Trading Estate
MARSTON
M85 4TB

FILE

For the attention of the Personnel Manager

Dear Sirs

Junior Shorthand-Typist

I am interested in your advertisement for a junior shorthand-typist, which I saw in last night's "Evening News", and give below details of my experience and qualifications:

Date of birth:	5 May 196-
Nationality:	British
Shorthand qualifications:	LCC certificate for 80 wpm
Typewriting qualifications:	RSA certificate Stage 3 (speed 50 wpm)
Other qualifications:	English CSE Grade 1
	Mathematics CSE Grade 2
	Office Practice RSA Elementary

Since leaving college in July 198- I have been employed as a typist in the Typing Pool at Griggs & Howe's Mail Order Company and would now like to move to a firm where I have an opportunity to use shorthand.

I am attending evening classes in shorthand at the college.

If you would like me to attend for an interview, I will be pleased to do so at any time to suit your convenience.

Yours faithfully

Elaine Knowles (Miss)

Release symbol

Filing point

A personal business letter

238

Personal business letters would still need release symbols to show that they had been dealt with.

In addition to letters, copies of outgoing letters, and other documents, there would be memos for the filing clerk to deal with. Many memos are not important enough to be filed, but occasionally there will be one which has to be kept for future reference.

```
Ref HH/OM
                              Filing point
15 February 198-

Miss Elaine Knowles
25 Avoncroft Avenue
St Andrews
MARSTON
M96 6TB

Dear Miss Knowles

Junior Shorthand-typist

Thank you for your letter dated 13 February in connection
with the above vacancy.

Would you please call at this office on Tuesday, 21 February
at 11 am? If you report just before that time at the Gate-
keeper's Lodge, he will arrange for you to be shown to the
Personnel Dept.

If this date and time is not convenient, would you please
let me know and I will arrange an alternative appointment.

Yours sincerely



H Hancox
Personnel Manager
```

The carbon copy of a letter sent to Elaine Knowles in reply to her application for the post of junior shorthand typist

As well as letters, memos and carbon copies of letters, filing would include invoices, quotations, orders, credit and debit notes coming into a firm. The 'filing point' on invoices, credit notes, debit notes and orders is usually a number, and these documents would be filed in order of the number (numerical filing). Letters are usually filed alphabetically, in order of the name of the sender, or the person receiving the letter.

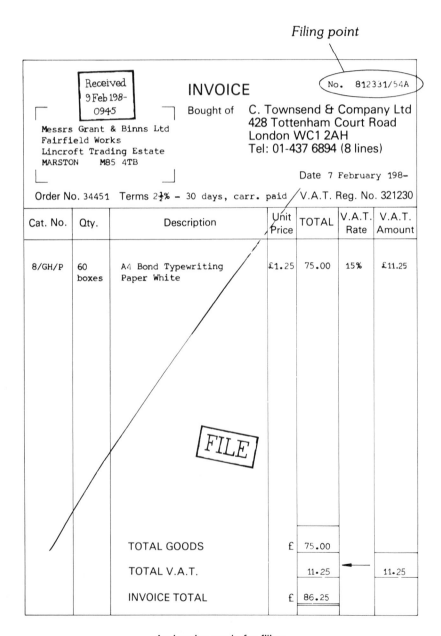

An invoice ready for filing

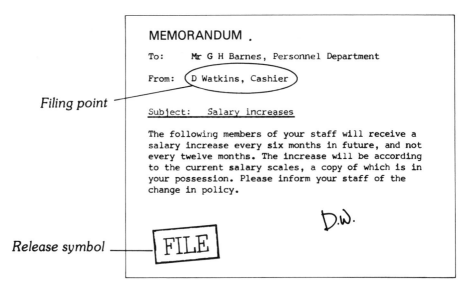

Filing point

Release symbol

A memorandum ready for filing

Copies of all these documents would be amongst a collection of filing, too.

A complete file borrowed should be replaced by an empty folder, ruled up and headed, known as an 'absent wallet'.

The wallet folder can then be used by the filing clerk for filing papers while the borrowed file is out.

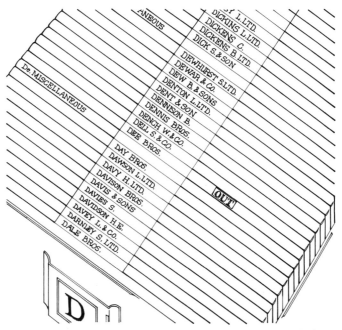

The file for Dee Bros. has been borrowed and is marked 'Out'

Miscellaneous files in a filing cabinet drawer

A miscellaneous file is used for storing papers when there is no file for them.

When four or five papers have been received from the same firm, the filing clerk should then make out an individual folder for them.

A convenient place for a miscellaneous file is at the front of each division of the alphabet.

Papers are placed in alphabetical order in a miscellaneous file.

Placing papers in the right files is only one part of a filing clerk's job. It is the most important part, but she will also have other duties to carry out.

One of these is the lending of files and papers.

"THE NEXT THING, OF COURSE, IS TO UPDATE OUR FILING SYSTEM"

An efficient filing clerk will not let her files, or papers, be taken away without first making a note of:

- name of borrower and his or her department
- title of file or paper
- date on which it was borrowed
- date on which it was returned.

One single paper taken out of a file should be replaced by an 'out' card, similar to the one below:

				OUT
Name of file	Borrower	Department	Date borrowed	Date returned

An 'out' card

Exercise 45

'OUT' CARDS IN FILING

Make a copy of an 'out' card and fill it in from the following details:

1) On 10 January 1978 Mrs K Lowndes of the personnel department borrowed the file of Mr H K Phillips. The file was returned on 12 January.

2) On 18 January 1978 Miss G Quinton, sales manager's secretary, sales department, borrowed the file of Shield Business Systems Ltd. The file was returned two days later.

3) On 21 January Mr B Simms, of the purchasing department, borrowed the file of Smallwood & Prince. He returned it on 24 January.

4) On 25 January Mr F Young, accounts department, borrowed the file of Stokes & Dalton Ltd. He returned it on 28 January.

5) On 30 January Mrs O Smithson, filing department, borrowed the file of Mr G Bailey and returned it the same day.

Cross out each name as the file is returned and before entering the next.

Cross-referencing

Firms may change their names, due to mergers or take-overs. People change their names, especially women when they get married, so a filing clerk has to organise a system in her files whereby anyone looking under an out-of-date name will be directed to the new name. This is done by means of a 'cross-reference'. A sheet is made out like the one below, and placed in the files under the *old* name:

Cross-referencing can also be used for goods and suppliers, e.g. for suppliers of typewriter ribbons, look under 'stationery'; for suppliers of carpets look under 'floorcoverings'.

```
┌─────────────────────────────────────────────┐
│                                             │
│   CROSS-REFERENCE SHEET                     │
│                                             │
├─────────────────────────────────────────────┤
│   FOR CORRESPONDENCE FOR:                   │
│   Waring and Simpson Ltd                    │
│                                             │
├─────────────────────────────────────────────┤
│   SEE:                                      │
│   Swift Engineering Company Ltd             │
│                                             │
├─────────────────────────────────────────────┤
│                                             │
│                                             │
└─────────────────────────────────────────────┘
```

Exercise 46

ASSIGNMENT ON CROSS-REFERENCE SHEETS

Rule up 6 cross-reference sheets as under:

```
┌─────────────────────────────────────────────┐
│                                             │
│   CROSS-REFERENCE SHEET                     │
│                                             │
├─────────────────────────────────────────────┤
│                                             │
│   FOR CORRESPONDENCE FOR:                   │
│                                             │
├─────────────────────────────────────────────┤
│                                             │
│   SEE:                                      │
│                                             │
├─────────────────────────────────────────────┤
│                                             │
│                                             │
└─────────────────────────────────────────────┘
```

Then fill in each cross-reference sheet with the following details (number each sheet):

1) The British United Airways file is often asked for under BUA.

2) For 'Upholstery firm' see 'Cattell & Guest, 1 Bromsgrove Road, Birmingham'.

3) The firm of Parker & Downs are now known as the Downs Export Co.

4) Correspondence from Feckenham of Barmouth is to be filed in future under 'Camping equipment: awnings' in a subject filing system.

5) For supplies of garden top soil see 'Greenfield Turf Supplies, 26 Driftwood Close, Southcrest, Deal'.

6) Miss Jane Heward is now married. Her married name is Slater, and correspondence will be filed under 'Mrs John Slater'.

Pending Papers

It is not always possible to deal with documents as soon as they are received. Some papers have to be kept while waiting for further information. These papers are known as 'pending' papers. 'Pending' means 'waiting for a decision'. A box file or lever arch file is useful for keeping 'pending' papers in, until they have been dealt with and can be filed in the main filing system.

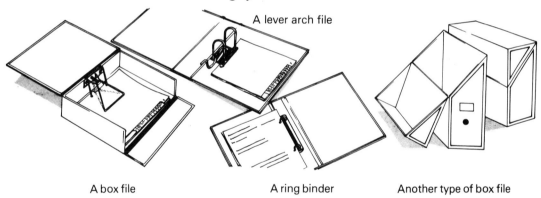

A lever arch file

A box file   A ring binder   Another type of box file

Ring binders are useful for 'pending' papers, too, as they have special cards in them called guide cards. These guide cards are used to divide the papers into different sections.

An expanding file, with sections sometimes called a 'concertina' file,

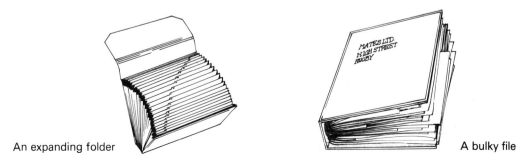

An expanding folder   A bulky file

could be used for 'pending' papers, and could also be used for pre-sorting papers, instead of a desk-top sorter with flaps. Another use for an expanding file would be for personal or confidential papers, which have to be taken around but still need to be arranged so that individual papers can be found quickly.

Eventually, some files become so packed with papers that they have to be 'thinned' out. This is done by taking out the oldest papers from the back of the file and transferring them to files which are stored out of the current filing system; they may still be needed for reference, so they should be labelled clearly, and dated, and a note of which papers have been removed placed in the current file.

These out-of-date files are called 'dead' files or 'transfer files'.

As papers cannot be kept for ever, they are eventually destroyed and the most efficient way of destroying papers is to 'shred' them in a special machine called a paper shredder. The shredded paper can then be used by the packing department – a very practical piece of recycling.

As well as making useful packing, shredded papers cannot be read by anyone who may be looking for confidential information.

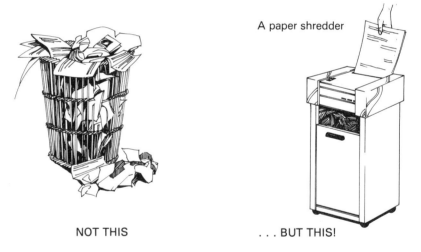

A paper shredder

NOT THIS   . . . BUT THIS!

The end of the filing system – but only after official instructions! No papers should ever be destroyed without authority to do so by a responsible person in a firm

The Filing Clerk's Job

- Collection of papers.
- Pre-sorting – checking for release symbols – noting filing point. Queries placed on one side for checking later.
- Placing papers in correct file, latest paper on top.
- Lending files or papers only when record of borrower has been correctly completed.

- Completing cross-reference sheets for any files where names have been changed.

- Organising miscellaneous files for single papers which have to be filed until four or five have been received from the same firm.

- Filing as frequently as possible – preferably several times a day.

The Supervisor's Job

- Arranging for 'dead' files to be made, so that bulky files are thinned out.

- Obtaining instructions from a responsible member of the firm for papers no longer required to be shredded.

FOR YOUR FOLDER

37. FILING

Write these notes in your folder, filling in the missing words and phrases.

1) Filing means _____ so that they can be found when they are needed.

2) Filing should be done _____ times a day so that files are _____.

3) The first step to be taken when preparing to file is to _____.

4) The filing clerk will know that documents have been dealt with and may be filed by special marks known as _____ on the papers.

5) Examples of these special marks are: line across the page

                                           large 'F' for 'file'

                                           _____.

6) The name under which a paper is to be filed is called the _____.

7) Papers should be fastened together with _____ as pins can be dangerous and paper clips gather up other documents.

8) Papers are placed in folders with the _____ on top.

9) The main reason for filing is to _____.

10) Equipment for collecting filing from different departments may be _____ or _____.

11) Pre-sorting filing saves frequent journeys to and from the filing cabinets and a _____ is useful for pre-sorting.

12) A great deal of filing consists of letters which have come into a firm and _____ of letters which have been sent out of a firm.

13) As well as letters, filing may also include invoices, quotations, orders and _____.

14) An OUT card is used for _____.

15) If a complete file is borrowed, it should be replaced by _____.

16) A miscellaneous file is used for _____.

17) If firms change their names due to mergers or take-overs, a _____ sheet is necessary, placed in the files under the *old* name.

18) A pending file is used for _____.

19) Suitable containers for pending papers are: lever arch file
box file
ring binder
_____.

20) When papers are no longer needed, they should be _____ (but only after official instructions!).

21) Files which have become bulky should have the excess papers removed from the back of the file and stored (dated and labelled) away from the current files in a _____ file.

Exercise 47

FILING

Copy the following passage, filling in the blank spaces with one of the words in the following lists. Each word or group of words is used once only:

dead	note	cross-reference
several	filing point	sheet
name of firm	collecting papers	up-to-date
recent	uncreased	placing papers in
find	release symbols	correct files
pending	miscellaneous	desk-top sorter
	expanding	absent wallet

It is important that files are _____, so filing should be done _____ times a day. Dealing with a pile of filing is divided into three steps:

1) _____.
2) pre-sorting.
3) _____.

A _____ helps with pre-sorting, as it saves unnecessary trips to and from filing cabinets. A filing clerk can tell that papers have been dealt with and can be filed by _____ which should be on all papers which have come into a firm. Carbon copies of documents which have been sent out of a firm will not have them. Carbon copies have no _____ printed at the top. While pre-sorting, the filing clerk may find it helpful to underline the _____ which is the name or title under which the paper will be filed. The most _____ paper is always placed on top of a file. Papers should be flat and square in a folder so that they remain _____. Filing is carried out in order to be able to _____ documents quickly. A record of borrowed files should be kept by placing an _____ with the file's details on it, together with the name of the borrower and the date borrowed. Papers for which there is no file should be placed in a _____ file. Out-of-date files are eventually taken out of the current files, dated, labelled and transferred to _____ files. A _____ of these out-of-date files must be made in the current filing system, so that anyone looking for them knows where to find them. A _____ should be made out and placed in the files when a firm, or person, changes its name. Sometimes documents cannot be dealt with at once and have to be put on one side for a short time, away from the main filing system. These are known as _____ files. An _____ file, sometimes known as a concertina file, would be suitable for filing these papers.

Exercise 48

MORE ON FILING

1) What is filing?

2) Why do firms file papers?

3) Why should filing be done as many times a day as possible?

4) What are release symbols?

5) Not all papers have release symbols on them, but can still be filed. What sort of papers could be filed without release symbols?

6) What equipment would be useful for the collecting of filing?

7) What equipment could be used for sorting filing?

8) Besides release symbols, what else does a filing clerk look for while sorting filing?

9) Besides letters, many other documents have to be filed. Amongst them would be memoranda – short notes sent from office to office in the same firm. Why has the example of a memo been headed 'memorandum'?

10) Explain the differences between an 'out card' and an 'absent wallet'.

11) What would be filed in a miscellaneous file?

12) What would be filed in a 'dead' file?

13) What would be filed in a 'pending' file?

14) What is a cross-reference sheet?

15) How are papers filed in a miscellaneous file?

16) Shredding papers is a very efficient way to make use of old files. Why is this a good way to destroy old files from a security point of view?

17) Who gives instructions in a firm to destroy old files?

18) A simple but not very efficient way of filing papers is on a 'spike'. What is wrong with this method?

Folders

Papers are usually kept in folders. One type is the wallet folder which has flaps and gussets so that it can expand.

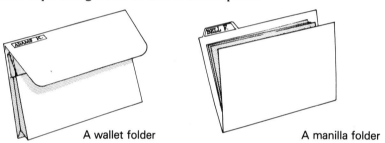

A wallet folder   A manilla folder

Alternatively papers may be kept in a simple folded piece of cardboard, with the back slightly longer than the front. This has no flap or gussets. It has the disadvantage of having no means of fastening papers in, so that they easily drop out. The name or title of the file is written on the longer, back portion of the folder. The thin cardboard used for folders is called 'manilla' and varies in thickness and colour.

Some folders have a spring, or metal clasp, which fastens the papers safely into the folder and allows them to be turned over like the pages of a book. This method ensures that papers cannot drop out of a folder accidentally, but slows down the process of filing, because the papers have to be perforated before they are placed in the folder.

A folder with a metal clasp

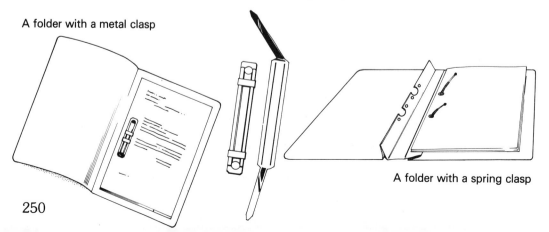

A folder with a spring clasp

Labelling Files

Labels for files can be flat, on the top edges of the pockets:

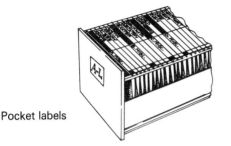

Pocket labels

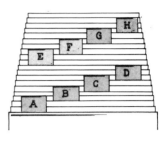

Guide tabs

Also, labels for files can be on projecting tabs, which are not directly behind each other, but are 'staggered' so that they can all be seen easily. These are known as 'guide' tabs.

Colour is useful to help the filing clerk to find files quickly.

Different types of documents, for example, could be in different coloured clear plastic folders.

Each section of an alphabetical filing system could have different coloured folders for easy identification of files.

Coloured guide tabs help the filing clerk to find files quickly, too.

Useful Filing Accessories

- Perforator – or paper punch – for perforating papers which are to be held in spring clip folders or ring binders.
- Staplers – standard size and long-arm.
- Embossing labeller – for labelling filing cabinet drawers.
- Clear adhesive tape – for repairing torn documents or folders.
- Labels – for labelling files.
- Cards – in various sizes, for card indexes.
- Reinforcing washers – for strengthening perforations.
- Treasury tags – for holding papers together loosely so that they can be turned over for reading easily.
- Bulldog clips – springs for holding papers firmly.

Bulldog clips   Treasury tags

Vertical Suspension Filing Cabinets

Files are conveniently stored in deep drawers in filing cabinets. The filing cabinets may have two, three, or four drawers.

Files stand upright – vertically – in the drawers and should be supported and held by pockets linked together. These pockets 'suspend' the files and prevent them from slipping to the bottom of the filing cabinet drawer. The correct name for this type of filing is vertical suspension filing. The weight of the files is taken by the rails, so keeping the files in perfect shape.

Vertical suspension filing cabinets. They need three times their actual floor space so that a clerk has room to stand in front of one when open. Note that filing cabinet drawers must be clearly labelled so that it is easy to find files quickly

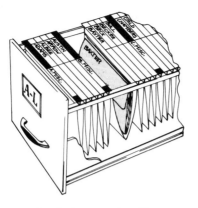

Vertical suspension filing

Files in a filing cabinet drawer without pockets

Lateral Filing Cabinets

These take up less floor space than vertical suspension filing cabinets, as there are no drawers to be opened – the files are arranged side by side, like books on a shelf. The word 'lateral' means 'from the sides'. Lateral filing cupboards can also be extended upwards towards the ceiling, but it will be essential to have a safe means of reaching the top shelves. Pockets in lateral filing cupboards are suspended in a similar manner to those in vertical suspension filing cabinets.

A sophisticated lateral filing system with horizontally sliding modules

253

Storing Large Documents

Maps, photographs, drawings, and charts are too large to be stored in the standard filing cabinets. They must, however, be kept flat. If they are folded, they will crack along the folds and if they are rolled up they are difficult to keep flat when they are taken out to be used.

A horizontal plan chest with wide, shallow drawers is one way to store large documents satisfactorily.

A vertical suspension plan chest is another way, where the documents are suspended from rods in a chest deep enough to hold them.

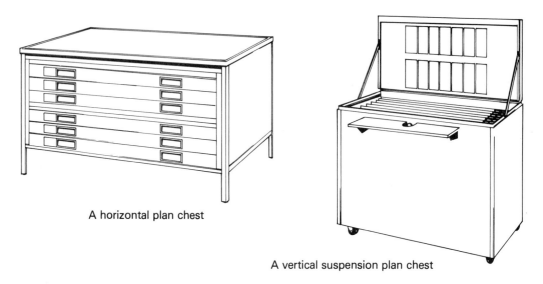

A horizontal plan chest

A vertical suspension plan chest

FOR YOUR FOLDER

38. FILING EQUIPMENT

Write these notes in your folder, filling in the missing words and phrases.

1) Thin cardboard used for folders is called ＿＿＿＿＿＿.

2) Labels for files can be flat, on top edges of pockets, or on projecting tabs which are 'staggered'. Staggered tabs are known as ＿＿＿＿＿＿ tabs.

3) Filing accessories include perforator, stapler, embossing labeller, labels, reinforcing washers, bulldog clips and ＿＿＿＿＿＿.

4) Filing cabinets containing files in vertical pockets, one behind the other, are vertical ＿＿＿＿＿＿.

5) The weight of the files is taken by rails, so keeping the files in ＿＿＿＿＿＿.

6) Files suspended in pockets arranged side by side is _____ filing.

7) The system of filing in No 6 is the one which saves _____.

8) Large maps, plans, photographs and charts should not be rolled or folded but filed in _____ chests either horizontal or _____.

Exercise 49

FILING EQUIPMENT

1) Describe the different types of folders used for filing.

2) What are 'guide' tabs?

3) Explain how colour could be used effectively in filing.

4) Vertical suspension filing cabinets need more space than lateral filing cabinets. Explain why this is so.

Safety

The top shelves in a lateral filing cupboard may be out of reach for some people, and a suitable step-ladder avoids accidents caused by standing on chairs or other makeshift objects.

Standing on a chair to reach the top shelf is dangerous!

A low stool on castors saves an aching back while filing in the bottom drawers of filing cabinets and is easy to move around.

Low filing stool

Vertical suspension filing cabinets usually have three or four drawers. These should always be closed after use. If the top drawer is left open while the bottom drawer is used, for instance, a nasty crack on the head could result, and if the top two or three drawers are all left open together, the filing cabinet could topple over on the unlucky filing clerk! Also, if the bottom drawer is left open, it may trip up an unwary passer-by.

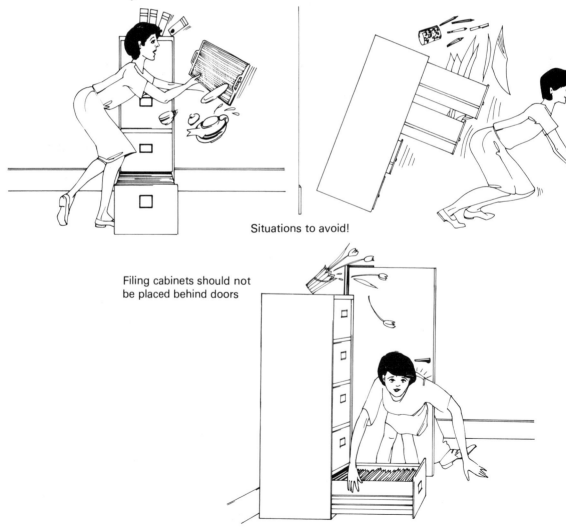

Situations to avoid!

Filing cabinets should not be placed behind doors

Security of Filing Systems

Special fireproof filing cabinets are obtainable, guaranteed by their makers to protect papers from severe fire hazards. Many fireproof filing cabinets preserved their contents against enemy fire bombs in 1940.

All filing cabinets which contain confidential documents should be locked whenever the office is left unoccupied, and at the end of each day before the staff go home.

Filing cabinets usually have protruding locks, as part of the structure. These lock all the drawers in a cabinet at once, when the lock is pressed in. The idea of the protruding lock is to show when the filing cabinet is *unlocked* – it makes it obvious to the filing clerk not to forget to lock up before she goes home.

FOR YOUR FOLDER

39. SECURITY OF FILING SYSTEMS

Write these notes in your folder, filling in the missing words and phrases.

1) Filing cabinets can easily cause nasty accidents if the bottom drawer is left _____ or the filing cabinet is placed behind a _____.

2) Top shelves in a lateral filing cabinet may be out of reach, and a _____ should be used, not a chair or other makeshift object.

3) To ensure that important documents are safe in the event of a serious fire, special _____ are obtainable.

4) All filing cabinets containing confidential papers should be _____ whenever the office is unoccupied.

5) Filing cabinets usually have protruding locks, which make it obvious when the cabinets have been left _____.

6) Filing in the lower drawers of a filing cabinet can cause an aching back. This can be avoided by using a _____.

Microfilming

An alternative to plan chests for very large documents is to reduce them in size by a process known as microfilming.

Microfilming reduces documents to the size of a postage stamp. Eight thousand A4 sized documents will go on to a roll of microfilm 100 feet long. A single storage cabinet 4½ feet high will hold microfilms of one and a half million documents.

Microfilm is available in several forms. The following are convenient for filing:

● *Microfiche* – a sheet of film which holds 98 micro-images. A micro-image is an A4 sized document reduced in size 24 times.

Microfiche

● *Aperture cards* have pieces of microfilm inset into them. They are usually punched cards for use in computers or punched card installations.

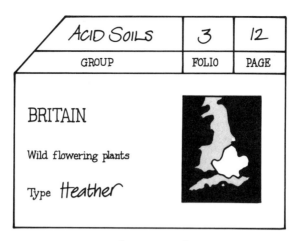

Aperture cards

JACKETING

Microfilm can be stored in a special protective transparent wallet or envelope, but it is difficult to remove the microfilms from this protective covering. This way of storing microfilms is known as microfilm 'jackets'. It has the advantage of making it almost impossible to lose a microfilmed document.

Microfilm on spools or reels is not suitable for filing and has to be stored in specially designed microfilm cabinets.

A reel of microfilm

Microfilm cassettes or cartridges are easier to handle and less likely to be damaged than reel film but are more expensive. Reel, cassette and cartridge films all suffer from the same disadvantage – it is difficult to locate any one particular section which may be required quickly.

EQUIPMENT

The following equipment is required for microfilming:
- camera
- platform
- jacketing machine
- reader or reader/printer.

The equipment is not cheap. The total cost would be about £5,000. Film is about £2 for 100 feet, which is relatively inexpensive.

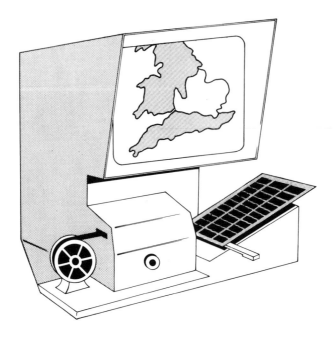

Viewing. Enlarging on to screen for reading off

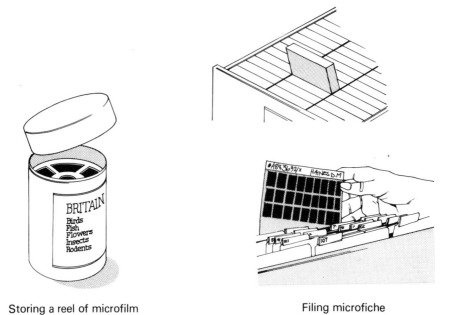

Storing a reel of microfilm

Filing microfiche

Storage. Microfiling takes under two per cent of normal film space

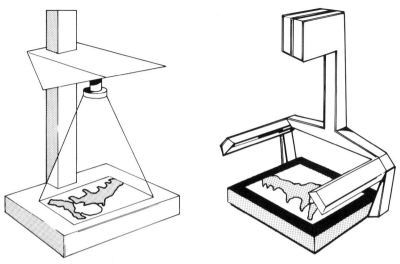

A microfilm camera

Prints from microfilm. Any number of copies can be made. Negatives are stored for future use

Microfilm can be produced directly from computer output, without any intermediate paper copy. This is known as COM, computer output on microfilm.

Firms use microfilming in many ways, including:

- for ordinary documents, to save filing space
- for large documents – maps, plans, photographs – to save space taken up by plan chests.

Libraries also use microfilming for back numbers of magazines and newspapers and to microfilm copies of thick, heavy books, so that they do not have the problem of carrying them from room to room.

Museums microfilm very old and valuable papers so that the originals need not be handled.

The other advantages of microfilming are, in addition to space saving:

- postage is cheaper than postage for originals, especially airmail
- duplicate copies of documents can be filed so that they are available in case of damage to originals by fire.

Apart from the cost of the equipment, the disadvantages are:

- a reader is needed to be able to see the documents
- any particular section on reel or cassette is not easy to locate quickly when needed.

FOR YOUR FOLDER

40. MICROFILMING

Write these notes in your folder, filling in the missing words and phrases.

1) Microfilming reduce documents to the size of a _____.

2) The most suitable forms of microfilms for filing are _____ and _____.

3) Microfilm on spools or reels has to be stored in specially designed microfilm cabinets. There is another disadvantage to this type of microfilm – it is difficult _____.

4) Equipment required for microfilms includes a camera, platform, jacketing machine and _____.

5) The reader/printer not only magnifies the microfilm so that it can be read easily, it also _____.

6) COM means _____.

7) As well as saving the space taken up by ordinary files, firms use microfilming to save _____.

8) Microfilms are also useful as duplicate copies of documents in case of _____.

9) The disadvantages of microfilming are the cost of the equipment, the necessity for a reader to be able to see the documents properly and _____.

Exercise 50

MICROFILMING

1) What is microfiche?

2) Explain jacketing microfilms.

3) What are aperture cards, and how are they used?

4) Microfilming is used by other organisations besides firms. Name two of them, and explain how they use microfilming.

Classifying Filing

Filing can be 'classified' in several ways. Classifying filing means the system by which it is stored. Most filing is in alphabetical order, because this is a simple system to follow. People's names are filed in alphabetical order of their surnames. Firms, societies, organisations and clubs are filed in alphabetical order of their registered names.

Alphabetical filing has one disadvantage – some letters will hardly be used at all (X and Z for instance) and so parts of an alphabetical filing cabinet may be half-empty. Also, a thorough knowledge of the alphabetical filing rules is necessary to use an alphabetical filing system.

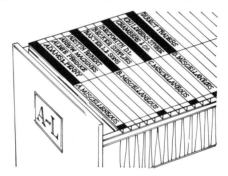

The top drawer in a filing cabinet, with the files arranged in alphabetical order of surnames or firms' names

General Rules for Alphabetical Filing

PEOPLE

Use surnames as filing points:

DOBSON   Michael
EVANS   Thomas
GRAYSON   Kate
HAYNES   Anne
MARTIN   Jane
OLIVER   William
QUENTIN   Carole
SIMMS   Margaret
WATKINS   Sarah
YEOVIL   Simon

263

Sometimes there are people with the same surname, in which case place the first names in alphabetical order:

HARRISON Elizabeth
HARRISON John
HARRISON Peter
HARRISON Theresa
HARRISON William

Occasionally, there may be identical first names and surnames. When this happens, file by second name, or initial, if full second name is not known:

BROWN Carole F
BROWN Carole Joanne
BROWN Carole W
BROWN Carole Yvonne
BROWN Carole Z

If there are identical first names and surnames, filing has to be done in alphabetical order of the towns in which the people live:

MARCH Roy Birmingham
MARCH Roy Coventry
MARCH Roy Huddersfield
MARCH Roy London
MARCH Roy Worcester

File names with prefixes such as: van, de la, O' under the prefix: (i.e. the prefix and the word is treated as part of one word name)

DE BRAY Martha
DE LA PARKE Laurence
O'TOURKE Patrick
VAN DE VEMEER Vera

'MAC' NAMES

File all Scottish names beginning with Mc, Mac or M' as if they were all spelt Mac:

McBETH Thomas
M'BRIDE Martha
McHENRY Ian
MACKENZIE Henry
MACMASTERS Janet
McPHERSON Martin

Some Irish names begin with M', Mac or Mc, too.

McNEIL Sean
MACMAHON Siobhan

St Genesius
patron saint
of secretaries

St Matthew
patron saint of
book-keepers
accountants
and tax-
collectors

St Gabriel
patron saint
of telephonists
and postal
workers

File all 'saint' surnames beginning with ST as if this were *spelt* Saint:

St Gabriel
St Genesius
Saint John Ervine
Saint Martin's Finance Co Ltd
St Matthew
St Philip's Benefit Building Society

Ignore titles altogether from the point of view of filing:

BROWN   Lady Jane
BROWN   Margaret
BROWN   Mrs Tina
GREY   Mrs Sally
GREY   Sir William
REDD   Alan
REDD   Lord George
SILVER Dr Mark
SILVER Noreen
WHITE   Lady Elizabeth
WHITE   Sir Harold
WHITE   Rev. Vincent

File a shorter surname before a longer one, when you have names like these.

MARCH   Andrew
MARCHE   Andrew
MARCHWARD   Andrew

Short before long!

File hyphenated names by the first part of the name (i.e. ignore the hyphen and treat whole name as one word):

CARTER-BROWN   James
SIMSON-ELLIS   Mary
TAYLOR-JACKSON   Richard
WILLIAMS-KING   Helen

FIRMS

Some registered names of firms include a first name. If so, file under the surname:

Ernest G Williams & Co Ltd
File as   Williams   Ernest G & Co Ltd

When the registered name of a firm includes two surnames, file under the first surname:

Hickson and Garrett Ltd
File as   Hickson and Garrett Ltd

File any firm's name which includes a number as if the number were spelt in full:

The 45 Club
File as   *Forty-Five* Club (The)

Ignore the words 'The' and 'A' in names of firms:

The O'Brien Steel Works Limited
A Modern Printing Company
File as   *Modern* Printing Company (A)
              O'Brien Steelworks (The)

Firms whose names consist of initials should be filed before firms whose names are written in full:

LKJ Engineering Co Ltd
Lamb's Furniture Co Ltd

unless it is known what the initials stand for, in which case the filing is done normally:

ICI Ltd file under: Imperial Chemical Industries Ltd
AA   file under: Automobile Association
RAC   file under: Royal Automobile Club

FOR YOUR FOLDER

41. FILING ALPHABETICALLY

Write these notes in your folder, filling in the missing words and phrases, and putting the names in the right order.

1) If there are two surnames which are identical, then the _____ names should be used as a filing point:

   Elizabeth Jones
   Robert Jones
   Deborah Jones
   Linda Jones.

2) If there are two names with the same surname and the same first name, then filing should be under _____.

   Peter Jackson, Coventry
   Peter Jackson, Hull
   Peter Jackson, Cardiff
   Peter Jackson, Sunderland
   Peter Jackson, Birmingham.

3) File hyphenated names by the _____ part:

   Martin Allan-Jenkins
   Donald Efans-Jones
   Peter Forbes-Robertson
   Claire Carter-Dobson
   Susan Simms-Anderson.

4) File names such as:

   de la Porte
   van Hagen
   O'Connor   under the _____ part.

5) Titles such as Mr, Mrs, Dr, Sir, should be _____
   Mr F K L Dixon
   Dr M Jenkinson
   Lady Sylvia Barker
   Mrs F J Dawson

6) 'A' and 'The' in the title of a firm or organisation should be _____.

   The Kleenwyte Detergent Co Ltd
   The Midlands Duplicating Co Ltd
   A Superior Office Cleaning Agency.

7) Scottish names, whether starting with 'Mc', 'Mac' or 'M' should be filed as if all spelt _____.

   McLellan
   McVitie

MacMillan
McMaster
M'Bride

8) Numbers in the names of firms or organisations should be filed as if the numbers were _____.

The 2001 Publishing Co Ltd
The 15th Century History Society
The 45 Club.

9) When it is not known what initials in the name of a firm stand for, file _____.

A & A Builders Ltd
LCP Fuels Ltd
GPR Developments Ltd
CK Sports Ltd
W & E Printing Ltd.

10) Names which begin with St are always filed as if spelt _____.

St Clair-Jones
Saint Clair-Johnson
St John's Antiques
St Paul's Printing & Label Co Ltd
Saint Simeon's Society.

11) When it is known what groups of initials stand for file _____.

TUC
MEB
BBC
ITV
NCB.

12) Names which have the same letters at the beginning such as:

Johnson
Johnston
Johns
John

should follow the rule _____ before long.

Exercise 51

FILING ALPHABETICALLY

1) Write the following names in the correct alphabetical order:

David Jones
D Jones
D A Jones
Dr D Montgomery-Jones.

2) Write the following firms' names in the correct alphabetical order:

Messrs Carter and Francis, Solicitors
The Midland Secretarial Agency
A L Carter and Company Limited
Middleton and Langdale, Sons and Co Ltd.

3) Write the following names of hotels in the correct alphabetical order:

The White Lion Hotel, Basingstoke
The White Lion Hotel, Alcester
The Angel Inn, Ipswich
The Angel Inn, Keswick
The Star Hotel, Ledbury
The Feathers, Ledbury.

4) Write the following names in the correct alphabetical order:

Jan van Meeren
William de la Pole
Peter O'Connor
Mary Mackintosh
Roberto di Lorenzo
Sarah O'Malley.

5) Write the following hairdressers' names in the correct alphabetical order:

The 20th Century Salon
Betty's Hairstyling Salon
Scissors
The Unisex Salon
11th Hour Shampoo and Set
A First-Class Hairdressing Salon.

6) Write the following names in the correct alphabetical order:

James St John
Mary Saint Claire
Michael Sinclair
Robert St John Ervine
Marie Sainte
Deborah St Nicholas.

Exercise 52

FILING POINTS

Make a list of all the above names in Exercise 51 in the correct alphabetical order and under each filing point. (Example: Littlewoods Organisation Limited (The).)

Exercise 53

FILING THE RIGHT WAY AROUND

Which name would be filed first in the following pairs of names:

1) G MacKnight
   L McKnight.

2) Thomas Jones
   T P Jones.

3) Sir Walter Appleby
   Andrew Appleby & Co Ltd.

4) Arnold & Co Ltd
   G T Arnold.

5) Mary Machin
   Martin Machin.

6) John Manning, Cardiff
   John Manning, Taunton.

7) Jean Hilton-Johns
   Jean Johns.

8) Donal Mackintosh, Glasgow
   Donal McKintosh, Edinburgh.

9) Michael O'Shea
   Michael Oliphant.

10) John Parsons & Co Ltd
    Johnson & Nesbit Ltd.

11) Lieut Col James Edmunds
    Right Hon Earl of Essex.

12) Dame Margaret Shaftesbury
    Mrs Margaret Shafto.

13) William Smith
    William Smithe.

14) Robert Smithers
    Robert Smithson.

15) W T C Transport Co Ltd
    Watson Transport Co Ltd.

16) BBC
    NBC.

17) F I O Craig
    Fiona Craig.

18) The 21st Century Supply Agency
    The Twisted Chimney Antique Shop.

19) Sainsbury & Co
    K P St Albans.

20) Dirk van Olesen
    Dick Vardon.

Numerical Filing

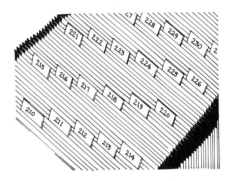

Numerical filing

This uses numbers instead of letters to divide the filing pockets of a filing cabinet. It is easy to use because each new file is given the next number and added to the end of the existing files. Numerical filing is especially useful in insurance companies, building societies and hospitals, where policy-holders, members or patients are each given a number. Numbers are difficult to remember, however, and an alphabetical index of all the names has to be kept, with the numbers of the files against each name. This is another example of 'cross-referencing'.

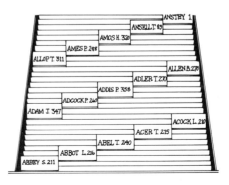

An alphabetical card index for a numerical filing system

Chronological Order

This is filing in order of the date. Most papers are placed in files in date order, with the latest paper on top, and the oldest at the back of the file.

Geographical Order

This is filing in alphabetical order of areas – either towns, countries, or continents. A travel agent would find geographical filing useful. Gas and electricity boards make use of geographical filing systems. Export departments and sales departments in firms file documents in this way.

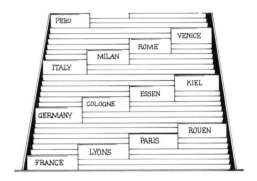

A geographical filing system

Subject Filing

This is a useful method of filing papers under topics. Each topic or 'subject' is filed in alphabetical order. It is especially useful for filing personal papers.

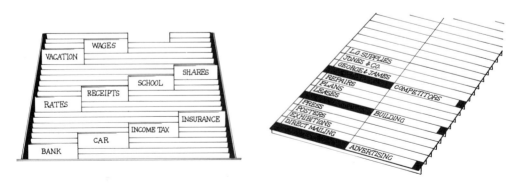

Subject filing systems

With subject filing, cross-referencing would be useful. For example: 'For salaries, see wages' and 'For PAYE, see income tax'.

FOR YOUR FOLDER

42. CLASSIFYING FILING

Write these notes in your folder, filling in the missing words and phrases.

1) 'Classifying' filing means the system by which it is _____.

2) Most filing is done in alphabetical order of _____ or _____.

3) Numerical filing uses _____ instead of letters to divide the filing pockets of a filing cabinet.

4) Numerical filing is especially useful in insurance companies, building societies and _____.

5) Because numbers are difficult to remember an _____ index has to be kept with the numbers typed or written against each name. This is an example of _____.

6) Filing in order of the date is _____ filing.

7) Geographical filing is filing in alphabetical order of _____.

8) Filing in alphabetical order of topics is _____ filing.

Exercise 54

CLASSIFYING FILING

1) Explain why the bottom drawer of a filing cabinet might be half empty.

2) Numerical filing is sometimes called 'open-ended'. What does this mean?

3) Geographical filing is still done in alphabetical order of areas. What would be the main sub-division and how would the filing be organised?

4) Explain how cross-referencing could be used in connection with subject filing.

Indexing

Textbooks, reference books, any books containing facts, have indexes at the back, arranged in alphabetical order. Newspapers and magazines have indexes, too, similarly arranged. Indexes are added to books, newspapers and magazines so that readers are able to find the information they want, quickly and simply, without wading through the entire book or magazine. Indexes are needed in offices for many reasons:

- Frequently used telephone numbers
- Internal telephone numbers – extension numbers
- Callers' business visiting cards
- Alphabetical index for a numerical filing system.

All the above indexes could be typed out, or written in a book with indexed pages. These methods are quite satisfactory until new numbers have to be added, or old ones taken out, which makes the list untidy and difficult to read.

Natham L.

Nicholas S.T.

Nixon P.

Norman M.

Norris M.

Nuttal S.

N O P Q R S T UV W YZ

An indexed book

Exercise 55

INDEXING NUMERICALLY

On the left, opposite, is a newspaper index. It is arranged in alphabetical order of topics. Rearrange it in numerical order of pages, putting the page number first, as below:

Page Number	Topic
20	Motors
21	Motors
22	Motors
23	Motors
24	Supermart
25	Supermart

Which would be the easiest, and quickest, method of classification to enable you to find the topic you wanted?

Exercise 56

INDEXING ALPHABETICALLY

On the right, opposite, is an index to the small advertisements in a newspaper.

Rewrite it so that the advertisements are all in alphabetical order, as below:

Description of
Advertisement   *Number*
Accommodation
   available   19
Accommodation
   wanted   20
Antiques for sale 57
Antiques wanted   58

THE DAILY NEWS CLASSIFIED INDEX

Appointments	26, 27, 29, 58, 59, 60, 61, 62, 64, 65, 66, 67, 68, 69
Posts in Education & Research	26
Accountancy & Finance	69
Overseas	58, 59, 60
Engineers	52, 64, 65
Sales & Marketing	66, 67, 68
Business to Business	54
Courses and Seminars	26
Entertainments	34, 35, 36, 37
Holidays & Travel	44, 45, 46, 50
Travel U.K.	50
Travel Overseas	44, 45, 46
Self Catering	45, 46
House & Garden	46
Motors	19, 20, 21, 22, 23
Personal	50-51
Collectors	50-51
Sale & Wanted	50-51
Swimming Pools	50-51
Tuition	50-51
Property	46, 47, 48, 49
Abroad	49
Country	46, 47
London & GLC area	47, 48, 49
Mortgages	47
Supermart	24, 25

GUIDE TO THE CLASSIFIEDS

(1) Situations Vacant (Professional & Trade)
(2) Situations Vacant (Office)
(3) Situations Vacant (Sales Representatives)
(4) Situations Vacant (Domestic)
(5) Situations Vacant (Agricultural)
(6) Situations Vacant (Part-time)
(7) Situations Wanted
(8) Business Opportunities
(9) Properties For Sale
(10) Properties To Let
(11) Properties Wanted
(12) Properties (Exchange)
(13) Financial/Money To Lend
(14) Land For Sale/To Let
(15) Land Wanted
(16) Business & Commercial Premises For Sale
(17) Business & Commercial Premises To Let
(18) Business & Commercial Premises Wanted
(19) Accommodation Available
(20) Accommodation Wanted
(21) Flats Available
(22) Flats Wanted
(23) Nursing Homes
(24) Travel & Holidays
(25) Caravans & Boats For Sale
(26) Caravans & Boats Wanted
(27) Caravans & Boats To Hire
(28) Motor Cycles & Cycles For Sale
(29) Motor Cycles & Cycles Wanted
(30) Cars & Commercial Vehicles For Sale
(31) Cars & Commercial Vehicles Wanted
(32) Car & Van Hire
(33) Trailers
(34) Driving Tuition
(35) Motor Spares & Accessories
(36) Motor Services & Repairs
(37) Motor Insurances
(38) Plant & Machinery For Sale
(39) Plant & Machinery Wanted
(40) Plant & Machinery For Hire
(41) Radio TV & Musical For Sale
(42) Radio TV & Musical Wanted
(43) Radio & TV Rental
(44) Radio & TV Repairs & Service
(45) Home Appliances For Sale
(46) Swap Shop
(47) Expert Services Offered
(48) Expert Services Wanted
(49) Home Improvements
(50) Photography
(51) Education & Tuition
(52) Personal
(53) Lost & Found
(54) Furniture, Furnishings & Carpets For Sale
(55) Furniture, Furnishings & Carpets Wanted

Card Indexes

A better method than a list or an indexed book is a card index. Separate cards are easy to add to, or to remove cards from, and the cards can be stored in boxes with lids or in small drawers.

A card index drawer

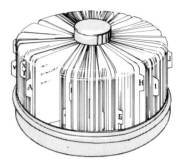

A small rotary card index

Another desk top method of storing card indexes is on a wheel which revolves. This is called a rotary card index. It stores more cards in a smaller space than that taken up by boxes or drawers and all the cards are within easy reach of the filing clerk.

Index cards can be typed on, or written on, and are large enough to contain several lines of information (e.g. name and address as well as a telephone number).

ROTARY CARD INDEX

This revolves so that all the cards are within easy reach of the filing clerk. It also stores more cards in a smaller space than would be taken up by boxes or drawers.

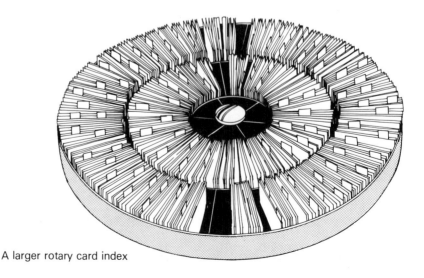

A larger rotary card index

Exercise 57

ASSIGNMENT ON CARD INDEXES

Below is an example of a card which is to be filed in a card index used in connection with a numerical file:

```
BAXTER       Mrs Linda Katherine          File No 4551

             13 Hill Top Road
             GREENFIELD
             Sussex

             Tel: 0864 778 437


             Account opened 5 March 1980
```

Rule up five similar rectangles, and then make out index cards as the above example for the following:

1) Mr John Edwards opened an account on 31 January 1979. His address was then 27 Temple Street, Birmingham. He moved to 28 Freeth Street, Walsall on 6 June 1980. His telephone number is now 0922 765 211. His file number is 4001.

2) On 12 February 1979 Miss Lorraine Austin opened an account. Her file No is 4325. She is not on the telephone. Her address is 22 The Square, Wilmslow, Cheshire.

3) File No 4440 was opened on 28 February 1979 for Mr Arthur West. His address is 65 Stanley Road, Wigton, Cumbria. His telephone number is 09654 334 865.

4) Mrs Jacqueline Saunders opened an account on 1 March 1979. Her file number is 4501. Her address is 10 High Street, Newark, Notts. Her telephone number is 0636 115 778.

5) Mr Frank Moreland opened an account on 3 March 1979. His address is 248 Grange Road, Weedon, Northants. His telephone number is 0327 668 343. His file number is 4548.

Exercise 58

ADDITIONAL QUESTIONS ON CARD INDEXES

1) Why is an alphabetical card index necessary for a numerical filing system?

2) What is the advantage of a card index over a written or typed list?

3) What other information, apart from an index for a numerical filing system, is often kept in the form of a card index?

4) Would an index card be typed, or written?

5) Card indexes are usually in boxes, or drawers, or on a wheel which revolves. This is called a rotary card index. What is the advantage of a rotary card index over an ordinary card index?

Exercise 59

ADDITIONAL ASSIGNMENTS ON CARD INDEXES

Make a card index of the surnames of your classmates.

Find an index to a newspaper or magazine, and make a card index from it.

Make a card index of all your singles or LPs.

Make a card index of all the hairdressers, or all the florists, in the Classified Trade Directory.

Make a card index of all the schools and colleges in your area.

Visible Edge Cards

Another method of storing cards is in a visible edge card index. Here the cards overlap, leaving the bottom edge of the card 'visible'. The bottom edge is used for the title, name of number of the card. Coloured markers or 'signals' are useful to draw immediate attention to any card which may need to be used frequently.

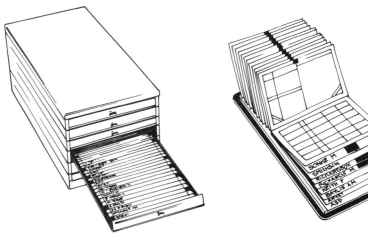

Visible edge cards in shallow drawers   Visible edge cards in a tray

Exercise 60

ASSIGNMENT ON A VISIBLE EDGE CARD

Below is a price-list for a special sale of camping equipment.

TERRIFIC PRE-SEASON SAVINGS ON CAMPING EQUIPMENT !!

	Sleeps	Rec. Price or Estimated Value	SALE PRICE				
CABANON FRAME TENTS				**TRAILER TENTS**			
Elvire	3	£113	**£89**	Rover Super	Everyman's	£659	**£399**
Emelia	4	£146	**£115**	Rapide	Everyman's	£749	**£599**
Emmanuelle	5	£165	**£129**	Popular	Conway	£645	**£550**
Pervenche	5	£300	**£235**	Campa Deluxe	Conway	£745	**£625**
Vis-a-Vis	6	£139	**£99**	Corsica	Conway	£845	**£725**
CROWN FRAME TENTS				**CONTINENTAL STYLE**			
Royal	4	£125	**£99**	**RIDGE TENTS**			
Regent	5/6	£177	**£129**	Ariel I	Octopus	£25	**£17.50**
Majestic	4	£197	**£139**	Ariel II	Octopus	£31	**£22.50**
Imperial	4	£194	**£149**	Panther	Selrig	£30	**£22.50**
BLACKS FRAME TENTS				Tradition III	Cabanon	£53	**£39.50**
Manitoba	5	£320	**£185**	Isabelle Sport	Cabanon	£109	**£69.50**
Columbia	4	£375	**£245**	Sirocco I	Lichfield	£34	**£22.50**
GOODALL FRAME TENTS				**ULTRA LIGHTWEIGHT**			
Chalet	4	£150	**£85**	**BACKPACKING TENTS**			
Quantock 4	4	£178	**£109**	Solite	Blacks	£56	**£39.50**
Quantock 6	6	£244	**£149**	Parklite	Blacks	£63	**£42.50**
Continental 4	4	£244	**£165**	Kamplite	Blacks	£69	**£49.50**
Continental 6	6	£310	**£195**	Monark	Blacks	£73	**£55.50**
WALKER FRAME TENTS							
Texas	6	£239	**£175**	**CARAVAN AWNINGS**			
Arbi Madrid	5	£295	**£199**	Popular 10'	Raleigh	£83	**£49.50**
El Patio Luxe	6	£376	**£269**	Popular 12'	Raleigh	£90	**£55.50**
Chalet Suisse Luxe	6	£390	**£279**	Popular 14'	Raleigh	£94	**£59.50**
Chalet Grande Luxe	6	£440	**£299**	Deluxe 11'	Raleigh	£96	**£67.50**
RINCO FRAME TENTS				Deluxe 14'	Raleigh	£104	**£75.50**
Costa Del Sol	6	£250	**£199**	Deluxe 16'	Raleigh	£110	**£85.50**

Later in the year, after the sale, the firm selling this camping equipment finds it useful to have a record on a visible edge card of the different price ranges of the tents. The edge of each card shows the price range, and the remainder of the card has on it the rest of the information about the tents, as below.

Type of tent	Grade	Name	Price
Continental Ridge		Octopus	
style	Ariel I	Octopus	£25
	Panther	Selrig	£30
	Ariel II	Octopus	£31
	Sirocco I	Lichfield	£34
	Tradition III	Cabanon	£53
Ultra Lightweight			
backpacking tents	Solite	Blacks	£56
	Paklite	Blacks	£63
	Kamplite	Blacks	£69
	Monark	Blacks	£73
TENTS Price range £25 – £100			

A visible edge card

Make out visible edge cards for tents from £100 to £200, and from those between £200 and £300. Then make out a separate visible edge card for the really large tents over £600 in price.

How could you mark the card giving details about the tents priced at between £200 and £300 so that you could find it quickly?

What is the main advantage of visible edge cards, which are held in frames, and a card index, where the cards are loose, in a box or drawer?

STRIP INDEXES

Strip indexing is a method of making an indexing list on narrow strips of thin cardboard. These strips are then mounted in a frame, and the frame can be placed in a holder on the desk top or mounted on the wall. So that it is possible to type on these narrow strips, they are attached to a backing sheet and can be peeled off when they have been typed on, and placed in a panel in the correct order. The strips can be moved easily up and down the frame or panel, or taken out and replaced by new strips, and are therefore especially useful for information which is constantly changing, such as prices, telephone numbers or addresses. As the strips are so narrow, only one line of information can be typed on them.

The strips are available in about six different colours, and effective use can be made of the different colours for easy identification of various groups of prices, or different sections of the alphabet.

It is also possible to obtain strips which are in a perforated sheet, and can be torn off, after typing.

Typing a strip index

Filing a strip index

Organisation of Filing

CENTRALISED FILING

With centralised filing all the firm's filing is stored in one large area under the supervision of trained experts in filing. The advantages of centralised filing are:

- Staff are engaged on filing and nothing else, and so are able to organise a smooth-running system.
- Junior staff are trained by the supervisor and so become efficient at filing.
- Equipment is used to the full.

There are two main disadvantages of centralised filing:

- Files may be out when needed.
- The centralised filing area may be a long way from some offices, causing inconvenience and waste of time when files are required.

Departmental Filing

Departmental filing means that each department carries out its own filing. It has the advantage of keeping all files near at hand and convenient for quick reference, but it means that many more filing cabinets are in use around a firm than are really necessary, thus wasting money as well as space. Also staff trained to carry out more specialised work (such as shorthand-typists) may be spending some of their time filing, when this could be done in a centralised filing office by filing clerks.

FOR YOUR FOLDER

43. ORGANISATION OF FILING

Write these notes in your folder, filling in the missing words and phrases.

1) Centralised filing is where all the firm's filing is stored in one large area and is looked after by _____.

2) Organisation of filing in this way is _____ because staff are engaged on filing and nothing else.

3) One of the disadvantages of centralised filing is that the files may be _____ when needed.

4) Another disadvantage is that the filing department may be a long way from some offices, causing _____ and _____ when files are needed.

5) Filing which is done by typists, shorthand-typists and secretaries in their own departments is called _____ filing. This is convenient for the office staff because papers are _____.

6) Departmental filing adds _____ to the jobs of shorthand-typists, secretaries or typists.

7) A disadvantage of departmental filing is that some of the filing cabinets may be _____.

Exercise 61

ORGANISATION OF FILING

1) Compare departmental with centralised filing and explain the advantages and disadvantages of each.

2) Why would the job of a filing clerk in charge of a centralised filing area be a very important one?

3) Filing is sometimes described as a boring job. Explain why this is a totally wrong description.

4) Filing is one of the most important clerical jobs in a firm. Explain why this is.

Exercise 62

CROSSWORD ON FILING

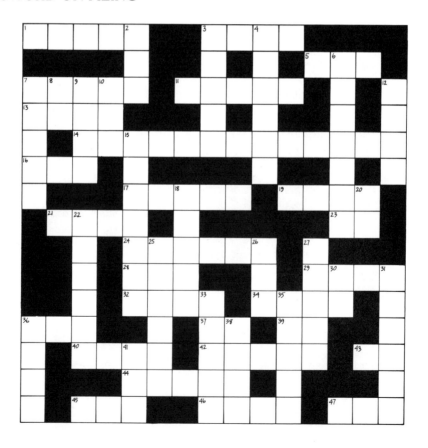

Across

1 When filing, it is very important to place papers in the _____ files (5)

3 When a file becomes too bulky, the correct procedure is to make a _____ file (4)

5 Besides answering the telephone, _____ of the most important office jobs is filing (3)

7 _____ filming reduces papers to a very small size (5)

11 This type of indexing is very useful for telephone numbers and price-lists (5)

13 Which is filed *last* – ONAT or ONAY? (4)

14 A special mark on a document showing it has been dealt with and may be filed, is called a _____ _____ (7, 6)

16 Which would be filed *first* – NOD, NED or NID? (3)

17 This should be clearly written on a file (5)

19 Before filing papers, pre_____ them (4)

21 Visible _____ cards are held in books or frames (4)

23 To file well is _____ efficient (2)

24 The most _____ paper is placed at the front of the file (6)

28 Which would be filed *first* – AUK, ANK, ASK, ART or AWK? (3)

29 Which would be filed *last* – ROOK, ROOD, ROCK or ROOB? (4)

32 A paper wrongly filed could well be _____ for ever (4)

34 Large maps, drawings or photographs are filed in _____ chests (4)

36 The efficient filing clerk should be able to _____ to the right file when a document is wanted (3)

37 File _____ soon _____ you can (2)

39 File papers _____ the correct files (2)

40 Which would be filed *last* – SEAT, SLAG, SNAG or SCAR? (4)

42 When sorting papers before filing, it is important to note the filing _____ (5)

43 Is De La Bere filed under De or La? (2)

44 One way to deal with papers no longer required is to _____ them (5)

45 _____ and Electricity Boards use geographical filing (3)

46 Which would be filed *last* – REES, REAS, REED or REEL? (4)

47 Do filing several times a _____ (3)

Down

2 Filing and answering the telephone are _____ of the most important office jobs (3)

3 Chronological filing is filing in order of _____ (5)

4 A filing clerk will be permanently _____ a state of chaos unless she files frequently (6)

6 Numerical filing is filing in order of _____ (7)

7 Loud _____ will be caused by lost files! (5)

8 Filing means storing papers _____ the right order so that they can be found quickly (2)

9 An out _____ should be placed in the files when a paper is borrowed (4)

10 Which would be filed *last* – ROE, RYE, RUE or RAE? (3)

12 It is necessary to _____ papers in order to find them (4)

15 The name of the filing system where the files are arranged like books on a shelf is _____ filing (7)

18 These could be 14 across (5)

20 _____ be an efficient filing clerk is to do a very important job (2)

22 Papers which are allowed to pile up instead of being filed at once will cause _____ if they are wanted urgently (6)

25 Filing just once a day may not be often _____ to keep it from piling up (6)

26 A desk _____ sorter is useful for pre-sorting filing (3)

27 Which would be filed *last* – GRANT, GRAIN, GRALL, GRANE or GRANO? (5)

30 Labels for files can be flat _____ the top edge of the suspension pocket (2)

31 Which would be filed *first* – KNIELY, KNEELY, KNELLY or KNOLLY? (6)

33 Which would be filed *first* – TYPER, TYLER, TAPER or TOPER? (5)

35 _____ across a document could be 18 down (5)

36 Filing papers keeps them _____, clean and uncreased (4)

38 Which would be filed *last* – SODE, SODA, SADE or SADO? (4)

41 You feel you are a complete _____ if you cannot find a paper you have been asked for! (3)

SECTION D   MONEY MATTERS

CHAPTER 14

Petty Cash

What is Petty Cash?

The word 'petty' means 'small'. Petty cash means, therefore, small amounts of money paid out, or received.

Every firm finds it necessary to have cash available for payment of small items, for which the services of a bank would not be convenient. Examples of payments by petty cash are:

- Tea, coffee, milk, sugar for the office staff
- Bus or taxi fares
- Parking meter fees
- Coins for charity-collecting boxes
- Postage stamps
- Magazines for reception
- Flowers
- Cleaner's wages
- Cleaning materials – polish, soap, dusters
- Small items of office stationery – labels, shorthand notebooks, envelopes.

Looking after Petty Cash

Money used for petty cash must be kept in a lockable cash box with a removable tray, so that bank notes can be stored safely under the tray. The box must be locked in a cupboard, out of sight, when not being used.

A lockable cash box

The person in charge of petty cash is sometimes a secretary, sometimes a senior clerk. He or she saves the chief cashier's time by paying out ('disbursing') money for small items.

The petty cash book is usually kept on a system called the imprest system. The word 'imprest' means 'advance' or 'loan'. Under the imprest system a sum of money to equal the amount which has been spent is disbursed by the chief cashier to the petty cashier at the end of a regular period – usually a week or a month.

Thus, if the clerk in charge of petty cash has started the week with £20, and spent £18.30 by Friday, she will ask the chief cashier for £18.30. This amount (the 'imprest') will bring the total in her cash box back to the original £20. The amount left in her cash box before going to the chief cashier for an 'imprest' is £1.70. This £1.70 is known as the 'balance' – that is, the amount *not* spent or paid out to other people to spend, out of the £20 imprest.

Monday 7th Jan

IN CASH BOX

£20

Friday 11th Jan

IN CASH BOX

£1.70

Monday 14th Jan

IN CASH BOX
£1.70 and vouchers totalling £18.30

Monday 14th Jan

IN CASH BOX
£1.70
+
£18.30
imprest

(cash received)

Petty Cash Voucher

Folio _____

Date _____ 19

For what required	AMOUNT	
	£	p

Signature _____

Passed by _____

Petty cash vouchers authorise the payments made from petty cash

288

Petty cash vouchers must be signed by the person *receiving* the money, and also by the person authorising the payment – e.g. a manager, supervisor or senior secretary. The clerk in charge of the petty cash must not pay out any money, however small the sum, without a petty cash voucher. In addition, a receipt should be produced for anything bought out of petty cash, when it is possible to obtain one. Bus and train tickets should be kept and handed to the petty cash clerk. VAT is reclaimable only when receipts can be produced.

The postage book (pp. 180–1) is kept as a record of stamps bought and used, and acts as a receipt – the Post Office does not normally give a receipt for stamps sold by them, although they will do so if it is required specially. A voucher would have to be signed for stamps bought for an office, of course.

At any time, the petty cash clerk can make a quick check of the petty cash by totalling the amount on the vouchers and adding to it the cash in her box. The final amount should equal the amount started with originally.

Filling in a Petty Cash Form

In petty cash account sheet No. 1 each item on the petty cash sheet has been entered twice – once under 'Total Paid' and once under its own special heading – one of the analysis columns.

'Stamps' under 'Postage'
'Tea, coffee, sugar' under 'Office expenses'
'Cleaner's wages' under 'Cleaning'.

Analysis columns enable the office manager, petty cash clerk and chief cashier to see at a glance whether too much is being spent on a certain item. Analysis column headings vary from office to office, which is why they are left blank for the petty cash clerk to fill in. It is useful to head one column 'Miscellaneous'. This can be used to enter any item which does not normally have to be paid for out of petty cash, i.e. does not fit under other headings.

A column headed 'Stationery' would be used for all items normally bought at a stationers – string, ball-point pens, shorthand notebooks, pencils, rubber bands, staples, adhesive tape, envelopes, A4 and A5 bond and bank, blotting paper, postcards, typewriter ribbons, typewriter erasers, liquid typewriter corrective, carbon paper, paper clips, rubber stamps and pads, glue, scissors, ink, bulldog clips, treasury tags, rulers, folders, index cards, and so on. Only occasional items should be bought with petty cash – most stationery is bought by the buying office and issued under stationery stock control in a large firm (see Chapter 11).

A column headed 'Travel' would be used for bus fares, train fares and taxi fares. Larger amounts would have to be authorised by the

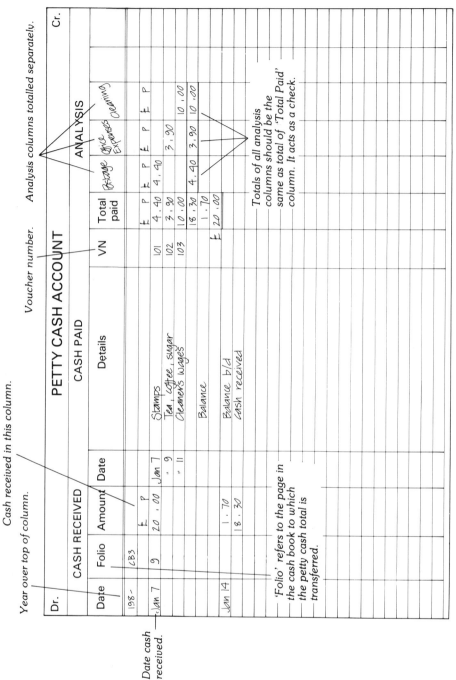

department dealing with travel and would not come out of petty cash (air fares, for example).

'Office Expenses' can be used for small items – tea, coffee, sugar, milk, flowers.

Any item which occurs fairly regularly would need its own analysis column heading – i.e. meter fees for parking or flowers for reception.

'Cleaning' would include soap, polish, dusters, window cleaning as well as the cleaner's wages.

'Postage' would include any surcharge paid on letters arriving understamped (see p. 175) and purchase of international reply coupons, registered envelopes and stamped envelopes, as well as stamps.

Each analysis column is totalled separately, and the combined totals should agree with the 'total paid'. If they do not agree, a mistake has been made. This 'cross-checking' ensures that any mistakes can be spotted and corrected.

The difference between the 'total paid' and the amount of cash received is the 'balance' – i.e. the amount remaining in the petty cash box.

The 'balance' is brought down first on the petty cash sheet, and the amount of imprest (i.e. cash to restore the balance to its original amount) is written underneath. The petty cash sheet is then ready for the next entries.

The folio number of the petty cash sheet refers to the page number in the cash book in which petty cash is entered – e.g. 'CB3' means 'cash book, page 3'.

FOR YOUR FOLDER

44. PETTY CASH

Write these notes in your folder, filling in the missing words and phrases.

1) The word 'petty' means _____.

2) Money used for payments out of petty cash must be kept in a lockable cash box with a _____ tray, so that _____ can be safely stored underneath.

3) The cash box must be _____ in a cupboard when not being used.

4) Petty cash book is usually kept on the _____ system.

5) Under this system a sum of money to equal the amount which has been spent is disbursed by the chief cashier to the petty cash clerk at the end of a _____ period – usually a week or a _____.

6) Petty cash is not paid out unless a voucher is produced, signed twice – once by the person _____ the money and once by the person _____ the payment.

7) In addition a _____ should be produced whenever possible.

8) At any time, the petty cash clerk can make a quick check of her petty cash by totalling the amount on the _____ and adding it to the _____ in her box. The final amount should equal the _____.

9) Each item on a petty cash sheet has to be entered twice – once under 'total paid' and once under its own special heading – one of the _____ columns.

10) Petty cash is used in offices for the payment of _____.

Exercise 63

ASSIGNMENTS ON PETTY CASH

1) Rule up your own petty cash sheet and call it no 2.

Make out five petty cash vouchers and number them 103, 104, 105, 106 and 107.

Date them for 1, 2, 3, 4 and 5 February respectively, 1980—. The folio is CB3. *(continued on p. 294)*

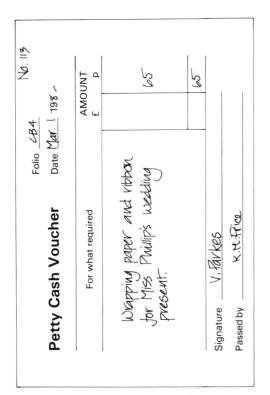

Petty Cash Voucher

No. 113

Folio CB4 Date Mar. 1 198–

AMOUNT £ p

For what required

Wrapping paper and ribbon for Miss Phillips' wedding present.   65

65

Signature V. Parkes

Passed by K.H. Price

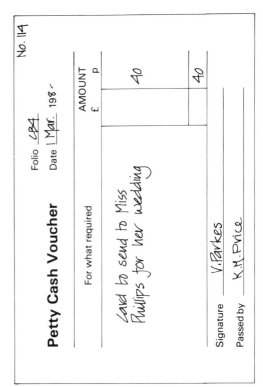

Petty Cash Voucher

No. 114

Folio CB4 Date 1 Mar. 198–

AMOUNT £ p

For what required

Card to send to Miss Phillips for her wedding   40

40

Signature V. Parkes

Passed by K.H. Price

Petty Cash Voucher

No. 115

Folio CB4
Date 3 Mar. 198-

For what required	AMOUNT	
	£	p
Sherry and biscuits for office party for Miss Phillips before her wedding	5	00
	5	00

Signature _____ V. Parkes
Passed by _____ K.M.Price

Petty Cash Voucher

No. 116

Folio CB4
Date 4 Mar. 198-

For what required	AMOUNT	
	£	p
Cleaner's Wages	10	00
	10	00

Signature _____ B.Black
Passed by _____ K.M.Price

Petty Cash Voucher

No. 117

Folio CB4
Date 5 Mar. 198-

For what required	AMOUNT	
	£	p
6 ball-point pens	1	80
	1	80

Signature _____ V. Parkes
Passed by _____ K.M.Price

Petty Cash Voucher

No. 118

Folio CB4
Date 5 Mar. 198-

For what required	AMOUNT	
	£	p
6 pints milk		96
		96

Signature _____ C. Downes
Passed by _____ K.M.Price.

Petty cash vouchers

Petty cash voucher no 103	Stamps	£10.00	Analysis column – Postage
Petty cash voucher no 104	Tea-towels	£2.50	Analysis column – Cleaning
Petty cash voucher no 105	Milk	64p	Analysis column – Office supplies
Petty cash voucher no 106	Bus fare	90p	Analysis column – Travel
Petty cash voucher no 107	Surcharge on letter	10p	Analysis column – Postage

Sign the vouchers yourself as the person receiving the money. Exchange with your neighbour for her to sign as person authorising the payment.

Enter the vouchers on a petty cash sheet and number the sheet 2. Your total amount of petty cash can be carried from petty cash sheet no 1 (p. 290).

The balance on petty cash sheet no 2 should be either £5.68 or £6.86 or £5.86.

Your petty cash sheet no 2 should show the correct figure.

2) Petty cash sheet no 3 (p. 295)

This petty cash sheet is unfinished.

Add up the analysis columns, check with 'total paid' and enter the balance.

Bring balance down on 15 February 198—and restore the imprest to £20.

3) Petty cash sheet no 4 (ruled by you).

Enter vouchers nos 113 – 18 (pp. 292 – 3) on petty cash sheet no 4, carrying down balance and cash received from petty cash sheet no 3, after you have completed it.

Finish off the petty cash sheet in the usual way, ready for the next week's entries.

4) Petty cash sheet no 5 (incorrect) (p. 296)

Two of the analysis columns have been totalled incorrectly.

The 'total paid' is wrong; therefore the balance is incorrect, too.

Copy out petty cash sheet no 5 and put the mistakes right.

5) Petty cash sheet no 6 (ruled by you).

Enter the following on petty cash sheet no 6:

Analysis column headings: postage, stationery, travel, office expenses, miscellaneous, cleaning

Balance brought down:	£9.52
Cash received	£20.48
June 8	Window cleaning	£5.00
June 9	Adhesive tape	£1.30
	Stamps	£10.00
June 10	Coffee and tea	£1.55

(continued on p. 297)

PETTY CASH ACCOUNT

Dr.   Cr.

| CASH RECEIVED | | | CASH PAID | | | | ANALYSIS | | | |
Date	Folio	Amount	Date	Details	VN	Total paid	Postage	Stationery	Travel	Misc.
198–	CB3	£ p	198–			£ p	£ p	£ p	£ p	£ p
		5 . 86		Balance b/d						
Feb 8		14 . 14		Cash received						
			Feb 8	Charity collection box	108	0.50				0.50
			9	Stamps	109	5.50				
			10	International Reply coupon	110	0.25				
			11	Envelopes	111	1.20		1.20		
			12	Train fare C.Downes	112	3.35				
						10.80				

Petty cash sheet no 3

295

PETTY CASH ACCOUNT

Dr.   Cr.

CASH RECEIVED			CASH PAID				ANALYSIS				
Date	Folio	Amount £ p	Date	Details	VN	Total paid £ p	Postage £ p	Travel £ p	Station-ery £ p	Office Expenses £ p	Misc. £ p
198- June 1	CB4	5. 80		Bal. b/d							
		24. 20	June 1	Cash received							
			June 1	Stamps	121	15.00	15.00				
			" 2	Taxi fare	122	2.50		2.50			
			" 3	Flag seller	123	0.50					0.50
			" 3	Parking meter	124	0.40					0.40
			" 4	String	125	0.35			0.35		
			" 5	Tea and sugar	126	0.83				0.83	
			" 5	2 new cups	127	0.90				0.90	
						20.58	15.00	2.50	0.35	2.63	0.50
		9.42		Bal. b/d		9.42					
		20.58		Cash received		£30.00					

Petty cash sheet no 5

296

June 11	Soap	90p
June 12	Cleaner's wages	£10.00
	Bus fare	40p
12	Flagseller	50p

Total, enter balance, bring down in usual way, restoring the imprest to £30 for 15 June 198—.

Exercise 64

BALANCING THE PETTY CASH

1) On 31 March 198—your balance of petty cash in hand was £5.25 and cash received was £24.75. Enter up the following, and bring down the balance on 14 April 198—.

April 1	Stamps	£5.50
April 1	Polish and dusters	£1.65
April 2	Taxi fare	£1.45
April 3	Envelopes	45p
April 6	Soap	70p
April 6	Stamps	£4.50
April 7	Train fare	£2.30
April 7	Pencils	£1.20
	String	35p
April 9	Surcharge on letter	24p
April 10	Coffee, tea	£1.75
April 11	Window cleaning	£2.00
April 12	Milk	32p
April 13	Bus fare	20p

2) Date for one week ago.

Cash received is £20

Travelling expenses	£1.60
Stamps	£2.00
Electric light bulbs	£1.05
Typing paper	£1.50
Tea, sugar and coffee	£1.75
Stamps	£1.00
Airmail letter forms	55p
Milk	45p
Fares	60p
Shorthand notebooks	£1.10

Balance the petty cash, show amount of cash received from cashier and take balance down to start again for the next day.

297

CHAPTER 15

Buying and Selling

Buying

An example of an ordinary, everyday 'business transaction' is when a customer goes into a shop, chooses what he or she wants to buy, pays for it (perhaps receives a receipt) and is given change. The exchange of goods for money forms part of everyone's lives – the shopkeeper makes a small profit on each transaction, which helps to pay the rent of the shop, lighting, heating, and the wages of any assistants he may have.

Similarly, all firms, large and small, make their profit by selling goods or providing services for which people are prepared to pay.

Employees of firms do not go 'shopping' for anything they want to buy on behalf of the firm. Instead, they write to the suppliers of these goods asking for details – price, delivery date, catalogues or leaflets giving any other information necessary. This is known as an 'enquiry' and it may be a short letter as below.

SHAW & SHORT LTD
Wholesaler

Whitaker Street
MANCHESTER
M96 8TB

Tel: 432 888   Telex: 990 111

Our Ref: PM/JK   15 November 198-

The Sales Manager
Office Equipment Supply Co Ltd
Knightley Road
BROMSWOOD   Lancs
T45 7BC

Dear Sir

I am interested in buying an addressing machine and noticed
in your recent advertisement in Office Equipment News that
you manufacture several models. Could you please send me details
of prices and delivery dates, together with descriptive leaflets
or catalogues?

Yours faithfully
SHAW & SHORT LTD

Peter Mason

Peter Mason
Purchasing Officer

A short letter of enquiry

Alternatively, an enquiry may be on a specially printed form, which asks for the same information, as below:

```
                    SHAW & SHORT LTD
                        Wholesaler

                     Whitaker Street
                      MANCHESTER
                       M96 8TB

   Tel:  432 888                          Telex:  990 111

   ENQUIRY FORM

   To: ........................         Date: .........
       ........................
       ........................
       ........................


   Dear Sir

   I am interested in buying ...............................


   Could you please send me details - prices, delivery dates,
   leaflets and/or catalogues as soon as possible?

   Yours faithfully
   SHAW & SHORT LTD


   Peter Mason
   Purchasing Officer
```

An enquiry form

The enquiry form, with its printed paragraph, saves the typist's time or can, when necessary, be filled in in handwriting, if no typist is available.

Peter Mason, the purchasing officer of the firm of Shaw & Short Ltd, made the first step in his 'shopping' for his firm — his intended purchase being an addressing machine.

A few days later Mr Mason received a reply from the suppliers he had written to, enclosing some leaflets illustrating several addressing machines, a price list and delivery dates.

Mr Mason, before making up his mind which one to buy, would probably want to see a demonstration of one or two machines, and even ask for one to be left with his firm for a week so that it could be tried out.

Then, the sales manager of Office Equipment Supply Co Ltd would be asked to send a quotation for the machine decided upon, to Shaw & Short Ltd.

QUOTATION

OFFICE EQUIPMENT SUPPLY CO LTD
Knightley Road
Bromswood
Lancs
T45 7BC   Tel 859 333   Telex: 674231

To: Shaw & Short Ltd   Date: 1 December 198-

     Whitaker Street

     Manchester   No: BAM 16

     M96 8TB

For the attention Mr Peter Mason, Purchasing Officer

Dear Sirs

In reply to your enquiry dated 15 November ... we have
pleasure in quoting you as follows:

Quantity	Description	Catalogue No	Price	VAT	Total
1	Addressing machine	HG 732-89	£190	£27.79	£217.79

Delivery: ex stock   Terms: $2\frac{1}{2}$% 30 days

P Benson
Sales Manager

A quotation

The quotation from Office Equipment Supply Co Ltd would be one of
several from different firms; the purchasing officer will then be able to
choose which addressing machine would be the most suitable, basing
his choice upon:

- Price.
- Delivery – whether it would be available immediately, or whether he
  would have to wait, possibly several weeks.
- Suitability for the work it would have to do. There are some very
  large addressing machines which also fold and insert letters into the
  envelopes. Mr Mason was interested in one which automatically
  printed envelopes only – he did not want the folding and inserting
  attachments.
- Terms of payment. Some firms offer more than others – some offer
  none at all.

After taking the above factors into account, Mr Mason and the mail
room supervisor decided to arrange a demonstration of the addressing
machine manufactured by Office Equipment Supply Co Ltd. After the
demonstration, it was left with them for a week, to try it out in the mail
room, and the decision was then made to buy it.

		SHAW & SHORT LTD	
		Whitaker Street	
Date 12 December 198–		MANCHESTER	
		Tel: 859 333 Telex: 674231	
To Office Equipment Supply Co Ltd			
Knightley Road			
BROMSWOOD Lancs			
T45 7BC		No. ___526___	

Please supply & deliver

Cat	Qty	Description	£ p
HG 732–89	1	Addressing machine	190
		+ VAT	27.79

Terms 2½% 30 days		Total £217.79
Delivery Ex stock	Signed _____	
		Purchasing Officer

An order form

The next step in this business transaction was to send an order. Orders have to be signed by the purchasing officer of a firm or one of his assistants with authority to sign. Orders are numbered, and dated, and copies are sent to:

- Accounts department
- Mail room supervisor (who will use the addressing machine)
- Purchasing department files.

Information on an order is based on the quotation.

Selling

When the order from Shaw and Short Ltd was received by Office Equipment Supply Co Ltd the details on it were checked by the sales department (price and delivery) before passing it to stock control. Delivery had been stated on the quotation as 'ex stock' which means that it could be taken out of stock and despatched at once.

Before sending the addressing machine, the sales department of Office Equipment Supply Co Ltd sent an 'advice note' to Shaw and Short Ltd, advising them that it would be sent that day. Packed into the box containing the addressing machine would then go a 'delivery note' which would have to be signed by the customer and given back to the driver of the van which brought the machine – any damage would be noted on the delivery note.

At the end of the month following the delivery of the addressing machine the 'invoice' would be sent by Office Equipment Supply Co Ltd to Shaw and Short Ltd. An invoice is a 'bill'. It is numbered, dated, quotes the customer's order number, and sets out the full price,

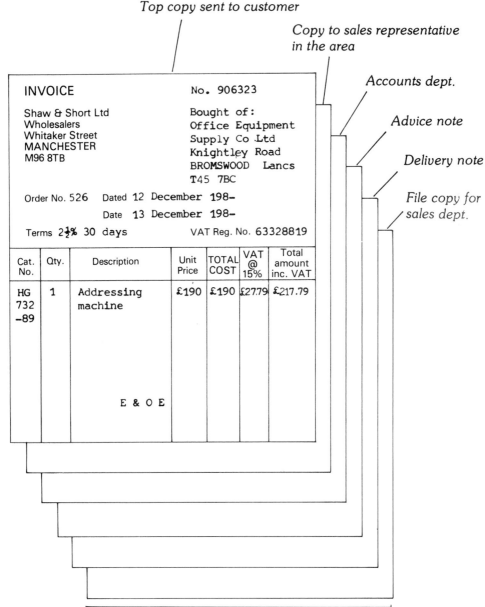

Top copy sent to customer

Copy to sales representative in the area

Accounts dept.

Advice note

Delivery note

File copy for sales dept.

INVOICE No. 906323

Shaw & Short Ltd
Wholesalers
Whitaker Street
MANCHESTER
M96 8TB

Bought of:
Office Equipment
Supply Co Ltd
Knightley Road
BROMSWOOD Lancs
T45 7BC

Order No. 526 Dated 12 December 198–

Date 13 December 198–

Terms 2½% 30 days VAT Reg. No. 63328819

Cat. No.	Qty.	Description	Unit Price	TOTAL COST	VAT @ 15%	Total amount inc. VAT
HG 732 –89	1	Addressing machine	£190	£190	£27.79	£217.79

E & O E

Note that VAT is worked out on £190 less 2 ½ % cash discount (i.e. £185.25).

These copies are different colours for easy identification. They would be NCR or one-time carbon and possibly continuous stationery to save time (see p. 209)

E & O E means 'errors and omissions excepted'. If the typist makes a mistake when typing the price, it does not bind the seller (in this case, the typist could have typed £19.00 which would have made a great deal of difference)

302

plus VAT and terms of payment. In this case, if Shaw and Short Ltd pay for the addressing machine within 30 days of receipt of the invoice, they are entitled to deduct 2½ per cent from the cost – 2½ per cent of £190 is £4.75 making £185.25 to which £27.79 VAT is added totalling £213.04, and so the amount of the cheque sent to Office Equipment Supply Co Ltd is £213.04 if sent within 30 days of receipt of invoice. VAT is added after all discounts are deducted, including cash discount for prompt payment whether the customer pays promptly or not.

All firms pay for goods after the goods have been received – no money is sent with orders. The 'terms' mentioned on the quotation are an encouragement to a customer to pay promptly. The terms can vary from firm to firm. Some firms do not offer any, in which case the terms are described on the invoice as 'net'.

When a large quantity of goods is being purchased, a firm may offer a trade discount to the customer. This is deducted by the seller when he makes out the invoice and is not affected by *when* the customer pays – it is quite separate.

Other printed forms

In addition to the forms already mentioned there are three others frequently used in business transactions.

PRO FORMA INVOICE

This is a special type of invoice sent *before* the goods are delivered if:

- Credit standing of customer is in any doubt (i.e. he may be a new customer)
- Goods are sent on approval (on a sale or return basis)
- Goods are sent to an agent or sales representative, who has goods on a sale or return basis.

DEBIT AND CREDIT NOTES

These notes are sent after the invoice. A 'debit note' indicates to the customer that he was undercharged on the invoice and owes the supplier more than was stated on the invoice. A 'credit note' indicates to the customer that he was overcharged on the invoice and owes the supplier less than was stated on the invoice. A 'credit note' would also be sent for packing cases returned, goods returned as damaged, or not as ordered.

STATEMENT

A 'statement' is sent to a customer at the end of each month by most firms, and shows how much he has paid to the supplier during the month, how much he has bought and any credit or debit due to him. The last figure in the right-hand column shows how much the customer still owes when the statement is made up, or if his account is clear.

DEBIT NOTE

Shaw & Short Ltd
Wholesalers
Whitaker Street
MANCHESTER
M96 8TB

No 387
12 December 198-

Dr to:

Office Equipment Supply Co Ltd
Knightley Road
BROMSWOOD
Lancs
T45 7BC

Order No: 433

VAT Reg No 63328819

Date	Description	Amount
198- 19 December	Undercharge on Invoice No. 906341	£ 12.00

CREDIT NOTE

Shaw & Short Ltd
Wholesalers
Whitaker Street
MANCHESTER
M96 8TB

No 423
21 December 198-

Dr to:

Office Equipment Supply Co Ltd
Knightley Road
BROMSWOOD
Lancs
T45 7BC

Order No: 487

VAT Reg No 63328819

Date	Description	Amount
198- 21 December	Packing cases returned against Invoice no. 906353	£ 7.00

```
STATEMENT

Shaw & Short Ltd                    Office Equipment Supply Co Ltd
Wholesalers                         Knightley Road
Whitaker Street                     BROMSWOOD    Lancs
MANCHESTER                          T45 7BC
M96 8TB

                                          Payments
                                             and
Date              Invoice No.       Purchases  Returns   Balance

198–                                   £                   £

13 December       906323            217.79     ─────     217.79
19 December       906341             12.00     ─────     229.79
21 December       906353            ─────        7.00    222.79


                                              The last
                                              balance in
                                              this column
                                              is the
                                              amount owing
```

FOR YOUR FOLDER

45. BUYING AND SELLING

Write these notes in your folder, filling in the missing words and phrases.

1) Usually the first step a firm makes in a business transaction is sending an enquiry to another firm. This may be a _____ or _____.

2) The department in a large firm which carries out the buying of goods for the whole firm is the _____ department.

3) The reply to an enquiry, sent from the _____ department of the firm supplying the goods, is a _____.

4) The choice of where to place an order depends upon price, suitability of goods and terms of payment, as well as _____.

5) Terms of payment vary from firm to firm. Some firms offer only net. Terms are an inducement to customers to pay _____.

6) After deciding which firm to buy goods from, the next step is to send an order. The information on the order is based on a _____.

7) An order has to be signed by _____ or his _____.

8) An invoice is sent after the goods have been delivered to the customer – usually at the end of the following month. *Before* goods are

despatched, a copy of the _____ as a goods advice note is sent to customer.

9) Another copy of the invoice is packed with the goods as a _____ note.

10) A detailed copy of the invoice is sent to customer after he has received the goods, usually at the end of the month following delivery. Other copies of the invoice go to _____ and _____.

11) An invoice gives details of the unit price (price each), total price, terms, and _____ is added.

12) E and O E on an invoice means _____.

13) Delivery 'ex stock' means _____.

14) The document sent to customer when he has been *undercharged* is a _____.

15) The document sent to customer when he has been *overcharged* is a _____.

16) At the end of each month, a customer receives a document setting out how much he has spent, how much he has paid, and how much he still owes. The name of this document is _____.

17) A *pro forma* invoice is sent before goods are delivered if credit standing of customer is unknown, for goods on approval (sale or return) or to a _____.

18) A trade discount is offered for _____.

Exercise 65

PRICE LISTS

Refer to the price list opposite.

1) What does 'delivery ex stock' mean?

2) What does 'trade discount on orders for 3 machines or over, 10 per cent' mean?

3) What does 'terms 2½ per cent 30 days' mean?

4) Why is the price list dated?

5) Work out the VAT on a standard 12 inch carriage typewriter, manual.

6) Work out the VAT on a standard 12 inch carriage typewriter, electric.

7) What would be the cost (not including VAT) of two portable typewriters with pre-set tabulators?

8) Work out the invoice price (i.e. 10 per cent trade discount deducted and VAT added) for five portable typewriters with variable tabulators (electric).

OFFICE EQUIPMENT SUPPLY CO LTD
Knightley Road
BROMSWOOD
Lancs
T45 7BC   Tel: 859 333   Telex: 674231

PRICE LIST

TYPEWRITERS

Catalogue No	Description	Price VAT <u>not</u> included
BG 78-21	Portable with pre-set tabulator Elite typeface. Manual.	£40.00
BG 79-22	Portable with variable tabulator Elite typeface. Manual.	£68.00
BG 80-23	Portable with variable tabulator Elite typeface. Electric.	£99.50
BG 81-24	Standard typewriter (12" carriage) Pica or Elite typeface. Manual.	£170.00
BG 82-25	Standard typewriter (12" carriage) Pica or Elite typeface. Electric.	£360.00
BG 83-26	Standard typewriter (15" carriage) Pica or Elite typeface. Manual.	£185.00
BG 84-27	Long carriage typewriter (20" carriage) Pica or Elite typeface. Manual*	£200.00

All machines supplied with a set of cleaning tools, a cover, and
a felt mat.
Portable typewriters have a carrying case with handle in addition.

TRADE DISCOUNT on orders for 3 machines or over - 10%

DELIVERY ex stock

* DELIVERY for long carriage (non-standard) typewriters
approximately 6 weeks.

TYPEWRITER ACCESSORIES

AT 100-28	Ribbons- all black, plastic carbon	£15.00 for 20
AT 100-29	Ribbons- black and red " "	£15.20 for 20
AT 101-30	Ribbons- all black, fabric	£12.00 for 20
AT 101-31	Ribbons- black and red, fabric	£12.20 for 20
AT 102-32	Ribbon cassettes, all black	£1.10 each
AT 103-33	Ribbon cassettes, black and red	£1.20 each
AT 103-34	Correcting ribbons	£3.20 each
AT 104-35	Typewriter covers (for 12" and 15")	£1.75 each
AT 105-36	Typewriter mats, black felt	80 each

TRADE DISCOUNT on orders minimum value £15.00 - 15%

Terms: (on all orders) 2½% 30 days

1 August 198-   (This cancels all previous price lists)

9) Then deduct 2½ per cent which customer would be entitled to subtract from the amount he pays if within 30 days of receipt of invoice.

10) Work out the price for 100 typewriter ribbons (black and red), fabric. Add VAT at 15 per cent and deduct trade discount of 15 per cent.

11) Work out the price for eight typewriter covers, adding VAT. Would this be of the minimum value for trade discount of 15 per cent?

12) What would be the VAT (15 per cent) on 250 ribbons, all black, plastic carbon?

13) What would be the trade discount on 250 ribbons, all black, plastic carbon?

14) Work out the VAT on one correcting ribbon.

15) What would be the trade discount on 20 typewriter ribbons, black and red, plastic carbon?

Office Routine for Purchasing Goods

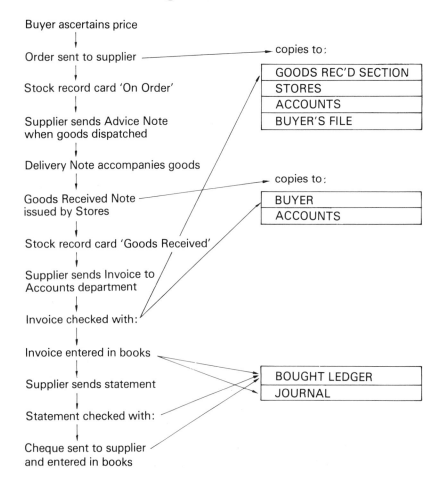

Credit Control

A sale is not complete until goods are paid for.

Credit (monthly account) is very convenient to businesses – payment is made at the end of each month.

Precaution must be taken to prevent bad debts.

Overdue accounts should be put on a stop list. Coloured flashes may be used to indicate a 'stopped' account. Flashes may also be used to indicate habitually slow payers. If shortages of goods occur, preference will be given to customers who pay promptly.

Persistent follow-up of overdue accounts is essential. First statement should be followed by a copy statement, then by a personal letter or telephone call. When everything has been tried, legal action may be taken – this may result in the debtor being bankrupted.

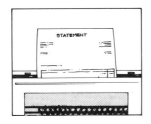

Dealing with overdue accounts

In the case of limited companies particular care is necessary in granting credit. The only safe way is to make preliminary examination of its affairs at Companies House in Cardiff. These will indicate size, profitability and rate of growth of company.

Firms must always take up references on new customers before granting credit. This may be a trader's reference (a supplier with whom the customer has been trading for some time) or a banker's reference. (The new supplier's bank will obtain this from the customer's bank.) A trade protection society may also be consulted.

When references have been obtained a strict control of credit levels must be exercised until customer is well known and well regarded (i.e. if £50 credit is allowed this should on no account be exceeded by the customer).

Delivery of goods may be withheld until enquiries are made.

If customer urgently needs goods, cash on delivery service may be used or a *pro forma* invoice (see p. 303).

Terms Used in Buying and Selling

Carriage fwd:	The buyer pays for carriage
Carriage paid:	The seller pays the carriage
Carrier's risk:	The carrier is responsible for loss or damage to goods in transit except under certain conditions
Cash discount:	An allowance, e.g. 2½ per cent, offered to a buyer to induce him to pay promptly. The rate and period are shown on the monthly statement of account
Ex stock:	From stock
Ex works:	The buyer pays carriage from the factory
F.o.b.:	The seller pays all expenses until the goods have been loaded on to the ship
Franco:	In addition to paying all carriage and insurance, the seller will pay customs duties
Loco:	The buyer takes the goods from their site and pays all subsequent charges
Owner's risk:	The owner can claim on the carrier only when misconduct by his servants can be proved.
Pro forma invoice:	Used for goods sent on approval, or as a form of quotation
Terms net monthly:	The full amount shown on the statement of account is due
Trade discount:	An allowance, usually expressed as a percentage, given to enable the wholesaler or retailer to make a profit. It is also given to encourage bulk buying, special displays, or to customers of long standing

Customer's Record Cards

A customer's record card is kept in some firms so that a quick reference can be made by clerical workers in the sales department to information which may be needed, such as:

- name of purchasing officer
- name of his assistant
- how long the firm has been a customer

- whether the customer has any overseas branches
- the name and telephone number of the sales representative in the area
- credit-worthiness.

CONFIDENTIAL

CUSTOMER'S RECORD CARD

Name ..... Shaw & Short Ltd., wholesalers ..... Account No ..... 60091 .....

Address ..... Whitaker Street ..... Telephone No ..... 859 333 .....

..... MANCHESTER M96 8TB ..... Telex No ..... 674231 .....

.....

Area ..... North West .....

Representative in area ..... Margaret Pratt ..... Telephone No ..... 576 311 .....

Name of firm's purchasing officer ..... Peter Mason .....

Extension No ..... 79 .....

Purchasing officer's assistant ..... Sandra Summers .....

Extension No ..... 78 .....

Average total value of goods purchased per month ..... £300 .....

Average total amount credited per month ..... £300 .....
Sales Representative seen with/~~without~~ appointment (delete whichever does not apply)

On Direct Mailing List   Yes/~~No~~ (delete whichever does not apply)

Other relevant information

First order placed ..... 8 February 1975 .....

Firm's overseas branches .. None .....

A customer's record card

Exercise 66

ASSIGNMENT ON A CUSTOMER'S RECORD CARD

Rule up a blank customer's record card and write (or type) in the headings. Then fill in with details overleaf:

Customer: Grosvenor Manufacturing Co Ltd
Grosvenor Works, Thorne Trading Estate, Nottingham
NS4 3IB
Tel 221 884   Telex 998 753

Representative in area: Simon Newman Tel 931 222
Name of firm's purchasing officer: Elizabeth Smith (Mrs) Ext 47
No purchasing officer's assistant.

Average total value of goods purchased per month: £1,000
Average total amount credited per month: £1,000
Sales representative seen without appointment (if prepared to wait about 30 minutes).
Not on direct mailing list.
First order placed: 10 August 1977.
Overseas branches in Paris and Milan.

Exercise 67

ASSIGNMENT ON PRICE LISTS

1) *An order*
   Make out an order for Grosvenor Manufacturing Co Ltd for:
   60 typewriter ribbons, black and red, fabric
    3 correcting ribbons

2) *Invoice*
   Make out one copy only for above. Supplier: Office Equipment Supply Co Ltd.

3) *Credit note*
   Make out a credit note for overcharge for one correcting ribbon on invoice.

4) *Statement*
   Construct a statement with the following information on:

   Opening balance owing £35.50
   Payment of £50
   Invoice as above
   Show final invoice owing
   Put in appropriate dates and invoice no.

Exercise 68

BUYING AND SELLING

1) Name two sources of information available to a purchasing department.

2) Trade discount is given for prompt payment. True/False?

3) Who pays the delivery and transport costs on goods purchased 'ex works'? Purchaser/Supplier?

4) After a quotation has been accepted what document will a purchasing officer send to a supplier of goods as confirmation?
5) What is received by a purchaser in reply to a letter of enquiry?
6) Who normally signs an internal requisition?
7) Why do firms allow cash discounts?
8) Who receives the top copy of a purchase order?

Exercise 69

MULTIPLE-CHOICE QUESTIONS ON BUYING AND SELLING

1) In reply to enquiries, a purchasing department will expect to receive:
   a a quotation
   b a credit note
   c an invoice.

2) 'Carriage forward' means:
   a the seller pays carriage
   b the buyer pays carriage
   c the carriage is included in the price.

3) 'Ex stock' means:
   a no stock available
   b within two weeks
   c immediate from stock.

4) Most firms will give credit to prospective customers without making enquiries or asking for references:
   a true
   b possibly
   c false.

5) If goods are returned, chargeable 'empties' returned or an invoice has been overcharged, the seller issues:
   a a debit note
   b a credit note
   c a consignment note.

6) A statement of account is sent out:
   a after each transaction
   b at fixed intervals, usually monthly
   c only once a year.

7) Cash discount is offered to buyers:
   a to enable them to make a profit
   b to encourage them buy in bulk
   c to encourage them to pay promptly.

8) 'F.o.b.' means:
   a the buyer pays all expenses
   b the agent pays all expenses
   c the seller pays all expenses until the goods are loaded on the ship.

9) If invoices were typed in sets with copies to various departments, which would be the odd man out?
   a accounts
   b sales
   c purchasing.

Exercise 70

MORE ON BUSINESS TRANSACTIONS

1) From the following particulars, rule up and complete an invoice form:

   On 15 February 1977, James Lyon & Co Ltd, of Sizewell, Kent, sold to William Walters, 271 Main Drive, Coventry, West Midlands, the following goods:

   10 reams ruled paper A4 @ £1.20 a ream
   25 reams plain paper A5 @ £1.10 a ream
   Trade discount allowed was 25 per cent
   Cash discount allowed was 5 per cent 7 days or 2½ per cent 30 days.

   Mr Walter's order no was 6073 and delivery was carriage paid. VAT applies at 15 per cent.

2) Explain the meaning of 'cash discount 5 per cent 7 days or 2½ per cent 30 days'.

3) What is the meaning of the abbreviation VAT?

4) Why does Mr William Walters need to have this invoice?

5) Who pays the cost of carriage for the goods in this particular transaction?

6) Invoices are usually typed with several copies. The top copy is sent to the customer, and one is retained for filing. Suggest where two other copies might go.

7) Hallamshire Supplies Ltd, Norfolk Road, Sheffield, a firm of wholesalers, supplied P Wells & Co Ltd, with the following goods on 18 January 198—:

4 refrigerators	@	£60 each
10 electric mixers	@	£15 each
10 electric fires	@	£12 each
6 spin dryers	@	£35 each
Trade discount	20%	
Cash discount	2½%	one month

314

On 20 January P Wells & Co returned one refrigerator and two spin dryers which had been damaged in transit. They also drew the attention of the suppliers to the catalogue price of the fires which was £10 each.

8) What action would Hallamshire Supplies take when the goods were returned and they received the complaint about the overcharge on the fires?

9) Using the above information, rule up a statement of account which would be sent by Hallamshire Supplies to P Wells & Co at the end of January 198—. Fill in all the necessary details.

10) Explain the difference between a cash discount and a trade discount.

Exercise 71

ASSIGNMENTS ON INVOICES

INVOICE			
WILTON, WATKINS AND IRVINE LIMITED, 93 BOWLING STREET, SHEFFIELD, 3.			
		Quote this number on all communications	
DATE	YOUR ORDER NO.		
QUANTITY	DESCRIPTION	RATE	£

1) On 1 May your company (Wilton, Watkins and Irvine Ltd) sold 20 tables to J Berry Ltd, 10 Lower Street, Sornborough at £15 each. You allow a trade discount of 15 per cent and 4 per cent cash discount within one month.

   a Complete the invoice above for this sale.

   b Distinguish between trade discount and cash discount.

   c What sum would J Berry Ltd pay if the account were settled on 15 May?

   d What would have to be paid if the account were settled on 15 June?

				Invoice Number

INVOICE
BARRY FABRICATIONS LIMITED
WALSALL   W3P 8YY

Tel: Walsall 236511
Telex: 646172

Date	Your order	Terms
	Despatch date	Carr Paid

Qty.	Description	Code Number	Unit Price	Price	VAT	TOTAL

TOTAL VALUE

Delivery address

2) Complete the above invoice from the following details: Porterhouse Printers Ltd, of Cantwell Road, Plymouth, Devon, ordered exactly one week ago (order no 92746) 24 three-drawer metal filing cabinets, 90 cm high, fitted with lock, colour ocean-blue, and six file cupboards with two folding doors 180 cm high and fitted with rails for five rows of lateral filing. For the first item the stock code is 12/07/0169, at £20.70 each totalling £496.80, and for the second item 12/06/0159, at £25.40

316

each totalling £152.40. Porterhouse want these goods sent to their Exeter branch, which is at 27 Totnes Road. Barry's will despatch today by British Rail and will give 12½ per cent 14 days discount, invoice no being 73/822353. *Include the total of the goods, but ignore VAT calculations and entries.*

List other documents likely to be made out at the same time as this invoice.

Exercise 72

INTERPRETING A STATEMENT

Answer the following questions on the statement below:

1) What is the name of the supplier?
2) What is the reference number of the customer's account?
3) How much did the customer owe at the beginning of the period?
4) How much did the customer spend during the month of September?
5) How much did the customer pay during the period?
6) How much did the customer owe at the end of September?

STATEMENT

Williamson & Co. Ltd.
16 George Street
BATH

Mr P Freeman
295 Portland Avenue
LONDON   W1D 9QX

A/c 6/F138

Date		Purchases	Payments and Returns	Balance
July 1	Balance forward			2.40
10	Cash		2.40	
Sept 18	Goods	17.32		
21	do.	5.91		
25	do.	29.18		
30	do.	51.77		
	Cash		20.50	
	Credit note		2.50	81.18

317

Exercise 73

ASSIGNMENTS ON WRITING ORDERS

1) Prepare an order for:

   10 reams no 64 Mill Bond Paper, A4 @ £1.20 per ream;
   10 reams no 50 Bank Paper, A4 @ 65p per ream;
   5000 Abermill Bond White Envelopes @ £4.50 per 1000.

   The supplier's terms are net, thirty days against statement and delivery is free of charge by their own delivery service.

2) You work for Stiggins and Bleach Ltd, of 49 High House, Chisleworth, London, W1, a firm with several branches, and are told to order six gross black lead HB pencils @ £1.57½ per gross and two dozen quality hexagonal pencils @ £1.80 per gross from Cowerby Stationery Supplies Ltd, 29–31 The Rise, Hilchester, Anyshire. You usually receive five per cent discount for orders over £6.00 from this company. Delivery is required at the head office: the stationery department.

   Draft a letter, ordering the above goods.

CHAPTER 16

Wages and Salaries

Wages or Salaries

The two words 'wages' and 'salaries' have exactly the same meaning, but over the years a tradition has been established of describing wages paid weekly (or hourly) as 'wages' and wages paid to non-manual workers (usually monthly) as 'salaries'. The advantage of having wages paid every week is that it is easier for the wage-earner to 'budget' – that is, pay for travelling, food and clothes. If the employee is paid monthly, he or she may spend a lot for the first two weeks of the month and then be in debt for the last two weeks.

Many years ago, employers often paid workers in 'kind' – that is, not with money but with goods of various types. A farm worker, for example, might receive milk, eggs, or a free cottage; a clothing worker might receive a piece of cloth. Another system paid the workers with vouchers which could only be exchanged at shops owned by the employers. Many such practices are now banned under the Truck Acts of 1831 and 1870. Employees must be paid in notes and coins of the realm or cheques or credit transfer into a bank account (see p. 348) under the Payment of Wages Act 1960.

Rates of Pay

There are several ways of calculating wages.

PIECE WORK AND BONUS SCHEMES

Under a piece work system of payment, workers are only paid for each article produced or operation carried out. Workers employed where bonus schemes operate (either individual or group) receive a flat-rate wage per week, below which their earnings cannot fall for a standard week, and earn bonus for all production over the set target figures.

TIME RATES

Under this arrangement a rate is set for each hour worked. A higher rate is paid for overtime – that is, any time worked beyond what is a normal working day. This system boosts the pay of workers who are punctual and are willing to work long hours. Deductions for lateness are usually made.

Each worker, when he arrives at work, 'clocks in' – that is, he puts his card in the machine attached to a clock and the machine stamps the time on the card. When he leaves, he takes the card out and another time is stamped on the card.

DAY	IN	OUT	IN	OUT	Total
am MON					
pm					
am TUES					
pm					
am WED					
pm					
am TH					
pm					
am FRI					
pm					
am S					
pm					
am SU					
pm					

CLOCKED	OVERTIME
SHIFT ALLOWANCE	OVERTIME ALLOWANCE
SHIFT ADJUSTMENT £	OVERTIME ADJUSTMENT £
OTHER ADJUSTMENTS	
EXPENSE CODE	AMOUNT £
	£
	£
ADJUSTMENT CODE	AMOUNT £
	£

The front and back of a clock card (also called a 'time' card)

The stamped time cards act as a record of attendance (many office workers who are not on 'time rates' have to 'clock in' for this reason). Also, the time cards are used to work out wages for those on time rates. Frequently, the worker is identified by a number which becomes his clock number.

COMMISSION

Many people engaged on selling the goods their firm makes receive a commission on sales and are paid a relatively small weekly or monthly salary because of this. A salesman who is good at selling is able to increase his salary far more than one who is less hard-working and this acts as an incentive to sell.

FOR YOUR FOLDER

46. WAGES AND SALARIES

Write these notes in your folder, filling in the missing words and phrases.

1) Wages paid to non-manual workers, usually monthly, are known as _____.

2) Weekly wages have the advantage of enabling the workers to _____ more easily.

3) Monthly salaries can encourage the worker to spend too much in the first fortnight of the month and then get into _____ towards the end of the month.

4) All employees – manual and non-manual – must be paid in notes and coins or cheque or _____.

5) Where workers are paid for each article they make, or each operation they carry out, this is known as a _____.

6) A time rate is where a rate is set for each _____.

7) Overtime is sometimes paid for at a higher rate. Overtime is any time worked beyond what is a _____ working day.

8) All manual workers on piece rates or time rates have to clock in and out. The stamped time cards act as a _____.

9) A salesman is able to increase his salary by selling large quantities of his firm's goods on which he is paid _____.

Gross and Net Pay, Deductions

The rate agreed with an employer (whether calculated on an hourly, weekly or an annual basis) is the *gross* wage or salary. Before any wages are paid to employees, certain deductions are required to be made by law – otherwise known as statutory deductions. Other deductions are agreed by the employee (i.e. they are voluntary) and when all deductions have been totalled and taken away from the gross pay, the remainder (known as net pay) is paid to the employee. The difference between gross and net pay can be quite large. It is often a shock to someone receiving their first pay packet.

STATUTORY DEDUCTIONS (REQUIRED BY LAW) FROM PAY

National Insurance contributions – scaled according to earnings (employers also pay National Insurance on behalf of each employee). National Insurance contributions are calculated on *gross* pay. The employer is responsible for forwarding both his contribution and his employee's to the Inland Revenue. Every person over 16 is liable to pay National Insurance contributions, whether still at school or not, if they earn over £27 a week (from April 1981). The percentage of gross salary to be paid is reviewed annually by the Department of Health and Social Security.

NATIONAL INSURANCE

There are three rates for National Insurance contributions:

- Standard – paid by most people.
- Reduced – paid by certain married women and widows.
- Nil – because a worker has reached pensionable age (*but* the employer still has to pay his contribution).

Self-employed people (those working for themselves, such as hairdressers, decorators, windowcleaners) pay less than standard contributions because the benefits to which they are entitled are less – no unemployment pay, for example.

National Insurance numbers are sent to all schools for school leavers by the Department of Health and Social Security, to whom application should be made if the number is lost.

PAYE (INCOME TAX)

The second statutory deduction from pay is income tax (known as PAYE – Pay As You Earn, because it is deducted weekly or monthly from everyone who earns a regular income).

The amount of income tax deducted from wages depends upon a code number which is allocated by the Inspector of Taxes, who works for the Inland Revenue Department. This code number is based upon the information contained in a form supplied by the Collector of Taxes (Form P1) to everyone earning money regularly. It is essential that this form be filled in and returned to the Collector of Taxes, otherwise the maximum amount of tax will be deducted under an Emergency Code Number allocated by the tax office. Form P1 is usually sent out each year to everyone who is a wage-earner.

Income for the purposes of Income Tax means:

- Wages (or salaries)
- Overtime
- Bonuses or Christmas gifts in money
- Interest from savings accounts
- Dividends from shares
- Pension
- Holiday pay
- Commission
- Rent from furnished lettings
- Profits from businesses and professions
- Social security benefits (after 1982)
- Tips received in connection with employment
- Perquisites (cars, houses, telephones), known as 'perks' when supplied as part of wage or salary.

**TAX
RETURN
1981-82**

**Income and Capital Gains
for year ended 5 April 1981**

**Allowances for year ending
5 April 1982**

Please fill in this form, sign the declaration below and send it back to me as soon as possible, using the enclosed envelope. If you do not do so you may pay an incorrect amount of tax.

Please read the introduction to the enclosed notes before you start to fill in the form; the notes are there to help you but they have been kept short and do not of course tell you everything about income tax or capital gains tax. If you need help or further information please ask me.

J. W. BARCLAY
H.M. Inspector of Taxes

DECLARATION
*(False statements can
result in prosecution)*

To the best of my knowledge and belief the particulars given on this form are correct and complete.

Signature . . . . Date . . . . .19. . . . .
(A woman should state after her signature whether she is single, married, widowed, separated or divorced)

Private address
*(Use BLOCK letters and
include postcode)*

Name and address
of employer

*If you or your wife were born
before 6 April 1922 please
enter date(s) of birth.*

SELF	
WIFE	

Nature of
employment

Branch, Department, etc.
and Works No. *if any*

P1 (1981)

page 1

The front of Income Tax form P1

Certain allowances can be offset against income tax. These allowances are given for the following, but must be claimed on Form P1 – the Tax Inspector will not know the wage-earner is entitled to them unless he is informed:

- Interest on mortgage repayments to a building society
- Dependants – (man) – earned income allowance, wife, any other dependent relatives not earning any money
  (wife) – earned income allowance – if she has a job
  (unmarried woman) – single person's allowance

323

- Any special protective clothing needed for a job – boots, overalls, spectacles, gloves
- Any special tools required for a job
- Books for teachers
- Subscriptions to trade unions and other official professional organisations connected with a job or profession
- Special income tax allowances for the blind
- Interest on bank loan which qualifies for tax relief (not all do).

Income which is completely tax-free

- Student grant or scholarship
- War widow's pension
- Child benefit allowance
- Maternity pay
- Sick pay
- Unemployment benefit (up to April 1982)
- Industrial injury or disablement pensions
- First £70 interest from National Savings Bank ordinary account

There is no tax relief for National Insurance contributions.

Some tax is paid direct on your behalf, e.g. Building Society interest.

Any of the above information which is relevant should be entered on Form P1 so that the correct code number can be allocated for an employer to know how much tax to deduct from the gross pay.

Employee's Tax Code. A tax code is the amount of annual income an employee may earn before paying tax – e.g. Tax Code 180 means tax-free income of £1,800 per annum.

At the end of every tax year Form P60 is sent to every employee, showing the total amount of tax which has been deducted during the previous 12 months. The year for income tax purposes starts on 6 April and finishes on 5 April of the following year.

When changing from one job to another, Form P45 must be obtained from the previous employer and taken to the new one. This shows how much income tax has been deducted up to the date of leaving and also the code number. If Form P45 is not taken, tax will be deducted on an emergency coding, and may be much more than is normally paid.

At the end of the Income Tax year (5 April) the following should be sent to the Collector of Taxes, by the employer:
- Deduction cards for each employee
- Form P35 (the employer's annual declaration and certificate) which shows both NI contributions and income tax
- Any balance of NI contributions and income tax due.

Form P11. This is the official deduction card for PAYE and NI. If an employee is earning too little to pay tax, a deduction card for NI purposes only should be completed to show the NI contributions payable. The amount of pay need not be entered.

No one pays tax on the whole of their income. Everyone is given a tax-free allowance to set against their income and tax is paid only on what remains after these allowances have been deducted. Income tax is worked out over a whole year and the tax-free allowances are also yearly – the PAYE system spreads the load over a year and prevents tax having to be paid in one big 'lump' at the end of the tax year on 5 April. The idea is that on 5 April each year each wage earner does not owe the taxman any money.

Voluntary Deductions from Pay

In addition to income tax and National Insurance contributions, which are compulsory by law (statutory) an employee may agree to have certain other deductions from his pay.

SAVINGS FUND

Usually this is money left in as a form of saving for a specific purpose, e.g. holidays or purchase of an expensive article such as a car. It may be contributions to SAYE (Save As You Earn), which is a savings fund operated by the Government and from which money cannot be withdrawn for a minimum of five years.

SOCIAL FUND

This goes towards the social activities organised by a firm, e.g. sports, drama, music.

TRADE UNION DUES

This is a regular (usually small, but it varies) contribution made by employees who agree to join a trade union.

CONTRIBUTIONS TO A PENSION SCHEME

The pension may be a private one (in which case the employee is known as 'contracted out') or may be the Government's scheme, in which case the employee is known as 'not contracted out'.

Contributions to a pension scheme provide security in retirement and every worker should make proper provision for old age. Every worker over the age of 18 has to contribute to a pension scheme – either the Government scheme or a firm's own scheme. Upon retirement, a worker will then be entitled to two pensions, one from his firm (or Government) based on his 20 best earning years, and one which will be his basic retirement pension based on his National Insurance contributions.

FOR YOUR FOLDER

47. DEDUCTIONS FROM PAY

Write these notes in your folder, filling in the missing words and phrases.

1) After deductions agreed by the employee together with statutory deductions have been made from pay, the remainder is known as the _____ pay.

2) Statutory deductions are those required by _____ to be deducted from pay.

3) Statutory deductions are National Insurance, income tax (PAYE) and _____.

4) National Insurance contributions are calculated on _____ pay.

5) Every person over _____ years of age has to pay National Insurance contributions, whether still at school or not, if they earn over £27 per week.

6) There are three rates for NI contributions – standard, reduced and _____.

7) The amount of income tax deducted from wages depends upon a _____ number.

8) This number is based upon the information contained in a form supplied to everyone earning money – Form _____.

9) There is no tax _____ for National Insurance contributions.

10) The form which is sent to every employee annually showing the total amount of tax deducted during the previous 12 months is Form _____.

11) When changing from one job to another Form _____ must be taken by the employee.

12) The end of the income tax year is _____ April.

13) Voluntary deductions from pay are agreed to by the _____.

14) The official deduction card showing PAYE and NI is _____.

15) PAYE spreads the load of tax due over a year and prevents tax having to be paid in one big 'lump' at the _____.

16) No one pays tax on the _____.

17) The form sent out to all employees annually which must be completed so that the correct coding can be worked out is _____.

18) If this form is not completed, an _____ code number will be

allocated and the amount of tax deducted may be higher than it should actually be.

Exercise 74

WAGES AND SALARIES

1) The words 'wages' and 'salaries' have exactly the same meaning, but over the years, they have come to have a separate meaning. Explain the difference between them.

2) What is payment 'in kind'? What is the importance of the Truck Acts in connection with payment in kind?

3) What is the difference between gross pay and net pay? Why is net pay sometimes quite a shock to a new wage-earner?

4) Explain the importance of Form P1.

5) Explain the importance of Form P45.

6) What has to be sent to the Collector of Taxes at the end of each tax year?

7) What is the importance of Form P11?

8) 'No one pays tax on the whole of their income.' Explain this statement.

9) What is the main object of the PAYE system?

Payment of Wages

Payment of wages can be done by cheque, credit transfer, direct debit (through a current bank account) by National Giro, or by cash (notes and coins). According to the National Westminster Bank in May 1980, over half of the British workforce still prefer to receive their wages in the form of cash. This means that firms must transport from a bank well before the day wages are paid out sufficient money and coins to make up into the exact amount for each pay packet.

In order to calculate exactly how many £50, £20, £10, £5, £1 notes and 50p, 20p and 10p coins will be needed a cash analysis has to be worked out as below.

When this cash has been received from the bank, it is possible for all the wage packets to be made up exactly to each worker's net amount. Not only does it take a great deal of time to pay wages in cash, but there is also an immense amount of risk involved while the money is in transit. This is the reason for the use of special security vans. It is also a good idea to vary the day, time and person if money is collected weekly from a bank to be paid out in wages.

```
WAGES CASH ANALYSIS

Clock No.  Name        Wage     £20  £10  £5   £1   50p  10p  5p   2p   1p

   351    BROWN J     £31.70    1    1    -    1    1    2    -    -    -
   352    WHITE E      39.75    1    1    1    4    1    2    1    -    -
   353    GREY S       42.20    2    -    -    2    -    2    -    -    -
   354    BLACK P      49.45    2    -    1    4    -    4    1    -    -

 TOTAL               163.10     6    2    2   11    2   10    2    -    -

                Summary of cash requirements        £      p
                        6 @ £20                    120.00
                        2 @ £10                     20.00
                        2 @ £5                      10.00
                       11 @ £1                      11.00
                        2 @ 50p                      1.00
                       10 @ 10p                      1.00
                        2 @ 5p                         10

                                              £   163.10
```

A wage cash analysis

In each wage packet is a slip, showing how the money is made up. If a worker does not agree with the contents of his wage packet (i.e. it does not agree with the wage slip) or he does not agree that his wage slip is correct, he must take it to the wages clerk and ask for an explanation. Some firms also use the outside of a wage packet on which to print details of pay instead of a separate pay slip.

PAY SLIP

Name: J Brown   Dept: Packaging   Works No. 351

Basic Pay	Overtime	Gross Pay	Income Tax	National Insurance	Pension	Others	Net Pay
50.00	----	£50.00	£10.00	£6.00	£1.00	£1.30	£31.70

A pay slip

The information for a pay slip is taken from the payroll, which will now be described.

Payroll

A payroll is the document which shows for all the employees:

- Gross pay and amount of income tax deducted
- Statutory deductions (e.g. income tax, pension contributions, National Insurance contributions)
- Voluntary deductions (e.g. SAYE, Trade Union dues)
- Overtime (if any)
- Net pay

and may also include a cash analysis for the purpose of obtaining the correct numbers of notes and coins from a bank to make up the wage packets.

PAY ROLL																	
WEEK OR MONTH NO **1** DATE		12	April														
	DETAILS																
EARNINGS	A																
	B																
	C																
	D																
	E																
	GROSS PAY	50	00	60	00	65	00	70	00								
PENSION/SUP'N.																	
GROSS PAY FOR TAX PURPOSES		50	00	60	00	65	00	70	00								
GROSS PAY TO DATE FOR TAX PURPOSES		50	00	60	00	65	00	70	00								
TAX FREE PAY		20	00	25	00	26	50	35	00								
TAXABLE PAY TO DATE		30	00	35	00	38	50	35	00								
TAX DUE TO DATE		10	00	12	50	13	25	12	00								
TAX REFUND		–	–	–	–	–	–	–	–								
DEDUCTIONS	TAX	10	00	12	50	13	25	12	00								
	Pension	1	00	1	25	1	50	2	00								
	NAT. INS.	6	00	6	20	6	35	6	45								
	1. SAYE	1	00	–	–	1	50	–	–								
	2. Trade Union		20		20		20		–								
	3. Social Club		10		10		–		10								
	4.																
	5.																
	6.																
	TOTAL DEDUCTIONS	18	30	20	25	22	80	20	55								
NET PAY		31	70	39	75	42	20	49	45								
F																	
G																	
TOTAL AMOUNT PAYABLE		31	70	39	75	42	20	49	45						163	10	
EMPLOYER	NAT. INS.																
	H																
	J																

NAME	BROWN J	WHITE E	GREY S	BLACK P					
£20								6	
£10								2	
£5								2	
£1								11	
50p								2	
10p								10	
5p								2	
2p									
1p									

A payroll

Exercise 75

WORKING OUT WAGES

1) Copy out three pay slips and make out one for E White, S Grey and P Black from the details on the payroll (pp. 328–9).

2) Work out wages cash analyses for the following wages:

a £66.41 A Marshall
  £73.59 D Kenwright
  £84.90 F Rhodes
  £59.37 L Denman
  £79.48 C Price

b £101.22 P Moore
  £144.91 C Parkins
  £56.87 D Dawson
  £73.54 G Martin
  £81.00 F Hines

c £55.39 C Snow
  £49.80 L Frost
  £59.11 J Iceland
  £61.34 M Fogg
  £77.61 W Rayne

CHAPTER 17

Money at Banks and Post Offices

How much do you know already? Try the following quiz.

True or false:

1) Banks always charge for looking after people's money?

2) It is difficult to find a convenient time to get to a bank when it is open?

3) It is more sensible to keep savings in a box in a cupboard at home?

4) A great deal of tiresome form filling is necessary to take money out of a bank account?

5) It is not worthwhile having a bank account unless one has a lot of money?

6) To own a cheque book, it is necessary to be over 16 years old?

7) Banks will lend money to anyone who asks them for it?

8) Banks *never* lend money, whoever asks for it?

9) A cheque will be accepted by a bank whatever it is written on – even the side of a large fish?

10) Writing a cheque makes spending money easier – it does not seem like 'real' money?

The answers are on p. 363. Don't worry if you got some wrong – just read this chapter.

Why Banks?

There are three major reasons for banks:
- keeping customers' money safe
- transferring money to and from their accounts
- lending money to them.

Banks provide many other useful services, too, which will be explained later in this chapter.

Types of Banks

There are several different types of banks – the 'big four' (as they are often described) have nationwide branches in England and Wales and are the largest Clearing House banks (see p. 353). In descending order of size, they are:

- National Westminster (NatWest)
- Barclays
- Midland
- Lloyds

There are other, smaller, 'clearing house' banks with fewer branches. All clearing house banks open at 9.30 am and close at 3.30 pm. The Trustee Savings Banks and Co-operative Banks are also clearing house banks which open earlier and close later than the big four. Co-operative banks open on Saturdays, too, which is a great convenience to customers.

A typical enquiry desk at a bank

In addition, there is the Post Office Giro ('Giro' means transmission of money) which also opens during normal shopping hours.

Bank accounts

There are two types of bank accounts – current and deposit (or savings). In order to encourage customers to leave their money in a deposit account, interest is paid at base rate. For example, if bank rate is 10 per cent, £100 left in an account for a year will 'grow' to £110.

Most banks allow customers to withdraw money from a deposit account on demand (after completing a withdrawal slip). Giving seven days notice of withdrawal avoids loss of interest.

A current account is quite different. It is the most widely used, although many bank customers have both a current and a deposit account. A current account enables the customer to write cheques to pay bills and to take out any cash needed for day-to-day expenses. *No interest* is payable on a current account, but a balance left (about £100) in a current account is set by the bank against any charges due, so it is worth keeping about that amount in excess of normal requirements in a current account.

Banks charge customers for a current account only if the balance falls below this amount (and it varies from bank to bank); the charges are based on the number of cheques written and the number of other 'transactions', i.e. standing orders and direct debits (see p. 347).

How to open a current account or a deposit account

Go into the nearest branch of the big four, or Co-operative Bank, or Trustee Savings Bank and find the enquiry counter.

Tell the clerk you wish to open an account (either current or deposit). You will then be asked for:

- a description of your occupation
- some money (it need only be a few pounds)
- a specimen signature (so that no one else can sign your cheques or withdraw money from your deposit account)
- a reference (your employer would be suitable, or a friend with a bank account).

You will be given (in about a week):

- a cheque book (for current account) printed with your name on each cheque (personalised) (see below)
- a book of paying-in slips (for paying in cash, cheques or postal orders) to your account (see p. 348).

All you have to do then is to use your account sensibly and, if a current account, avoid writing too many cheques and spending more money than is left in your account (this is known as 'being in the red' – in which case the bank manager will write to you letting you know that he is aware of what you have done and is not pleased with you!).

SPECIMEN ONLY Issued by Bank Education Service.

_____ 19___   **00-00-00**

BANK OF EDUCATION

HOMETOWN

Pay _____*or Order*

_____ £_____

_____ B HOPEFUL

⑈000651⑈ 00⑈0000⑊ ⑈0475375⑈ ⑈⑈

A personalised cheque

Cheques

WHAT A CHEQUE IS

A cheque is an order in writing addressed to the bank to pay, when required, a sum of money to the person named on the cheque. It is quite legal for a plain piece of paper to be used, or even a tablecloth or fish (this has actually happened) but it is now the practice for the banks to issue special cheque forms, in books.

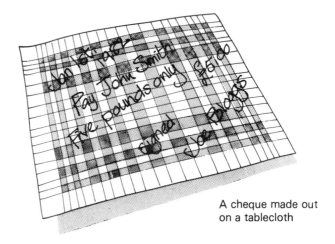

A cheque made out
on a tablecloth

A cheque is not legal tender — as a bank note is — and anyone is entitled to refuse a cheque in payment of a debt, but a cheque is a legal document recognised by Acts of Parliament.

REASONS FOR CHEQUES

One very good reason is that a cheque takes up far less space than a quantity of coins and bank notes. It is also very suitable for posting or carrying and is much safer.

Banknotes and coins . . .

. . . attract thieves

WRITING CHEQUES

Cheques must be written in ink or ball-point and *not* in pencil.

Each cheque is attached to the cheque-book by a 'counterfoil'. The counterfoil is left in the cheque-book after the cheque has been made out and removed, as a record for the customer, so it is sensible to fill it in as a copy of each cheque.

Date counterfoil also   Drawee   Date here

Sept. 10 19 8‒	SPECIMEN ONLY Issued by Bank Education Service.
	September 10 _____ 19 8‒ **00-00-00**
	BANK OF EDUCATION
	HOMETOWN
	Pay _____ *or Order*
	£_____
	B HOPEFUL
£ _____	
000658	⑈000658⑈ 00⑈0000⑆ 10475375⑈ 11

Counterfoil

The person receiving the money represented by a cheque is the 'payee'. The name of the 'payee' is written clearly on the cheque against the word 'Pay' and should also be written on the counterfoil, with the date and the amount.

Name of 'payee' on counterfoil

Sept. 10 19 8‒	SPECIMEN ONLY Issued by Bank Education Service.
	September 10 19 8‒ **00-00-00**
Miss Joanne Phillips	**BANK OF EDUCATION**
	HOMETOWN
	Pay Miss Joanne Phillips _____ *or Order*
	£_____
	B HOPEFUL
£ _____	
000658	⑈000658⑈ 00⑈0000⑆ 10475375⑈ 11

Name of person who will
receive cheque — 'payee'

A cheque must be dated with the date on which it is written. Banks will not accept post-dated (dated in advance) cheques, for immediate withdrawal of cash.

On the line beneath the payee's name the amount to be paid is written *in words*. It is written again in figures in the 'box' provided. The two amounts must be the same – if not, the bank will not pay out the money. Any space left should be ruled up so that no one can dishonestly add any figures. 'Noughts' are best avoided as they can look like sixes if written badly. Dots must not be used either – write long dashes instead. The word 'only' may be added after the amount in figures as an extra safeguard (see below).

Sept. 10 19 8-

Miss Joanne Phillips

£ 10 —

000658

SPECIMEN ONLY Issued by Bank Education Service.

10 September   198-   **00-00-00**

BANK OF EDUCATION

HOMETOWN

Pay Miss Joanne Phillips _____ *or Order*

Ten pounds only — ___ £ 10 ___

B HOPEFUL

"000658"   00"0000:   10475375" 11

Sept. 10 19 8-

Miss Joanne Phillips

£ 10 —

000658

SPECIMEN ONLY Issued by Bank Education Service.

10 September   198-   **00-00-00**

BANK OF EDUCATION

HOMETOWN

Pay Miss Joanne Phillips _____ *or Order*

Ten pounds only — ___ £ 10 ___

B HOPEFUL

B. Hopeful

"000658"   00"0000:   10475375" 11

The counterfoil does not have to be signed; it remains in payee's chequebook

Signature of 'drawer'

SIGNATURE

The customer signs his (or her) name always in the same way, and it should agree with the specimen signature he gave to the bank when he opened his account. The signature is at the foot of the cheque. This signature is the name of the 'drawer' of the cheque.

CHEQUE-SIGNING MACHINE

This machine saves the time of managers and supervisors who may have many cheques to sign – the signatures are printed on the cheques by a metal plate. Security is provided by a key locking system, and special ink.

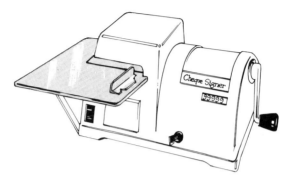

A cheque-signing machine

'STALE' CHEQUES

A cheque is 'valid' (that is, it will be cashed by a bank) up to 6 months after it has been made out. After 6 months, it is out of date, and is 'invalid' and will be returned to drawer marked R/D (refer to drawer).

CHEQUES WHICH 'BOUNCE'

Cheques which 'bounce' are dishonoured cheques, for any one of the following reasons:

- if the drawer of the cheque has no money in his current account
- if the amount in words does not agree with the amount in figures
- if drawer's signature looks different from his specimen signature
- if an alteration has not been initialled
- if cheque is postdated (dated in advance)
- if cheque has been 'stopped' by the drawer
- if cheque is 'stale' (see above).

COMPLETING THE COUNTERFOIL

It is useful to the 'drawer' if he has a record of what he wrote a cheque out for as well as to whom and also he may like to deduct the amount of the cheque from his current account balance and make a note on the counterfoil.

CORRECTING MISTAKES ON CHEQUES

Providing it is a simple one, a mistake on a cheque may be crossed through (once only, not scribbled over) and the correction initialled by drawer of cheque. If the error is a large one (the wrong payee's name for example), it is better to tear up the cheque, cancel the counterfoil and start again.

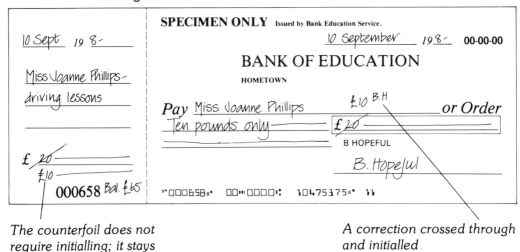

The counterfoil does not require initialling; it stays in the chequebook

A correction crossed through and initialled.

What cheque was made out for

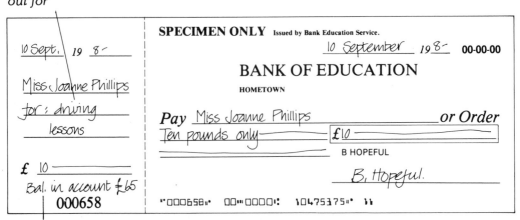

Balance in account on 10th September 198-

The completed cheque and counterfoil

Bank/branch number

SPECIMEN ONLY Issued by Bank Education Service.

_____ 19 _____   _____ 19___ **00-00-00**

BANK OF EDUCATION
HOMETOWN

Pay _____ *or Order*

£ _____

B HOPEFUL

£ _____

000651

"000651" 00"0000: 10475375" 11

The cheque number is
repeated on the counterfoil

The cheque number

The Bank/Branch number

The customer's account
number

The meanings of the numbers on a cheque

'Stopping' a cheque

The bank should be informed at once if a customer has lost his cheque-book, or a cheque which he has posted has not been received. The bank should be telephoned if possible giving date, number and amount. Then, later, it will be necessary to complete the 'stop instruction' form shown at the top of p. 340.

Stopping payment

After Mrs Mary Jenkinson had posted her cheque in payment of an account, she was very surprised when, later, the bill was sent to her again. Upon enquiry she found out that her cheque had never been received and must have gone astray.

She immediately went to her bank and found out that the cheque had not been presented for payment. Mrs Jenkinson therefore immediately completed the form overleaf authorising the bank to stop payment of the missing cheque should anyone present it at the bank. She then made out a second cheque in payment of the still unpaid bill. The staff of the bank keep a careful watch for the lost cheque among those which are presented for payment, and a record of the 'stop' is placed on Mrs Jenkinson's computer records. The computer automatically rejects the cheque if it is eventually presented for payment. *But cheques guaranteed by a cheque card cannot be stopped.*

THE BANK OF EDUCATION

Hometown _____ Branch

STOP INSTRUCTION

Please stop payment of the undermentioned cheque(s):

Note: Cheques drawn under Cheque Card arrangements cannot normally be stopped

Date _26 September_ 198-   Numbered _000779_

Account _Mary Jenkinson_   Account Number | 0934150 |

Payee _Mark Tyme_   Amount £ _50_———

Lost/~~Stolen~~ Cheque(s) ~~or Cheque Book~~-Number(s) of Cheque(s) _1_

Has a Cheque Card also been lost? Y~~es~~/No

Date _30 Sept_ 198- Signature _Mary Jenkinson_

A 'stop payment' instruction form

Withdrawing cash from a current account

This is very simple. A cheque has to be made out by the customer to 'Self' or 'Cash' where the name of the payee is normally written. If it is a crossed cheque, the crossing has to be 'opened' by signing and adding the words 'please pay cash' otherwise the bank will not cash the cheque.

Oct. 4 19 8-

Cash

£ 20 ——

000651

4 October 198-   **00-00-00**

BANK OF EDUCATION

HOMETOWN

Pay _Cash_ _____ _or Order_

Twenty pounds only —— | £ 20 ——— |

B HOPEFUL

Please pay cash B. Hopeful   _B. Hopeful_

"000651" 00"0000: 10475375" 11

A crossed cheque made out to 'Cash'. The crossing has been 'opened' by signing

Most banks have a quick service counter for customers who only want to cash a cheque. This avoids standing in a queue for a long time behind people with other business to transact.

An 'open' cheque has no crossing. It will be cashed by a bank, and is therefore not as safe as a crossed cheque, which has to be paid into a bank account.

If a crossed cheque which has been lost or stolen is later paid into a bank account illegally, it is always possible to trace the person who stole or found the cheque.

10 July 19 8-	SPECIMEN ONLY Issued by Bank Education Service.
	10 July 198- 00-00-00
Cash	BANK OF EDUCATION
	HOMETOWN
	Pay Cash or Order
	Fifty pounds only £ 50
	B HOPEFUL
£ 50	B. Hopeful
000654	⑈000654⑈ 00⑈0000⑈ 10475375⑈ 11

An open cheque made out to 'Cash' (for withdrawing money in cash from a current account)

An 'open' cheque can be crossed simply by ruling two parallel lines from top to bottom across the middle, but banks issue cheques already printed with a crossing for people who prefer them. A bank customer may choose which type of cheque book to have. Cheque books are provided free to holders of current accounts.

10 July 19 8-	SPECIMEN ONLY Issued by Bank Education Service.
	10 July 198- 00-00-00
Cash	BANK OF EDUCATION
	HOMETOWN
	Pay Cash or Order
	Fifty pounds only £ 50
	B HOPEFUL
£ 50	Please pay Cash B. Hopeful B. Hopeful
000654	⑈000654⑈ 00⑈0000⑈ 10475375⑈ 11

All cheques sent by post should be crossed, as a safeguard against theft.

It is extremely foolish to sign a cheque and leave the amount blank. The cheque could be filled in for any sum of money and the bank would accept it, even though the writing would be different from the signature. Because the latter is genuine, the cheque would not be queried.

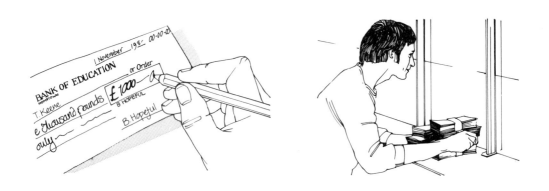

A 'blank' cheque (amount is not specified). Anyone could fill in any amount in words
and figures . . .

SPECIAL CHEQUE CROSSINGS

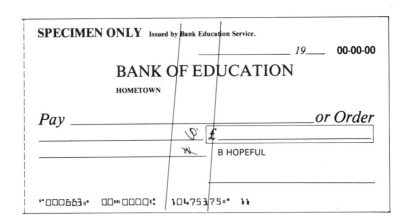

An ordinary cheque crossing (printed on by the banks) consists of two parallel lines
which usually has '& Co' printed between the lines, but this is not essential. This is
known as 'general crossing'

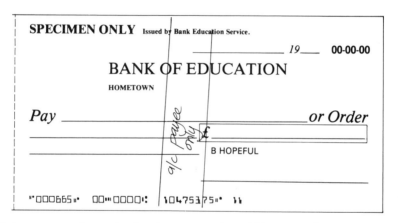

SPECIMEN ONLY Issued by Bank Education Service.

19____ 00-00-00

BANK OF EDUCATION

HOMETOWN

Pay _____ or Order

£

B HOPEFUL

Under £20

"000664" 00"0000": 10475375" 11

This cheque must be for an amount under £20 – it is a safeguard against anyone altering the amount by adding an extra nought

SPECIMEN ONLY Issued by Bank Education Service.

19____ 00-00-00

BANK OF EDUCATION

HOMETOWN

Pay _____ or Order

£

B HOPEFUL

a/c payee only

"000665" 00"0000": 10475375" 11

This is an extra safeguard – the cheque must be paid into payee's account and no other

SPECIMEN ONLY Issued by Bank Education Service.

19____ 00-00-00

BANK OF EDUCATION

HOMETOWN

Pay _____ or Order

£

B HOPEFUL

Lloyds Bank Ltd. Carlisle

"000666" 00"0000": 10475375" 11

This cheque must be paid into Lloyds Bank, Carlisle

343

FOR YOUR FOLDER

48. BANKS AND BANK ACCOUNTS

Write these notes in your folder, filling in the missing words and phrases.

1) The three major services provided by banks for their customers are:
   - keeping their money safe
   - transferring money to and from their accounts
   - _____.

2) The Big Four banks are:
   - National Westminster
   - Barclays
   - Midland
   - _____.

3) The banks which open during normal shopping hours (which the big four do not) are Post Office Giro and _____.

4) The two types of bank accounts are current and _____.

5) The one on which interest is paid is _____.

6) To open a bank account it is necessary to provide:
   - a sum of money
   - a reference
   - _____.

7) Cheques are useful because they take up far less space than a quantity of notes and coins and are suitable for _____ or _____ and are much safer.

8) A cheque must be written in ink or ball-point and not _____.

9) The amount of money to be paid by cheque should be written in _____ and figures.

10) Any correction on a cheque should be _____.

11) Crossing a cheque is a _____.

12) Withdrawing cash from a current account is done by making out a cheque to _____ or _____.

13) A 'personalised' cheque is _____.

14) Another name for a cheque counterfoil is a cheque _____.

15) The payee of a cheque is the _____.

16) The person signing the cheque is the _____.

17) The drawee of a cheque is the _____.

344

18) A stale cheque is _____.

19) A cheque which bounces is _____.

20) A post-dated cheque is _____.

21) Stopping a cheque means _____.

Cheque cards

Current account holders may have a cheque card, if they wish (after they have had a current account for about six months and proved that they can handle it responsibly). A cheque card enables them to cash a cheque for up to £50 at any branch of any bank, or write a cheque for goods bought up to the value of £50 in the UK and in the major cities of Europe. A cheque card is an undertaking by the bank issuing it to honour the cheque written in association with it.

There is one disadvantage to a cheque card – a cheque written in conjunction with it cannot be 'stopped' (see p. 339).

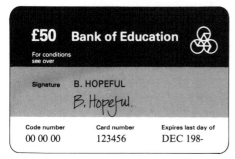

A cheque card

Cash Dispenser Cards

A cash dispenser is a machine set in the outside wall of a bank and stocked with packets containing notes. The customer is given a card which she inserts into the machine; she then taps a personal number on the keyboard. If the number is correct, the machine 'dispenses' the notes. Some dispensers are available 24 hours every day and night. Some banks now have arrangements with their customers to be able to take out up to £200 in any one week from their current account.

A cash dispenser

Credit Cards

A credit card (Access is a well-known example) can be used for shopping or paying for meals in a restaurant simply by signing for the goods or the meal. A statement is then sent out at the end of each month to the credit card holder (who must have a current account at a bank). If the amount owing is paid at once no interest is charged. If it is not, interest is charged.

A credit card

Access cards are accepted by over one million places abroad.

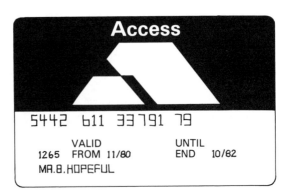

Access is National Westminster's, Midland and Lloyds bank credit cards

Barclaycards are credit cards and cheque cards combined, issued by Barclays bank.

The minimum age for anyone to hold a credit card is 18 years.

A Barclaycard (credit card and cheque card combined)

Standing Orders

A standing order is an instruction in writing to a bank by a customer (usually on a printed form – see below) to pay on his behalf, from his current account balance, amounts which are paid regularly (insurance premiums, mortgage payments, TV rental, hire purchase payments, savings into a building society or SAYE savings scheme, and subscriptions to clubs). This avoids the possibility of forgetting to pay these amounts at the right time.

```
                                         Standing Order
  TO  COLLEGIATE BANK                    Specimen Only
  Branch  Hometown
                        Date  25th February 198-

  Please make payments and debit my /our  current    account, No. 57367401
  in accordance with the following details, to:
  Bank    Bank of Education
  Branch  Newtown
  Sorting code number  00 - 00 - 04
  For account of  XYZ Insurance Co.
  Account number, if any  1047537S
  Reference, if any
  Amount      £ 15 —
  Payments to be made          weekly / monthly / quarterly / half-yearly / annually*
  Date of first payment  14th March 198-
  Date of final payment  14th March 19--
  This order cancels the existing one * for £
  * Delete as appropriate

                        B. Hopeful.
```

A standing order form

Direct Debit

This is similar to a standing order except that the amount may be varied by the payee without reference to the current account holder. It is a great help to building societies and organisations such as the AA, because a direct debit avoids having to ask for the customer's permission to change (usually increase) the amount payable. Notification that a direct debit is to be changed is sent to a customer by the bank.

Paying Cash in

Money may be paid into a bank by using a paying-in slip such as the one below. Here Mr Hopeful is paying notes and coins and a cheque for £2 into his own account.

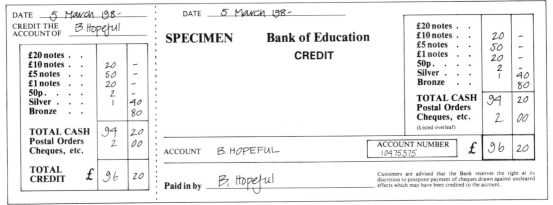

A bank credit paying in slip

CREDIT TRANSFER

By writing one cheque, a customer is able to pay several bills at once; he makes out the cheque for the total amount. The cheque and the credit transfer form is handed in to the bank. This saves postage and writing a number of cheques. It is also useful for paying salaries.

FROM BANK OF EDUCATION

bank giro credit

HOMETOWN   BRANCH

DATE 25 February 198–

CODE NO	BRANCH AND BRANCH TITLE	ACCOUNT	AMOUNT
20–00–00	BARCLAYS BANK ANYTOWN	A J Smith	£28.24
		A/C No. 213478	

By order of Bloggs & Co Ltd

Ref. JME/5480/22/9

A bank Giro credit paying-in slip

Bank Statements

These are sent to a holder of a current account at regular intervals, or when he asks for one. It shows all money paid into his current account (money paid in sends the balance up), all cheques written (which send the balance down) and all credit transfers, standing orders and direct debits – as well as any dividends paid into the account. The last figure in the right-hand column is the amount in the account when the statement is made up.

When a customer has overdrawn his account, the letters DR or OD are printed at the right-hand side under 'Balance'. DR and OD mean 'overdrawn balance', i.e. being 'in the red'.

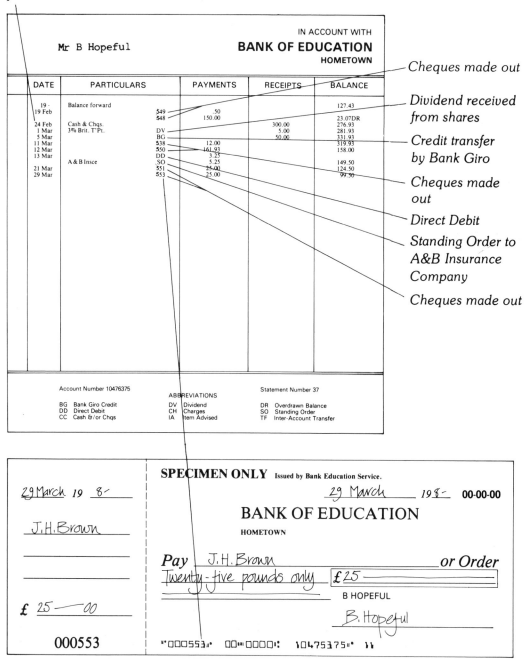

Cash and cheques paid in to the account

Cheques made out

Dividend received from shares

Credit transfer by Bank Giro

Cheques made out

Direct Debit

Standing Order to A&B Insurance Company

Cheques made out

Bank statement of account

349

Other Bank Services

FOR TRAVELLERS

Traveller's cheques are a world-wide form of international currency. Anyone (not just bank customers) can buy traveller's cheques from a bank, in denominations of £2, £5, £10, £20 and £50. The bank makes a small charge.

When bought each cheque must be signed at the foot (where it says 'signature of drawer'). A passport has to be taken to the bank and the total sum (currency and traveller's cheques) being taken out of the country overseas is entered on the passport.

When being cashed, each traveller's cheque has to be signed again (endorsed) by the same person who signed when they were collected from the bank. This endorsement has to be made in the presence of the cashier at the bank. Therefore it is necessary to make sure that when traveller's cheques are collected in this country from the bank, that they are signed for by the person most likely to cash them when abroad. It is possibly a good arrangement for a husband and wife to sign half each.

Traveller's cheques are a safe way to carry money abroad (or in this country) as if lost, they will be replaced. Many hotels, shops and restaurants will accept traveller's cheques in payment.

Drawer has to sign here when presenting his traveller's cheque for cashing; an 'endorsement'

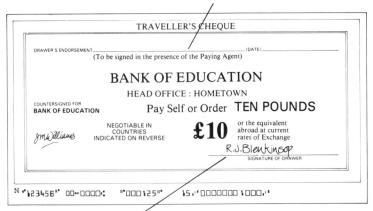

Drawer has to sign here when collecting his traveller's cheques from the bank. He must also take his passport if he is going overseas.

A traveller's cheque

FOREIGN CURRENCY

Banks will provide foreign currency in exchange for pound notes (or debit a current account for the value of the foreign currency). It is always useful to carry some foreign money for a journey abroad, so that some money is available for small items on arrival (drinks, bus fares, telephone calls).

SAFE CUSTODY OF VALUABLES

Rather than go on holiday and leave jewellery or other valuables (foreign stamps, silverware) in the house, ready for burglars it is more sensible to take it to a bank and ask them to look after it. This service is provided free of charge to bank customers, but it is the customer's responsibility to insure the articles deposited at the bank and they must be handed in in wrapped and sealed packages.

NIGHT SAFES

A night safe is built in to the outside wall of a bank. The customer has a bag given to him by the bank. The bag has two keys – one held by the customer, the other kept by the bank. The customer completes a paying-in slip (see p. 348) in the usual way and puts it in the bag with the money. He locks the bag and puts it into the night safe. The next day, while the bank is open, the customer goes into the bank, collects the bag, which is opened in his presence and the money it contains is counted and credited to his account. A night safe is of great use to shopkeepers, restaurant managers, and bingo hall organisers, who have large sums of money to take care of after banks are closed.

A night safe

For Families and Businessmen

INSURANCE

Banks will advise on the best type of insurance to take out for children, wives, husbands, and businesses.

WILLS

A will is an instruction to carry out wishes regarding the distribution of his property after his death. These instructions are written down in his will. A bank will act as an executor or trustee (a trustee is someone who looks after property or money left in a will to someone who may only be a child, until they are grown up). The bank makes a charge for acting as an executor. An executor carries out the instructions in a will.

INVESTMENTS

Banks employ specialists who will give advice to customers about the best ways of investing their money. The bank cannot force customers to take their advice, and if someone wishes to buy shares in a diamond mine on a remote island that cannot even be found on a map, the bank cannot stop him! Banks charge for advising about investments too, in some cases.

Bank Drafts

A bank draft is a means of transferring money from the account of one bank customer to another, and is preferred by customers to a cheque where a large sum of money is involved. A bank draft is considered to be as good as cash, as the customer pays for it in advance.

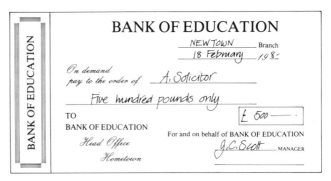

A bank draft

A bank draft is guaranteed by the bank and is useful when two strangers are involved in a business transaction (e.g. selling a car).

The buyer may wish to drive the car away immediately and not wait for the seller to wait for the cheque he has received in payment to be 'cleared' (see p. 353) as it may 'bounce' (see p. 337).

Getting Cash Out of a Branch of Another Bank

A cheque must be written 'Pay cash' or 'Pay self' in the usual way, and when handed in to cashier, a cheque card has to be used for indentification. At present, there is a limit of £50 per day.

By special arrangement in advance, through the customer's own branch, cheques can be cashed up to an agreed amount (i.e. £20 daily) at another specified branch, without producing a cheque card. This is especially useful to bank customers on holiday.

Confidentiality

All transactions with a bank are confidential. No information will be given to *anyone* about a customer's account without the customer's written permission. The only exception to this, of course, are the executors of a will (*see* p. 352).

Clearing Banks

When a cheque is received by payee, he pays it into his own bank account. The procedure after this is as follows:

The bank collects payment from drawer's bank – this collection process is called 'clearing' and usually takes three or four days.

All banks which issue cheques are involved in 'clearing', which is why they are called clearing house banks.

Lending Money

This is one of the three chief reasons for banking, and it is the way banks make their profits – by lending customers' money at interest to other customers in need of it. So that the money is absolutely safe, they will not lend without security (collateral) which means that if a customer wishes to borrow a large sum of money he has to deposit at the bank something of great value, such as the deeds to a house, an insurance policy on which he has paid the premiums for a number of years, or share certificates. If, for any reason the loan cannot be repaid, the bank then has the right to take possession of the collateral. Thus customers' money is safeguarded.

An overdraft is the cheapest way to borrow money – the interest is slightly lower than that for a personal loan, which is the other way to borrow money from a bank. An overdraft means that a current account is overdrawn to a maximum amount and for a maximum period, both agreed with the bank manager.

A personal loan which is borrowed for a certain purpose (buying a car, for instance, or some hi-fi equipment) has to be repaid within a certain period, agreed with the bank manager (the limit is usually 3 years). A personal loan is normally repaid in monthly instalments from a current account. There may be a limit to the amount of cash advanced.

A budget account may be arranged with a bank so that a set sum is paid into the account each month to cover such bills as telephone, electricity, gas, car insurance and tax, calculated over a year. These bills unfortunately have a tendency to come in all at the same time and if payment can be 'spread out' over 12 months, it helps people to 'budget' their expenditure.

Interest is charged on overdrafts, personal loans and budget accounts – the actual amount of interest varying from bank to bank. Bank interest on loans is always much lower than that of other moneylenders.

Bank Note Counting Machine

This piece of electronic equipment counts both new and used banknotes at the rate of 100 in approximately 7 seconds. It is operated by a photo-electric cell.

FOR YOUR FOLDER

49. BANK SERVICES

Write these notes in your folder, filling in the missing words and phrases.

1) A cheque card enables a current account holder to cash a cheque for up to _____ at any branch of any bank, or to write a cheque at a shop for goods bought up to the value of _____.

2) The machine set in the outside wall of a bank which dispenses packets of banknotes after the customer has tapped out his or her personal number is a _____.

3) Two well-known credit cards are _____ and _____.

4) A credit card can be used for _____.

5) _____ are credit cards and cheque cards combined.

6) A regular payment made by a bank on behalf of a current account holder (e.g. insurance premiums, mortgage payments, TV rental or hire purchase) is a _____.

7) A direct debit is similar to the above except that the amount may be _____ by the payee without reference to the _____.

8) Bank Giro No 1 may be used for paying money into a bank account by a customer or a _____.

9) Bank Giro No 2 enables a customer to pay several bills at once by _____.

10) Credit transfer is another name for _____.

11) A safe way to carry money around (either abroad or in this country) is by _____.

12) While you are on holiday, it is sensible to arrange for valuables to be taken care of by a _____.

13) The information sent out to a current account holder about the amount of money he has in his account and the amount he had paid out, is in the form of a _____.

14) Bank services for families and businessmen are advice on insurance, investments and acting as an _____ or trustee.

15) A means of transferring money from one bank customer to another which is useful when two strangers are involved in a business transaction is a _____. A customer pays for a _____ in advance, so it is considered to be the equivalent of cash.

16) No information will be given to anyone about a customer's bank account without the customer's written permission; all transactions with a bank are _____.

17) The way banks make their profits is by _____.

18) The cheapest way to borrow money from a bank is by _____.

19) Another way of borrowing money from a bank is by personal loan; this has to be repaid within a certain period, agreed with the bank (limit _____).

20) When a set sum is paid into a separate account each month to cover such bills as telephone, electricity, gas, oil, car insurance and tax, this is known as a _____ account.

Postal Orders

The postal order is the most commonly used Post Office remittance service. It is especially useful for transferring small amounts of money to someone who has no bank account, as it is encashable over the counter of any Post Office. It could, for example, be used to send money as a birthday present.

The maximum amount for which a postal order may be sent is £10. The minimum amount (at the moment – shortly due to be raised) is 10p. As well as the value of the postal order, there is a small additional charge payable to the Post Office, called 'poundage'. There is a scale of poundage which increases with the value of the postal order.

Postal orders may also be sent overseas – the *Post Office Guide* gives full details.

A counterfoil is provided with each postal order for the use of the sender. It should be filled in and kept as a record. It should not be sent with the postal order.

The sender of the postal order should fill in the name of the person (payee) who will cash it and the name of the office where it will be cashed. If the office is not known the name of the town or village should be written here. The postal order will then be cashed at any Post Office in that town or village.

The person cashing the postal order must sign it and the signature must match the name at the top. If it is crossed it must be paid into a bank account (a Post Office Savings account is suitable or another bank account).

Postal orders are valid for six months, after which the Post Office will not cash them without reference to the District Postmaster.

Small amounts – up to 4½p – may be added to the value of the postal order by sticking on stamps.

CROSSED POSTAL ORDERS

Postal orders may be crossed in the same way as cheques, after which they have to be paid into a bank account – they cannot be cashed over the counter at a Post Office. Postal orders should always be crossed when they are sent away as payment for goods ordered by mail order, or to a football pools firm – uncrossed postal orders are a great temptation to a thief as they are so easily cashed.

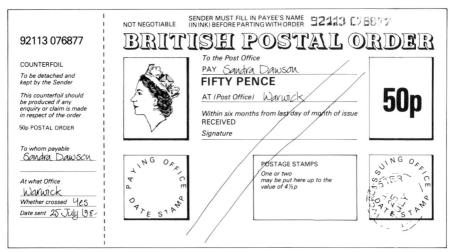

A crossed postal order with counterfoil

FOR YOUR FOLDER

50. POSTAL ORDERS

Write these notes in your folder, filling in the missing words and phrases.

1) The maximum amount for which a postal order may be sent is _____.

2) As well as the value of the postal order, there is a small additional charge called _____.

3) Postal orders may be sent overseas – the _____ gives full details.

4) It is safer to cross a postal order before sending it. If it is crossed, it must be paid into a _____.

5) Postal orders are valid for _____.

6) Small amounts may be added to the value of a postal order by _____.

7) The counterfoil provided with each postal order should be filled in and _____.

8) The counterfoil _____ be sent with the postal order.

9) The postal order is the most commonly used Post Office _____ service.

10) It is especially useful for transferring _____ to someone who has no bank account.

National Girobank

The National Girobank is the Post Office bank which now offers many of the same services as the clearing banks:

- cheque books and cheque accounts
- deposit accounts
- personal loans
- standing orders
- budget accounts
- bridging loans
- cheque card (holder must be over 18)
- free bank statements
- traveller's cheques and foreign currency.

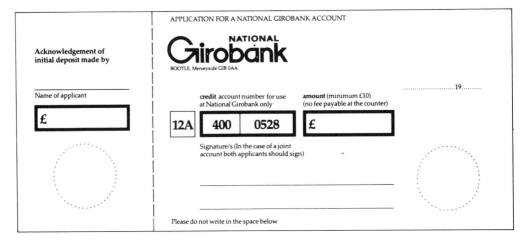

The National Girobank application form (front)

The National Girobank application form (back)

There are no bank charges as long as a customer's account remains in credit. When the customer is overdrawn (in the red) 10p is charged for each payment from the cheque account.

The National Girobank is cheaper than the clearing house banks, and also many post offices are open on Saturdays, which is convenient for withdrawing and paying in money. All post offices are open during normal shopping hours, so that National Girobank services are available outside normal banking hours (which are 0930 to 1530, Monday to Friday only).

If you want to open an account, you need to complete an application form like the one opposite.

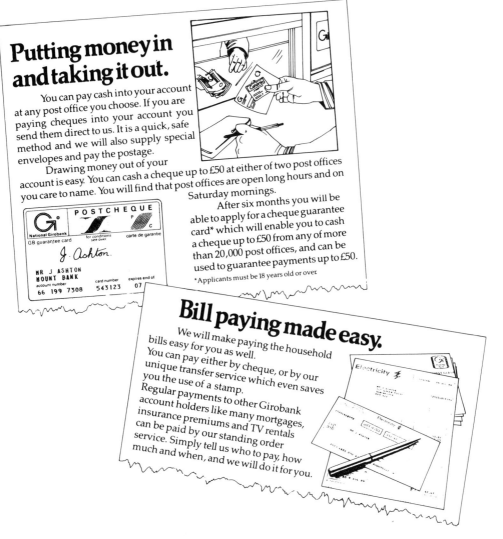

Extracts from National Girobank application booklet.

Exercise 76

NATIONAL GIROBANK

1) The National Girobank has several advantages over the clearing house banks. Give two of them.

2) What services are available to clearing house bank customers and *not* to National Girobank customers?

3) At what age is it possible to open a National Girobank account?

4) At what age is it possible to have a cheque guarantee card?

5) How much is it necessary to pay in to open a National Girobank account?

6) Where is this amount paid in?

7) What does the application form mean by 'joint account'?

8) Why does the form ask for details of a previous address if the applicant has moved within the last year?

9) How is bill paying made easy by National Girobank?

10) What is a 'guarantor'?

Exercise 77

ASSIGNMENTS ON CHEQUES AND PAYING-IN SLIPS

1) The balance in your current account stands at £20. Make out a cheque to withdraw cash for your own use (date it for today) for £5. Make a note of the balance remaining in your current account on your counterfoil (cheque 'stub'). (See p. 335.)

```
┌──────────────────────┐ ╎
│                      │ ╎
│  _____ 19 _____    │ ╎
│                      │ ╎
│  _____     │ ╎
│                      │ ╎
│  _____     │ ╎
│                      │ ╎
│  _____     │ ╎
│                      │ ╎
│  £ _____     │ ╎
│                      │ ╎
│     000651           │ ╎
└──────────────────────┘ ╎
```

2) You wish to pay some cash and a cheque and a postal order into your current account. Make out a paying-in slip (see p. 348) for the following:
- 2 £1 notes
- 3 50p coins
- 4 10p coins
- 3 5p coins
- 1 cheque for £1.50
- 1 postal order for 50p.

Make a note on the counterfoil in your cheque-book of the balance now in your current account.

3) Make out a cheque to Newtown Corporation for £2 with today's date. This will be for an examination entry fee for June 198—. Note balance in your account on the counterfoil.

4) Make out a cheque to R W Phillips Esq for £7.75 with today's date. This will be for a deposit on a record player. Make a note of the balance in your account.

5) Make out a paying-in slip for the following:
- 1 £1 note
- 1 50p coin
- 4 2p coins
- 3 1p coins
- 1 cheque for £1.30
- 1 postal order for 50p.

Make a note on the last counterfoil in your cheque-book of balance remaining in your current account.

6) Make out a cheque to withdraw cash from your current account for your own use for £3. Make a note of balance remaining in the account.

Exercise 78

BANKING ASSIGNMENTS

1) You will need:
- five cheque forms (crossed cheques)
- paying-in slips (three)
- a bank statement form.
- The bank account is in the name of 'F Martin'.
- The account no is 108976.
- F Martin runs a small boutique. Its name is 'The Chic Boutique' and the address is: 74 High Street, Hometown.
- F Martin's account had a balance of £750 on 1 March 198—.

a *3 March 198—*
F Martin makes out a cheque for £65.50 to 'The Glen Tweed Co' for 30 yards of cloth.

b *5 March 198—*

The day's cash takings at the boutique are £78.95. Make out a paying-in slip to pay this into the bank. It is made up as follows:

£10 notes 3
£5 notes 8
£1 notes 5
50 pence pieces 4
10 pence pieces 10
 5 pence pieces 12
 2 pence pieces 15
 1 pence pieces 5

On the same paying-in slip, include two cheques: one for £10.50 and the other for £9.64.

c *6 March 198—*

F Martin makes out a cheque to 'Thompson Trimming Co' for £34.81 for buttons, braid and buckles. Takings on 6 March are £108.95, which is paid into the bank on the same day, made up as follows:

£10 notes 9
£5 notes 3
£1 notes 3
50 pence pieces 1
10 pence pieces 4
 5 pence pieces 1

d *7 March 198—*

Make out a cheque for 'Cash' for wages amounting to £349.65 and a cheque for £56.11 for NHI and one for £127.31 for PAYE—both made out to the Inspector of Taxes.

e *8 March 198—*

The day's takings are £234.67. Make out a paying-in slip for this amount (divide it up into suitable notes and coins).

Make out a bank statement showing how much money F Martin had in his account on 10 March 198—. This statement should show all the above transactions.

If your calculations are correct, his balance should be £559.33.

2) You have received a private loan of £250 from K G Holding to enable you to buy a car. The cheque is reproduced opposite:

```
SPECIMEN ONLY   Issued by Bank Education Service.
                                Todays date    19___   00-00-00
              BANK OF EDUCATION
              HOMETOWN

Pay --- Your own name                        or Order
Two hundred and fifty    £250
pounds only               K. G. HOLDING.

                              K. G. Holding

"000851"  00"0000:  10475375"  11
```

a Prepare a paying-in slip or bank giro credit slip for paying the cheque into your bank current account.

b As you will be repaying the loan by banker's order, fill in a standing order form requesting 24 monthly payments from your account, commencing the first day of next month. (The total amount to be repaid over the two years – with interest – is £300.)

c Complete a bank statement showing the state of your current account, assuming £255.75 was the balance brought forward and including the above transactions, i.e. the cheque paid into your account and the first standing order payment.

d You have also paid:
   ● a local garage £225 for the car
   ● an insurance company £60 for insuring the car
   ● £38.50 for Road Fund Vehicle Licence.
   All three cheques have been presented at your bank and your account debited accordingly.
   Show one of the cheque counterfoils.

Answers to Quiz on Banking

1) No, they do not always charge – only for current account transactions when the account balance falls below a certain amount (see p.333).

2) Yes, some Banks do have rather restricted opening hours (see p. 332).

3) No – too easy for burglars to get at!

4) No – all that is needed is a cheque made out to 'Self' or 'Cash' for money from a current account (see p. 340).

5) It is worthwhile to have a Deposit Account – for saving even small amounts.

6) No – there is no minimum age limit.

7) No (see pp. 353–4).

8) Not true (see p. 354).

9) True! (see p. 334).

10) No, not if a record is kept on the counterfoil (see p. 335).

Exercise 79

METHODS OF PAYMENT

1) Describe the services provided through the Post Office for making and receiving payments.

2) State briefly what the following terms used in connection with cheques mean:

   a post-dated **b** stale **c** stopped

3) What action should be taken when:
   a You discover that a cheque sent by you in today's post has been incorrectly made out for £100 more than the amount owed,
   b a cheque which you have paid into the bank is returned 'words and figures differ (R/D)'.

4) What is a 'current account' and how is it used?

5) A cheque which has been sent by you appears to have been lost in the post. What action should be taken?

6) Explain how the credit transfer (Bank Giro) system operates for settling accounts.

7) Complete a blank specimen bank paying-in slip, using the following details:

4th June 1976	1	£20.00	notes
Creditor: A. Brown	3	10.00	notes
Paid in by: A. Brown	4	5.00	notes
A/C no. 10476375	30	1.00	notes
	30	50p	coins
	50	10p	coins
	15	5p	coins
Postal Order (value)		£ 3.60	
Cheques		£50.00	
Cheques		£15.25	
Cheques		£10.40	

Insert amount of total credit.

General Revision

Exercise 80
MULTIPLE-CHOICE QUESTIONS

Copy out the question, and write the correct letter underneath.

1) A filing clerk in an office would be responsible for:
a opening the mail
b dealing with all the callers to a firm
c filing all papers.

2) An audio-typist would:
a type from written notes
b type from shorthand notes
c type after listening to the dictation through headphones.

3) A copy-typist would:
a have to have accurate typing with a good speed
b have to be able to type in a foreign language
c have to know all about computer programming.

4) One of the following is an essential quality for an office worker:
a high shorthand speed
b conscientiousness
c good looks.

5) One of the following is a *qualification* which a secretary should have:
a excellent English
b initiative
c pleasant manner.

6) The following would be sent by Recorded Delivery:
a gold bracelet
b passport
c £50 in notes.

7) The following would be sent by Registered Post:
a driving licence
b a set of valuable foreign stamps
c worked examination papers.

8) An International Reply Coupon would be used to:
a prepay a letter for a reply from a pen friend in Germany
b send the postage to a mail order firm for a catalogue
c save buying a postal order for 25p.

9) Post Restante enables:
a people to collect their letters from a post office in a town where they will be staying, when they are not sure of their exact address
b people to have their letters collected by a postman instead of posting them in a letter box
c people to obtain a meal at a post office.

10) Private boxes at a Post Office sorting office are for:
  a confidential letters
  b firms who wish to collect their mail at their own convenience during the day
  c private detectives.

11) An airmail letter form is:
  a the cheapest seat in an aeroplane
  b a special form sold by the Post Office which is the cheapest way of sending an airmail letter
  c a rubber stamp with the words 'airmail' on it.

12) The airmail service to Europe is called:
  a the 'all-up' service
  b Express post
  c Datapost.

13) The telephone alphabet is:
  a The special language in which telephone directories are written
  b the order in which the *Yellow Pages* is set out
  c for a telephonist to spell out names which the caller cannot hear.

14) A fixed time call is:
  a when the length of the call is set beforehand and the caller is disconnected when the end of the call is reached
  b when a trunk call is booked in advance so that caller is connected at a pre-arranged time
  c a call which wakes you up in the morning.

15) A release symbol is:
  a a message of hope to a man in prison
  b a key
  c a special mark on a document which indicates it can be filed.

16) Spirit duplicating is a method of producing several hundred copies by means of:
  a ghosts who do the typing in the dark
  b hectograph carbon
  c photography.

17) Ink duplicating is:
  a copying by pen and ink
  b many different colours of ink
  c producing copies by stencil on an ink duplicator.

18) An agenda of a meeting is sent:
  a to all those entitled to attend the meeting
  b to all those who don't belong to the Society
  c to old age pensioners.

19) A trade discount is:
  a allowed when goods are returned

b allowed when goods are exchanged

c allowed to certain traders because of the quantity they purchase.

20) A cash discount is:

    a allowed for prompt payment

    b allowed only when payment is in cash

    c allowed only when payment is made personally

21) A statement of account is:

    a a story in serial form

    b evidence given in court

    c an account sent to a customer at the end of each month.

22) A cheque card enables the holder to:

    a shop without money

    b write a cheque or obtain cash from a bank up to a maximum of £50

    c obtain money from a service till outside a bank when it is shut.

23) The following account does not pay interest:

    a savings

    b deposit

    c current

24) The payee of a cheque is:

    a the person signing it

    b the bank on whom it is drawn

    c the person to whom the cheque is made out.

25) The drawee of a cheque is:

    a the person signing it

    b the bank on whom it is drawn

    c the person to whom the cheque is made out.

26) The most usual method of organising Petty Cash is:

    a inquest system

    b imprest system

    c outlet system.

27) Gross wages are:

    a wages in a very large pay packet

    b the amount of wages before deductions

    c the weight of a pay packet.

28) Net wages are:

    a wages actually received, after deductions

    b wages in a very small pay packet

    c wages made up in an envelope with a net pattern on it.

29) PAYE means:

    a pay as you enter

    b pay as you earn

    c pass all your earnings.

30) Statutory deduction is:

    a one required to be made by law

    b one which a wage-earner can refuse to have made

    c one made only from people earning over £10,000 a year.

Appendix 1   Making the Tea

In small firms, it is often the job of the junior typist to include making tea amongst her other duties, for other members of staff, for her boss and also, possibly, for visitors to the firm. It sounds a simple, familiar job, but is often done badly, resulting in a poor cup of tea.

The following rules help to make a good cup of tea the norm, rather than the exception:

- Fill the kettle with fresh water – don't boil up the contents left from the last tea-making.
- Make sure the cups and saucers are perfectly clean.
- Wash the milk jug and refill with fresh milk.
- When the water is almost boiling, pour about a cupful into the teapot and leave it until the kettle has boiled.
- Then empty the teapot and place the tea leaves in – one spoonful for each person and 'one for the pot' is a rule which results in a good, strong tea. It can always be made weaker by adding more boiling water, but it cannot be made stronger by any means at all.
- Make sure the water is brought back to the boil and while it is still boiling pour it into the pot. The amount of water depends upon the size of the pot – only trial and error can determine the exact amount, but a mental note should be made of the level the water reaches in the teapot (i.e. below the spout or above the spout) which results in a really good cup of tea, then results will always be the same.
- After pouring on the boiling water, replace the teapot lid and cover the teapot (ideally, with a cosy but anything will do which keeps it warm) and leave for about 3–5 minutes.
- Then stir, allow the tea leaves to settle, and it is ready for pouring into the cups.

Some people prefer to add milk after the tea has been poured; some prefer the milk poured into the cup first, this is not very important. The use of a tea strainer will prevent tea leaves being poured into the cups along with the tea and is quite important. Sugar should be left to the drinkers to add themselves – some people like sweet tea but because of weight control will add their own saccharines.

A little more *boiling* water may be added to the teapot after pouring out the tea, in case anyone would like another cup of tea, but the teacosy must be replaced or it will rapidly go cold. Tepid tea is revolting. Teabags can be used instead of loose tealeaves and they are easier to dispose of but they do not make such a good cup of tea as the leaves are contained inside the bag in a confined area.

Tea should be served attractively on a tray, with sugar basin and milk jug. There should be no tea slopped into the saucers – this spoils the whole effect!

Appendix 2 The Office of the Future

One of the meanings given in a dictionary for the word 'office' is a 'room for conducting business' and a recent (1980) TV programme showed an office of the future as a room containing electronic equipment but no people – the need for people to 'conduct business' is apparently going to disappear in the office of the future.

How soon this is likely to happen is very difficult to forecast. In small firms, existing equipment which provides adequate service at present is not likely to be put on the scrap heap and replaced by expensive equipment which no one will know how to use. It will take some years for the completely 'electronic' office to evolve and even then it should not mean a wholesale loss of jobs. As the cost of the latest equipment falls and salaries rise, word processors, for example, will become more favourably considered by employers, and this could mean that a firm could be more productive with the same staff, increasing their efficiency and training them to take on new duties – which, one hopes, will make jobs more interesting.

Already, a great deal of technology is available which could replace filing cabinets, carbon copies and mailing procedures. Documents needed for information can be recalled on a display screen, and distributed through computerised telecommunication services or computer print-outs. Telex and facsimile transmission, which have been available for many years, are now obtainable in a form whereby texts are transmitted from screen to screen, eliminating paperwork entirely.

Prestel and Viewdata are already relatively inexpensive and installed in offices in many places all over the country. If they are accepted by firms on a general level, the whole principle of buying and selling will change. With Prestel, there will be no need to leave the office to make purchases. An order will simply be placed in the data base of the seller and, at the same time, debit the bank account of the buyer. With financial accounts fully computerised much of the drudgery of book-keeping and accounting will be eliminated.

The latest development in word processors is the pocket-sized word processor, called a microwriter, which enables the report writer to put his work directly into a microprocessor.

Dictation directly into a word processor, obviating the need for keyboards, is still in the experimental stage, but is obviously the next development.

'Input' from a Palantype machine on to a word processor is already a possibility.

The completely electronic office could be not so far distant — if employers and employees want it!

Appendix 3   Commercial Abbreviations

These are just *some* of the abreviations you may come across! There are, of course, many more in the dictionaries.

&	and
AA	Automobile Association
a/c	account
AD	*anno domini* – in the year of Our Lord
advt	advertisement
am	*ante meridiem* – before noon
asst	assistant
appro	approval
bf	brought forward
BR	British Rail
Bros	Brothers
Bucks	Buckinghamshire
CA	Chartered Accountant
Cantuar	of Canterbury
caps	capital letters
cc	cubic centimetre *or* copies (to)
cent	centigrade
cf	compare
cm	centimetre
Co	Company, county
c/o	care of
COD	cash on delivery
cif	cost insurance and freight
Cr	creditor
cwo	cash with order
cwt	hundredweight
dept	department
do	ditto
Dr	doctor, debtor
E & O E	errors and omissions excepted
EEC	European Economic Community
Esq	Esquire
ex div	ex dividend
fahr	fahrenheit
fas	free alongside ship

fig	figure
fob	free on board
for	free on rail
ft	feet, foot
GATT	general agreement on tariffs and trade
GB	Great Britain
GMT	Greenwich mean time
GPO	General Post Office
Hon	Honorary, honourable
Hon Sec	Honorary Secretary
HP	Hire Purchase
HRH	His (or Her) Royal Highness
i.e.	*id est* (that is)
Inc	Incorporated
inst	instant (of the current month)
JP	Justice of the Peace
Jr	junior
lc	lower case (small print)
Ltd	Limited
MC	Master of Ceremonies; Military Cross
memo	memorandum
m/c	machinery
misc	miscellaneous
Mme	Madame
MO	Medical Officer; money order
MP	Member of Parliament
mpg	miles per gallon
mph	miles per hour
MS	manuscript
MV	motor vessel
NB	note well
np	new paragraph
no	number
nos	numbers
ns	not sufficient (funds to meet a cheque)
OHMS	On Her Majesty's Service
pa	per annum
PAYE	Pay As You Earn
pd	paid
pm	*post meridiem*—afternoon
pp	*per procurationem* – on behalf of
PRO	Public Relations Officer
pro tem	*pro tempore* – for the time
prox	*proxima* – next month
PTO	please turn over
PWD	Public Works Department
RD	refer to drawer (of cheque)
recd	received

RSVP	*répondez s'il vous plaît* – please reply
Ry	railway
SAYE	Save As You Earn
sec	secretary, second
soc	society
sq	square
supt	Superintendent
TUC	Trades Union Congress
uc	upper case (capital letters)
ult	*ultimo* – last month
VAT	Value Added Tax
wk	week
yd	yard
Yrs	Yours

Appendix 4   Sources of Further Information for Teachers

Telephone

Publicity Division, Education Service, Cheapside House, London EC2.

Marketing Executive, British Telecom, Seal House, Swan Lane, EC4R 3TH.

The above will supply posters, films and leaflets.

Mail Handling

Films Officer, Room 436, Postal Headquarters, London EC1A 1HQ.

Royal Mail Film Library, Park Hall Trading Estate, London SE21 8EL.

Schools Officer, Room 448, Postal Headquarters Building, St Martins-le-Grand, London EC1A 1HQ.

All main Post Offices have up-to-date supplies of (free) leaflets on packing, safeguarding and sending mail. Some Postmasters are co-operative about letting schools and colleges have copies of recent posters for display in classrooms.

Banking

The Bank Education Service, 10 Lombard Street, London EC3V 98T will arrange for a speaker to come and talk to schools or colleges, with a film, if requested.

The Bank Education Service will also send supplies of booklets, and facsimile banking documents.

Safety

ROSPA (The Royal Society for the Prevention of Accidents) publish a useful booklet *Care in the Office* as well as a picture competition, both of which are reasonably priced. Address: Cannon House, The Priory Queensway, Birmingham B4 6BS.

Miscellaneous Publications

Two monthly publications which give up-to-date information about all types of office machinery and furniture are *Business Systems and Equipment* (Circulation Department, Maclean-Hunter Limited, 30 Old Burlington Street, London W1X 2AE) and *Office Equipment News* (109–119 Waterloo Road, London SE1 8UL). These are issued free to lecturers and teachers.

The Inland Revenue office in most large towns and cities will supply out-of-date tax forms upon request, for practice purposes.

The AA or RAC have, on occasions, out-of-date copies of their handbooks which they pass on to schools and colleges, upon application, free of charge.

It is also worthwhile to get into touch with local librarians, with a request for out-of-date copies of any reference books they may be replacing.

Index